THEOLOGY
THROUGH THE
THEOLOGIANS

THEOLOGY
THROUGH THE
THEOLOGIANS

Selected Essays 1972–1995

Colin E. Gunton

T&T CLARK
EDINBURGH

T&T CLARK LTD
59 GEORGE STREET
EDINBURGH EH2 2LQ
SCOTLAND

First published 1996

ISBN 0 567 08527 9

British Library Cataloguing-in-Publication Data
A catalogue record for this book is available from the British Library

Typeset by Fakenham Photosetting Ltd, Fakenham
Printed and bound in Great Britain by Hartnolls Ltd, Bodmin

For Carolyn and Peter

CONTENTS

PREFACE

It was once said, on the occasion of the early death of a theologian, that it is good that members of the guild are often given long lives. It is a trade that takes much learning, and this in turn means that those who have done it well are often the best teachers. And how many of them there are! There is no excuse for Christians to be anti-intellectualist, or for those we call 'the world' to accuse the great tradition of being so. To read even those of the Fathers who are sometimes held to be chiefly servants of the liturgy is to enter a fiercely argued world, ever proficient in the development of new concepts and new ways to use old ones.

One of the ways of learning to write theology is therefore to sit at the feet of other theologians. Karl Barth, on whose theology a number of the following essays are centred, illustrates this in two ways. The first is that his *Church Dogmatics*, whatever else it is – and by virtue of its depth and richness, it is many things – is an education both in the history of dogmatics and in the thought of many of those who have pioneered the various loci. Barth rarely distorts, or perhaps it would be more accurate to say rarely misleads, because he makes his presuppositions all too clear. We know why and where he agrees and disagrees with Athanasius, Luther, Descartes, Schleiermacher and Heidegger, but in the process of learning we also learn much about those he discusses.

The second way is in his view that those we read, however long ago they wrote, are living voices to which we must listen, even if finally to disagree. In a culture which has tended to think that anything written before, say, the seventeenth, or perhaps a more recent, century is useful only for the exercise of critical powers, this is a salutary attitude. The best way to enter on the study of systematic theology is by a study of some of its

leading proponents. And this book is intended as an introduction of a kind to systematic theology. It will not introduce all of
theology's central topics, but many of them will be found here.
More than that, by being based on the writings of major
thinkers in our past and present, the chapters present the
topics through a consideration of the writings of those who
have made major contributions in what is under review.

Most of the essays have been published before, but some
have not. Thanks for permission to reproduce them here are
due to Mowbray (for ch. 4), T. & T. Clark (5, 13) and Oxford
University Press (2); to the Congregational Memorial Hall
Trust (11); and to the editors of *Journal of Theological Studies* (6),
Modern Theology (12) and *Scottish Journal of Theology* (1, 3, 9). The
earliest have been revised, especially when that enables greater
engagement with the topic of theology under consideration.
Two of the essays on Barth have received most revision, partly
because they were written rather long ago, and partly because I
have over the years attained a measure of distance from Barth's
theology. As time passes, the oft-repeated judgement that he is
the theologian of the twentieth century seems to be yet more
securely established. At the same time, however, certain aspects
of the content and structure of his *Church Dogmatics* have come
to appear problematic. Some of the reasons for this judgement
are spelled out in the added final section of chapter 6.

As I have read the collection through, what has struck me is
how many of the chapters, including the earliest, raise the
question of the doctrine of the Holy Spirit. I hope that this will
justify the inclusion of the longest of the chapters (7), the only
one not directed to the thought of one or two theologians. It
begins with Augustine, who represents one end of a tradition
still to be seen in Barth. Throughout its long history, with some
exceptions that are noted, that tradition manifests a common
doctrinal weakness which is explored in that chapter and
illustrated in many places in the book. That things look
different when compensation is attempted is one of the main
unifying themes in the collection. As the chapter devoted to
Edward Irving shows, christology is one of the central doctrines
to require radical reshaping when emphases change.

While it cannot be claimed that the doctrine of the Spirit
provides a unifying thread to all the chapters, neither is this
simply a selection of papers that happen to have been written

about theology and theologians. The provenance of many of the chapters in particular commissions for conferences, public lectures and books makes the collection in a sense accidental. But while the chapters do not cover anything like the doctrinal spectrum that would require treatment in a complete Christian dogmatics, those selected do provide an introduction to many matters of method and content in such a project. The logic of the arrangement, which has changed during the period of editing, should be apparent from the order of presentation. Matters of the method and character of Christian theology are treated first, with Coleridge and Newman providing interestingly contrasting illustrations of the English response to modernity in the nineteenth century. There follow two chapters on Barth, one treating the development of doctrine, the other the question of the knowledge of God. While the content of theology is absent from none of these first four chapters, it is visible at the back of the stage, and begins to come to the forefront with a set of chapters concerned with the divine attributes, the doctrine of God and the person of the Spirit. The latter, seventh, chapter forms the midpoint of the book in both senses, for it provides the entry point into various specific loci: creation, Christ, the atonement, the Church and theological anthropology. The completion of that which began with the contribution of two English theologians is provided by a Scot who, like this author, taught in London. Placing the question of authority at the end rounds off the collection appropriately, because Forsyth reminds us that the basis of all we do, and not only in theology, can be found only in that which has the authority to grant it. As he reminds us, unless the God made known in the cross and resurrection of Jesus of Nazareth forms the basis of thought, action and social life, they all alike build upon the sand.

I am grateful to those, commissioners of essays, public lectures and organisers of conferences, who have made me look carefully at writers whose thought is so rewarding to explore; and to Lavinia Harvey, who has by various means put on to disks usable on my current machine and edited those several papers which belong to an era before Macintosh.

Colin Gunton
King's College, London, October, 1995

CHAPTER 1

THE NATURE OF SYSTEMATIC THEOLOGY

Anselm of Canterbury, Samuel Taylor Coleridge and the possibility of an English systematic theology[1]

I *The nineteenth-century background*

Early in his career Edward Bouverie Pusey paid visits to Germany, as a result of which he wrote a book, revealing the influence of both Hegel and Schleiermacher, on the development of German theology. Then came some form of personal crisis, as a result of which he repudiated the book, seeking out second-hand copies in order to destroy them, and in his will requiring that it never be republished. The event was tragic not merely for Pusey's personal life, but because it can be taken as symbolic of the fate of English theology since then. As one commentator remarks, it was an attempt to answer modernism by ignoring it. 'If modernism could not be defeated by intellect, it must be defeated by piety.'[2] Stephen Sykes has pointed out that it was for essentially nationalistic reasons – for it is the nationalist tendency of some Tractarianism which is here the point – that a breach between the different European traditions was opened, and this has meant that English systematic theology, never very strong, has suffered injuries from which it has not yet recovered.

The nationalism was already becoming apparent in the middle of the third decade of the nineteenth century. At the

[1] First published as 'An English Systematic Theology?' in the *Scottish Journal of Theology* 46 (1993), 479–96.
[2] H. C. G. Matthew, 'Edward Bouverie Pusey: from Scholar to Tractarian', *Journal of Theological Studies* 32 (1981), 101–25 (122, 118).

1

very time when, in London, Coleridge was engaging with the challenges of modern thought and his friend Irving was preaching against it in sermons of astonishing intellectual brilliance, at Oxford the response was chiefly rhetorical. Hugh James Rose, against whom the early Pusey wrote in defence of German thought, was seeking to protect the Church of England from the 'caprices of madness', while expressions like 'German unbelief' filled the air and the pages.[3]

The disastrous outcome of all this is a tendency in many an English, and particularly in Anglican, theology to find it extremely difficult to appropriate material from any tradition other than its own deriving from the period between the Middle Ages and the mid nineteenth century. Indeed, it was Pusey's strategy to seek pure authority in the Fathers, and to cross the intervening developments, which once he had interpreted in rather Hegelian fashion, by a historical leap. Leading representatives of the Oxford Movement rarely appear to make serious distinction between the Reformation and subsequent individualistic rationalism, with the result that an unscholarly view of theological history often remains deep-seated. Another outcome of the tendency is the odd isolation of English theological thought, signalled by its utter unpreparedness for Darwinism, and by other odd quirks, of the kind noted by Peter Fuller: 'Pre-Raphaelitism depended, in part, upon a kind of biblical literalism which was perhaps only possible in England'.[4] Germany had moved on.

The steadfast ignoring of anything after the Fathers is only a tendency, and by no means universal. My own appropriation of Calvin's theological legacy was helped to no little degree by the teaching of an Anglo-Catholic, the late G. V. Bennett. Yet such catholicism is by no means universal, as two illustrations will show. The first is found in Alister McGrath's claim that Newman, possibly deliberately, misrepresented Luther's views on justification.[5] We all have blind spots, and for the Tractarians

[3] Albrecht Geck, 'The Concept of History in E. B. Pusey's First Enquiry into German Theology and its German Background', *Journal of Theological Studies* 38 (1987), 387–408 (388).

[4] Peter Fuller, *Theoria. Art and the Absence of Grace* (London: Chatto & Windus, 1988), p. 66.

[5] Alister McGrath, *Justitia Dei* (Cambridge: Cambridge University Press, 1986), volume 2, p. 127.

the theology of the Reformers was clearly one of those. Yet, whatever one's views of the value of Reformation theology, it does one's own tradition no service to ignore the historical fact of its constitutive presence in the English tradition. Deliberately to ignore what has in fact happened in one's past is to fail to understand the present. (In chapter 3 below something will be said about how it is possible see the Reformation's place in a rather more balanced reading of the history of theology.)

The second illustration is to be found in a remark made by Alasdair Heron, appropriately enough in one of the two volumes published in celebration of the centenary of *Lux Mundi*. Professor Heron is worth citing at some length because he is writing of a time when the tendencies that I am lamenting were in full force. Speaking of *Lux Mundi* itself, he writes:

> ... the aversion of the authors to what they regarded as 'Protestant' does seem to betray a certain narrowness of view. In the two generations before *Lux Mundi* appeared, a major group of Scottish and English theologians, some Reformed, some Anglican, had vocally and powerfully proclaimed the integral relation between incarnation and atonement as the axis upon which all Christian theology turns ... The contributors to *Lux Mundi* betray little if any awareness of these men, or of their North American counterparts ... Nor do their strictures on 'Protestantism' betray familiarity with or appreciation of the strongly incarnational theology of English Methodism.[6]

It is surely ironical that, as some older Tractarians complained at the time, *Lux Mundi*, in terms of its content, very much represented the re-establishment of Anglo-Catholicism on an essentially modernist basis. In retrospect, that is certainly how the development looks. Such is the result of cutting oneself off from intellectual developments: one appropriates them unconsciously and without due awareness of the price to be paid. Already, a mere generation later, the intellectual chickens are coming home to roost.

Another price that was paid with this development was that the concentration on the incarnation in relative abstraction

[6] Alasdair Heron, 'The Person of Christ', *Keeping the Faith. Essays to Celebrate the Centenary of* Lux Mundi (London: SPCK, 1989), pp. 99–123 (p. 119).

from the atonement which began there is one of the causes of the later disrepute into which, in some circles, the former doctrine has fallen. What point the incarnation if it is merely a dogma to be defended, with little to do with human flourishing? It is a strange irony, and one of the most unfortunate outcomes of nineteenth-century insularity, that a concern to resist continental and 'Protestant' scepticism has led to both the scepticism of recent exercises and the sawing off of the intellectual branch upon which Christian theology rests. If there is to develop, as theologians like Stephen Sykes have urged, a genuinely English systematic theology, the chief assistance to be gained from the recent English past is a cautionary lesson.

II *The intellectual demand*

The evidence for the absence of an English tradition of systematic theology is to be found in the fact that apart from John Henry Newman there has been for nearly two centuries very little talent of the kind that will place English theologians in important – or even serious – places in future histories of theology. Here a distinction must be drawn between talent and genius. Genius is inexplicable, and it is not necessarily to the discredit of the English that they have produced no one of the ability and impact of Barth or Tillich. But talent is another matter, and can be developed and trained. The weakness of the English tradition is that it has produced few of the ability of Scotland's P. T. Forsyth and T. F. Torrance, both of whom are at the very least – like or dislike the content of their theologies as you may – theological talents whose intellectual achievement will continue to live, and on whom a continuing stream of secondary works is to be expected, rather than, say, the occasional doctoral thesis.

However, it may be objected that such a lament makes a number of assumptions, among them that systematic theology is important; at least as important, say, as the historical and exegetical skills on which our English tradition tends to rest its laurels. Why should not the English stick to what they are good at, instead of trying to ape foreign customs? Indeed, one could further add that we do not necessarily want too many of this odd guild about us. Did not Barth himself warn us of our limitations in his tribute to his teacher, Wilhelm Herrmann, who 'was not ashamed of the gospel. So even his physical appearance was wholly lacking in that trait of worldly wisdom and cunning which too often makes the "systematic" theologian recognisable even at a distance'?[7] We must accept that there is a case for arguing that theology can be too clever, using intellectual skills to evade the true challenges to Christian integrity. The protest of the liberation theologians against unpractical philosophical abstraction is a case in point.

How should we reply to suggestions that the English would be better to stick to their last? One *ad hoc* reply to suggestions of the dubious nature of the discipline is that England is as a matter of fact beginning to recognise the importance of the subject, sometimes by courses on 'modern theology' – not, however, quite the same thing – but more significantly by the presence in a number of universities – Durham, London and Cambridge among them – of lectureships explicitly dedicated to the subject. But *ad hoc* arguments do not establish the rights of a subject to consideration. What is the subject, and what justifies the fuss?

Let me begin by attempting a definition, and then proceed to say something about justification. Simply, we can say that systematic theology is the articulation of the truth claims of Christianity, with an eye to their internal consistency, on the one hand; and, on the other, to their coherence with Scripture, the Christian tradition and other truth – philosophical, scientific, moral and artistic. How these different dimensions might be supposed to hold together will, I hope, be shown somewhat more clearly as the conversation with various intellectual allies and opponents takes shape in this chapter.

But, before that, a move towards a justification, with the help of a contrast. It is possible to profess Christian doctrine as a discipline, as I do, and yet at the same time fall short of a concern to be systematic in theology. For example, one could teach Christian doctrine as an authoritative given, as a physicist

---

[7] Eberhard Busch, *Karl Barth. His Life from Letters and Autobiographical Texts,* translated by John Bowden (London: SCM Press, 1970), p. 45.

might teach the laws of motion or the theory of relativity; or as a historical fact in our past, as some histories of theology do. But those very examples are instructive about the need for a systematic theology, for they remind us that our culture calls theology into question in a way that it does not with physics or history. Already, then, we have a reason why theology must of necessity – in this case, external necessity – be systematic. Culture, the intellectual and generally humanist atmosphere in which we live, requires some account, certainly from the university theologian, but also from the Church, of the intellectual credentials of what they profess. When the culturally successful pursuits of an era are neutral, indifferent or actively hostile to Christian claims, some account of the latters' consistency with other truth is unavoidable. A faith that presumes to continue in being in the light of, for example, the Enlightenment's critique of dogma or modern philosophy's preoccupation with knowledge claims will find demands for intellectual justification made upon it. It may reject the form that those claims take, but unless it is to have recourse to intellectual sectarianism it must at least face the question of the way in which it relates to other claims for truth. And so the justification of systematic theology derives in the first place from the particular intellectual situation of Christian theology in the modern world. It is there that is to be found the pathos of Pusey's attempt to evade intellectual challenges by ignoring them.

The second justification is more important, because it is internal, and arising from the nature of Christian faith. Christianity is of its nature a faith claiming to be true and so to involve truth claims about God, the world and human life within it. It therefore requires that attention be given to its systematic structure, that is to the interrelation of the various levels and dimensions of its truth. We may take Anselm of Canterbury as one model exponent of the internal demand for being systematic in theology, calling upon one who would count as a model also for many a nineteenth-century Tractarian, although it is as a matter of fact a twentieth-century Reformed theologian who has achieved the crucial reappropriation. 'Anselm wants "proof" and "joy" because he wants *intelligere* (understanding) and he wants *intelligere* because he believes', says Barth of

Anselm, and quotes him as saying that it is because we believe that we seek reasons.[8] Christianity is a faith that has had, since the beginning of its theological tradition, both outer pressures and an inner drive to be systematic.

Anselm is particularly interesting in our context for reasons over and above that appeal to the inner drive of Christian faith to rational expression. First, he accepts the challenge of the sceptic and the one who denies the intellectual respectability of Christianity. The two works that are given most attention today are dedicated to the defence of the rationality of the creed against sceptics. Second, and perhaps more important in the English context, he is one who adopted a conception of the relation of theology and philosophy which can be called conversational rather than parallel. By this I mean that he did not keep the two disciplines on parallel lines to each other – meeting only at infinity – or in relatively separate compartments, as has tended to be the case in England, certainly since Paley, but integrated the two pursuits in a unified approach to theological truth. The result is that what appears to us to be the more strictly doctrinal topic of the atonement is treated in the same kind of way as is the proof of the existence of God, something we tend to locate in a separate genre of the philosophy of religion. Anselm thought and wrote systematically about both of them.

Anselm is also interesting for a further reason, and it is that he reminds us of the important distinction between a systematic theology that aims at system, and one that more modestly aims at being systematic. For him, the topics of theology were treated in relative independence of one another. One can, in that sense, be systematic without aiming at the development of a complete system. The framers of systems, like Origen and Schleiermacher, from ancient and modern worlds respectively, tend to be oversystematic: to treat Christianity as containable in a complete and logically watertight system, on the analogy of Spinoza's geometrically ordered philosophy. The weakness of their approach is that it tends to overlook the limits to the possibilities of systematisation of this kind set by the nature of

---

[8] Karl Barth, *Anselm: Fides Quaerens Intellectum*, translated by I. W. Robertson (London: SCM Press, 1958), pp. 15f.

God, of human finitude and of the world itself. Without doubt, both Origen and Schleiermacher were aware of the dangers of being oversystematic, but that does not detract from the truth of the judgement that they, like Barth in a different way on some occasions, found the innate human intellectual drive to system too much for them.

It is here that we are well advised to take the more modest example of Irenaeus. According to Brunner's magnificent characterisation of Irenaeus, to be a systematic theologian is 'to perceive connections between truths, and to know which belongs to which'. On this account, then, systematic theology is any activity in which an attempt is made to articulate the Christian gospel or aspects of it with due respect to such dimensions as its coherence, universality and truth. 'No other thinker was able to weld ideas together which others allowed to slip as he was able to do ... ' That is the point. While not wishing to say everything every time, systematic theologians will have in mind the implications of what they are saying on one occasion for what they may want to say on others. Irenaeus' theological unity was, we might say, a free and open unity: 'he did not take any trouble to articulate into a theological system the sets of ideas which were connected in their own groups; this cannot have been in the least accidental'.[9] As a modern example of such a kind I would take Samuel Taylor Coleridge rather than Barth, for reasons to do both with the uncomprehending reception the latter tends to receive in England and with his own tendency to be oversystematic against all his own canons. After all, we are seeking for an English systematic theology, and of Coleridge as a model there will be much to say. But first a contrast.

III   *Coleridge as example*

The third section of this chapter begins with another Tractarian blind spot. In his *Apologia*, John Henry Newman damns with faint praise – perhaps patronises with faint praise would be a

[9] Emil Brunner, *The Mediator. A Study of the Central Doctrine of the Christian Faith*, translated by Olive Wyon (Philadelphia: Westminster Press, 1947), p. 262.

better description – the theology of Coleridge, a teacher whom he tends to repudiate rather as Pusey had repudiated the Germans from whom he had once wanted to learn: 'a very original thinker, who, while he indulged a liberty of speculation, which no Christian can tolerate, and advocated conclusions which were often heathen rather than Christian, yet after all instilled a higher philosophy into enquiring minds than they had hitherto been accustomed to accept'.[10] Such remarks are of ill omen. As we shall see in the chapter devoted to him, had Newman listened more carefully, it might be that some of the major flaws in this otherwise important theologian would have appeared less glaring. Newman's chief and interrelated faults are, first, a tendency to authoritarianism, to see dogma as a given to be defended, rather than a relatively open body of tradition with which critically to engage; and, second, a tendency to see theology and philosophy as externally related, to be held more in parallel than in genuine mutual enrichment.

Now, it might be objected that to treat Newman in this way is to be anachronistic, to behave as if he had lived in the age of Barth and of revelation conceived dynamically and personally. That is true for a large part of the point, but not for all, and it is here that Coleridge is so important, for he is an example of a genius who to a large measure succeeds in being systematic without succumbing to system, however much he hoped one day, as he hoped for so much else, to develop a system of thought. The crucial differences between the two emerge in their treatments of the Trinity. For Newman, talk of the oneness of God is one thing, the product of philosophical reflection, while the threeness is a matter of authoritative revelation. Speculation about the relation of the one and the three is forbidden:

> the Catholic doctrine of the Trinity is a mere juxtaposition of separate truths, which to our minds involves inconsistency, when viewed together; nothing more being attempted by theologians, for nothing more is told us.[11]

[10] John Henry Newman, *Apologia pro Vita Sua*, edited by M. J. Svaglic (Oxford: Oxford University Press, 1967), p. 94.
[11] John Henry Newman, 'On the Introduction of Rationalistic Principles into Revealed Religion', *Essays Critical and Historical* (London: Longmans, Green & Co., 1907), volume 1, p. 52.

That is a refusal to face the question of systematic rationality, and it is significant that in that same tract Newman chastises an opponent for seeking to do very much what Anselm of Canterbury had once sought to do. But can we really, in a world such as ours, take seriously a conception of Christian theology as involving 'a mere juxtaposition of separate truths'? The implication is that the Trinity is little more than a dogma to be taught, so that it is little wonder that it is widely represented as pointless antique speculation. To make the main point, however, it is now time to compare that tendency to authoritarian dogmatism with Coleridge's use of the doctrine of the Trinity. He did indeed use the doctrine speculatively, and, indeed, in relation to pagan thought. But it was as a way out of pagan thought, and as a means of integrating a vast range of human concerns, especially those thrown up by modern thought, that Coleridge grew into trinitarian theology.

Why is it that I wish to recommend the odd figure of Coleridge as a model for an English systematic theology? The first reason is that his whole life was marked by a theological quest which took in so many other dimensions of culture and thought. Coleridge wished to see things whole, and in this respect, as in so many others, his history is rather different from that of Pusey. He did indeed go to Germany, and was indeed enthralled by the challenges of its thought. His life was, indeed, fraught with personal disasters and changes of direction. But otherwise the story is a very different one. His life had an intellectual unity of the kind that makes it possible to see it as a model for the present. One way of putting this is to say that Coleridge was obsessed with truth, and with truth as an essentially theological quest – a quest which puts him in a long tradition, stretching back to the pre-Socratic philosophers of ancient Greece. His recent biographer, no theologian, nevertheless notes the early development of this orientation.[12] Contrast that with the more functional view of the discipline represented by Paley on the one hand and Pusey on the other: theology in defence of a more or less fully defined package.

Yet Coleridge's quest for truth was not one which divorced it

[12] Richard Holmes, *Coleridge. Early Visions* (London: Hodder & Stoughton, 1989).

from practical concerns. Far from it, for in many ways a moral concern was very much at the centre, as we shall see. One form the quest for truth took was in his engagement with the thought of that prince of modernity, Immanuel Kant. Kant, as we are often reminded, stands at the watershed of modern thought, as is revealed above all else in the breach he engineered between the truth of being and the truth of doing. Coleridge took up his moral thought, and developed from it the possibility of a unified – and theological – view of reality. Of course, there was an element of wish-fulfilment in his assertion that he could not believe Kant really meant what he said about the impossibility of metaphysics. But Kant served as a first step, as a liberator from the mechanistic view of reality that threatened to sweep all human values off the face of the earth.

Freedom, human freedom, was Coleridge's concern, as it was Kant's. But rather than assert it against the blank wall of the empty universe – as the Kantian Sartre was later to do – he used it as a starting-point in a search for a universe containing the possibility of personal truth. But that is to begin at the end. What began it all was a quest for human freedom somewhat on the model of the Enlightenment: unitarianism, a new political order, human self-improvement – all very English. But, as is well known, the decline of the French Revolution into violence and repression had a deep effect on both Wordsworth and Coleridge. In a recent review of a biography of Wordsworth, Paul Foot repeatedly used the word 'apostate' of Wordsworth's change of allegiance. (It would be interesting to hear the cries of outrage from some political libertarians if such a word were to be used in its original context.) It would be less easy, even for a socialist, to use the word of Coleridge, for whom there was no 'handful of silver'. In any case, whatever the truth about his former associate, there can be no doubt of the integrity of Coleridge's later development: freedom, human freedom, both personal and social, continued to be his preoccupation.

That matter, however, was complicated by the Augustinian and Reformation contribution to Coleridge's thought. He was, and knew himself to be, shaped by the consequences of the Fall. His addiction to opium, alongside failures in both personal relations and literary achievement, gave him a strong sense of the bondage entered by those who misuse their freedom – all of us – and of the need of redemption. The question of human freedom, and indeed of all human being, was bound up with the question of God. That is one of the bases of his concern to be systematic: to think things together. But even from the heady days of his optimistic youth, the matter of God was never far absent. As he developed, it became central, and for two reasons. The first we have seen: that without redemption, there can be no freedom. The second, and it is the one we shall pursue here, is the broader philosophical and theological question of the way things are: the nature of our world, and whether it is indeed a place within which human beings have the right to expect to be free.

It is here that Coleridge faced the question of the inter-relation of the Hellenic and Hebraic determinants of Western culture. Christian theology, from the very beginning, has always worked out its salvation in the context of the Greek inherit-ance. It is still doing so, and a careful observation of the debates about the character and status of modern science will reveal that it is still at the heart of the question of being. One contrast will suffice. The concepts which Jacques Monod took for his theme and title in his influential book came, directly or indirectly, from Hellenistic thought. *Chance* and *Necessity* are not the products of pure science – nothing is – but reaffirma-tions of two Greek divinities.[13] Indeed, it is an essentially Hellenic and pantheistic vision that Monod provides, albeit with existentialist and irrationalist overtones. By contrast, in a more recent account of the cosmos, Ilya Prigogine and Isabelle Stengers call on concepts still recognisably Greek, but imbued by tradition with far more Hebraic overtones: their title is *Order out of Chaos,* and they present us with a universe more consistent with Christian doctrines of a contingent universe which is the product of an act of free creation.[14] The dispute between them – and the many other weird theologies that are emerging from the pens of scientific cosmologists – is not a purely scientific one. It is theological, to do with the nature of the world and which divinity makes it what it is.

[13] Jacques Monod, *Chance and Necessity. An Essay in the Natural Philosophy of Modern Biology,* translated by Austryn Wainhouse (London: Collins, 1972).

[14] Ilya Prigogine and Isabelle Stengers, *Order out of Chaos. Man's New Dialogue with Nature* (London: Fontana, 1985).

What Coleridge saw, and saw clearly, is that in all thought there is a choice of divinity to be made. Others have seen that it is so: Irenaeus with his argument that if God does not create out of nothing, then it is the world that is in effect the deity; and Kierkegaard with his remark that the only real alternative to Christianity is pantheism. Coleridge's point is that only a God conceived trinitarianly – that is, in terms of his personal otherness to and free relation with the world – is consistent with a universe that is a fit place for human beings to live their lives. It is such a concern for the interrelatedness of things, of world and life, of theology and ethics, that founds the necessity for being systematic in theology, for thinking things together.

Such an argument may, to be sure, be accused of wishful thinking, especially in view of the character of the one from whom it came. But the point is that it was first hammered out in conversation with representatives of the tradition from the pre-Socratics through the Bible and its higher critics, the Fathers, mediaevals, Reformers and moderns; and second that it converges with all the other factors that Coleridge had in view: the fallenness of humankind, the fact of redemption, the philosophies of perception and of aesthetics which were so important in his overall concern for systematic truth. It was partly, not only, because Coleridge had become an orthodox Christian that he pondered the doctrine of the Trinity; rather, he became an orthodox Christian because he came to see the doctrine of the Trinity as the foundation of a systematic quest for truth: as the 'one substrative truth' underlying all truths.[15] Thus it was not for him primarily a dogma to be accepted, but a truth to be brought into relation to all other truths in an attempt to show systematically something of the nature of the world and of human life within it.

In all of this Coleridge had a number of strengths that enabled him to transcend while being true to his Englishness. It may be that one of his strengths was his lay status, so that it was not professionally incumbent upon him to refrain from rocking the Anglican ecclesiastical boat. (Not that he was unconcerned with central questions of the English establishment, and in a

[15] Samuel Taylor Coleridge, 'Notes on Waterland', *The Complete Works of Samuel Taylor Coleridge*, edited by W. G. T. Shedd (New York: Harper & Brothers, 1853), volume 5, p. 407.

positive way.) But another was a way of seeing things whole that
enabled him to elude the worst traps of the Enlightenment and
particularly to see through the ways of the Paleys of this world.
His refusal of an approach to Christianity based on 'evidences'
indicates the integrated nature of his thought, in this respect
poles apart from that which would hold philosophy and theology merely in parallel. Here, as in so much else, what he says
is key to the matter of systematic theology in general.

IV   *The present age*

What, then, are the problems of the English tradition in the
light of all this? Historically, the form they have taken derives,
as we have seen, from an essentially nationalist fear of continental thought. What then happens is that nationalist isolation tends to institutionalise, so to speak, the typical problems,
just as incest can inbreed genetic ones. Strengths, uncriticised,
become weaknesses, while weaknesses are magnified. English
theology tends to reflect the weaknesses of English thought in
general: a suspicion of intellectuals of all kinds, allied to a
tendency to naturalism and moralism. Daniel Hardy has
observed that these are the reasons why English theology has
found it so hard to come to terms with the theology of both
Schleiermacher and Barth. They seem to say things that it is
simply not possible to say.[16] Because of inbred tendencies the
English simply fail to understand what these seminal thinkers
are doing.

It is from such tendencies that Coleridge can help to free us,
because he faced and thought them through. He is therefore a
model for an English systematic theology, not necessarily for all
of the content of his thought – though I believe that his mature
thought in particular has much to offer in terms of content –
but because of the way in which he approaches the subject. He
is interesting because he is in many ways a very English thinker,
especially perhaps in his concern for the centrality of the

[16] Daniel W. Hardy, 'The English Tradition of Interpretation and the
Reception of Schleiermacher and Barth in England', *Barth and Schleiermacher.
Beyond the Impasse*, edited by J. Duke and R. Streetman (Minneapolis: Augsburg
Fortress, 1988), p. 147.

practical and ethical. The later Coleridge, once he had thought his way out of his youthful unitarianism and poetic flirtation with pantheism, also belongs very much within the Anglican tradition, as his essay *On the Constitution of the Church and State* makes clear.[17]

And yet he was to distance himself from the trends that have marked so much later English theology. Of the ways of Paley, he is rightly impatient, as he would be with contemporary obsession with historical evidence, narrowly conceived. More important, his use of his experience in Germany remained with him as a positive influence to the end. Not only did he continue to wrestle with Kant, but he also engaged with the fundamental epistemological problems underlying the myth theory of Eichhorn and others. Would he have been among the pious who resisted the publication in English of Schleiermacher, Strauss and Feuerbach, leaving the latter two to be left to the unbelieving George Eliot? It must be doubted. Whatever the truth of that, he was neither an Englishman for whom all things German were to be revered, nor an insular nationalist of the kind still lying behind if not actually within Austin Farrer's slighting reference to 'German profundity' as something not quite healthy.[18] He is a model for English systematic theology because, like Irenaeus, Coleridge saw things whole, and yet in their parts as well.

Where shall we go from here? The possibilities for any tradition lie in developing its own strengths in conversation with other related traditions of theology and with thought in general. The heart of the matter lies in making connections. The strategy attributed to Pusey was to disavow connection in favour of 'a strict, dogmatic and closed view of faith and scholarship'.[19] Here we may not disavow an engagement with modern culture, and may indeed find that it offers more encouragement than the reverse. There are many signs that culture is recognising in itself, and with little enough help from

[17] Coleridge, Samuel Taylor, *On the Constitution of the Church and State. The Collected Works of Samuel Taylor Coleridge, Volume 10*, edited by John Colmer (London: Routledge and Kegan Paul, 1976).

[18] Austin Farrer, 'An English Appreciation', *Kerygma and Myth. A Theological Debate*, edited by H.-W. Bartsch, translated by R. H. Fuller (London: SPCK, 1972), volume 1, p. 212.

[19] Matthew, 'Edward Bouverie Pusey', 115.

theology, that the crisis of modernity is in large measure a theological crisis. A few swallows do not make a summer, yet the fact that philosophers – notably Alasdair MacIntyre – art critics and playwrights are asking questions of basic theological importance should alert us to the fact that the outside world is not as blankly secular as may sometimes be supposed.

And yet the situation in theology remains one of fragmentation and confusion. This is to be observed at two levels. The first is between the disciplines that make up the typical degree in theology, with students of the Bible and systematicians tending to regard each other's programmes as being in tension, if not worse (though even here there are signs of a change in co-operative enterprise and a widespread broadening of interests). Similarly, there is a tension between what can be called the antiquarian and constructive dimensions of the disciplines, with some concerned to lay out – the corpse of? – history, others to engage with it with more intent to interact with problems of modern social and other thought. And the tension is not only between antiquarians and those oriented towards the contemporary. There is a similar breach between the orientations of many philosophers of religion and systematicians, although here again conversation is in many areas taking place.

The second level at which there is fragmentation is within the discipline of Christian systematic theology itself. This is widespread and serious, with a large measure of mutual incomprehension. There are those for whom questions laid open by trinitarian conceptuality are the very heart of the matter, opening up vistas and possibilities of almost infinite promise; there are others for whom the question is simply a piece of dead tradition, to be left on one side while the real questions are decided. Each side of this, admittedly extreme, characterisation feels a responsibility to the modern world. Where they differ is in their analysis of what the modern world is and what it requires if it is to be taken seriously in the appropriate way.

Two factors, however, make this picture less bleak than it may appear to be. The first is that a plurality of positions can be, in the right conditions, productive of truth and light through dialectic and debate. While this cannot take place through the blank dismissal of opposing positions, as often happens, it can be recognised as a sign of promise, not necessarily of terminal fragmentation. The second mitigating factor is that divisions in theology are reflected in the debates in other disciplines, as, for example, a reading of the art criticism of Peter Fuller, an observation of the internal politics of faculties of English at our ancient universities, or the debates about the nature of science will demonstrate. As a part of culture, theology will necessarily share its problems. There is nothing wrong with reflecting the divisions of culture so long as we do not merely reflect them. Whether theology can help to heal them is another matter, and the crucial question; and it is here that we must come to some suggestions for a way forward.

What are the strengths in the English tradition? Historical studies and a concern for practicalities.[20] Whence do these need to be supplemented? The simple answer is for an integration into wider patterns of thought, where the often unquestioned assumptions about method and the nature of being remain unprobed. It is here that thought attempting to integrate cannot remain an optional dimension. Partly through our own most grievous fault we have allowed others to do most of the interesting work, and we are now required to listen to them. English music has enjoyed something of a renaissance in the twentieth century, but it has not achieved this by ignoring the great tradition of German music. There is no reason why we may not learn our lesson, and use it to enter into conversation with our own tradition. Here, our own traditions of historical scholarship can be brought into play with great profit, for a modern systematics done in ignorance of the past will fail to understand what it is doing. And there is much to be found. If we reach back beyond the nineteenth century there is a rich tradition of – to name but two examples – Anglican and Puritan theology to be mined. Similarly, the nineteenth century is not merely reaction, nor, as the remark of Professor Heron quoted above indicated, merely Anglican.

I believe that the lessons are already being learned. Research

[20] There is something else, too. As was pointed out to me by Christoph Schwoebel when this lecture was given there is a long tradition in England of the communal preparation of books – *Lux Mundi, Essays and Reviews* and the like – which has saved this tradition from the excesses of individualism to which some continental and American theologians have succumbed.

students in the discipline continue to come forward in good numbers, and will increase if good teaching and writing in the subject are offered. There is much to be hoped for. In the midst of the fragmentation, new alliances are waiting to be made and new lines of connection drawn. With modern culture itself beginning to question the total propriety of its rejection of its Christian past, and with new talents in systematic theology beginning to make their mark, there is every reason to hope that an English but not at all insular systematic theology can begin to be taken seriously outside our own tradition. In the next chapter, we turn to the related question concerning the nature of dogmatic theology.

CHAPTER 2

THE NATURE OF DOGMATIC THEOLOGY

Dogma and reason in Newman's 'Seventy-third Tract for the Times'[1]

I *The dialectic*

Like all thinkers, Newman is what he is by virtue of what he made of the influences that formed him. Two in particular appear to have given shape to his questions and answers. The first is – despite Newman's interest in Athanasius and his opponents – the dominating mind of the West, Augustine of Hippo. To Augustine must go much of the credit – if that be the word – for the unique combination of rationalism and authoritarianism which was long the mark of Western theology. The leaning towards authoritarianism derived from Augustine's experience, and is well expressed by Harnack. Augustine's encounter with Manichaeism, he holds, shook for ever his confidence in the rationality of Christian truth, so that he acquired a compensating tendency to fall back upon ecclesiastical authority:

> The thousand doubts excited by theology, and especially Christology, could only be allayed by the Church ... *The Church guaranteed the truth of the faith, where the individual could not perceive it* ... Openly he proclaimed it: I believe in many articles only on the Church's authority; nay, I believe in the Gospel itself merely on the same ground.[2]

[1] First published as 'Newman's Dialectic: Dogma and Reason in the 73rd Tract for the Times', *Newman After a Hundred Years*, edited by Alan G. Hill and Ian Ker (Oxford: Oxford University Press, 1990), pp. 309–22. Revision is chiefly of the closing paragraphs.

[2] A. von Harnack, *History of Dogma*, translated by J. Millar (London: Williams & Norgate, 1898), volume 5, p. 80.

19

Both the experience and its outcome have parallels in Newman so long afterwards, and it is a noticeable feature of the *Grammar of Assent* that, where argument fails, a last resort is appeal to the authority of the Church. 'That the Church is the infallible oracle of truth is the fundamental dogma of the Catholic religion.'[3]

The other side of Augustine is to be found echoed in Newman also, and that is a relentless drive to prove, within the limits of Catholic authority, the truth or at least conceivability of the doctrines of the faith. The dialectic of faith and reason, of trust in authority and drive for understanding, that marked Augustine's thought became the pattern for Western theology until the Reformation and Enlightenment. And that takes us to a second formative influence on Newman. In the Enlightenment, the Western dialectic received a one-sided radicalisation. For Locke, reason and revelation were indeed two sources of thought, but the latter became subordinate to the former, and its credibility was to be assessed entirely by the light of reason. In place of the authority of the infallible Church there was posited the authority – at least in principle – of infallible reason. Thus was formed the anti-dogmatic principle which Newman rightly repudiated as the enemy of Christianity.

From such a point of view, Newman's programme can be read as a return to Augustinianism: the *Grammar of Assent* to move behind Locke, the *Lectures on the Doctrine of Justification* to move behind Luther, in both cases back to Augustine. The result is that, as with Augustine, we meet the appeal to authority and the free use of argument side by side – again as in Augustine not always very well co-ordinated. An examination of Newman's encounter with Thomas Erskine of Linlathen and others in Tract Seventy-Three 'On the Introduction of Rationalistic Principles into Revealed Religion' will enable us to appreciate something of the shape the Augustinian dialectic of authority and reason, of acceptance and argument, took in Newman's thinking.[4]

---

[3] J. H. Newman, *An Essay in Aid of a Grammar of Assent* (Notre Dame and London: University of Notre Dame Press, 1979 (1st edition, 1871)), p. 131.

[4] 'On the Introduction of Rationalistic Principles into Revealed Religion', *Essays Critical and Historical* (London: Longmans, Green & Co., 1907), volume 1, pp. 30–101. Further references to this work are placed in parentheses in the main text.

II   *The critique of rationalism*

The brilliance of Newman's 1835 contribution to *Tracts for the Times* is that it pinpoints with great clarity the inner logic and weakness of his opponents' positions, and at the same time allows his own conception of dogma and revelation to come to the surface. Despite its brilliance, however, the Tract is only half successful, because it fails to deal with the underlying strength of the position it is concerned to attack. It has been suggested that the reason for a fundamental disagreement between two opposed positions may often be found in their sharing of a false premiss,[5] and there is something to be said for that being the case here, too. Although the objects of Newman's polemics were harbingers of the depressing reductionism which has come to full flower in the century since his death, there is also much reason to be dissatisfied with the rather dualistic Augustinian theology which continues to dominate his thought.

First, then, a critique of the rationalistic theologies of Newman's adversaries. His general objection to rationalism is that it wants to know too much and so dismisses too easily that which cannot be exhaustively known. In his polemics, as in some of the points made in the *Grammar of Assent*, it is possible to hear anticipations of the arguments of Michael Polanyi in this century against the Enlightenment's demand for totally explicit and formal systems of knowledge. According to Polanyi, all knowledge is personal, which is not to say unreal but rather a function of the way in which finite persons engage with the world.[6] He would agree with Newman that 'Rationalism is a certain abuse of Reason; that is, a use of it for purposes for which it never was intended and is unfitted' (p. 31). Human knowledge, being human, may not claim too much. The trouble with the theological rationalists is that they do precisely this, at once trespassing on the domains of mystery and falsifying the Christian revelation.

On the face of it, the programme of Thomas Erskine of Linlathen was an admirable one. Erskine was in salutary reaction

---

[5] R. W. Newell, *Objectivity, Empiricism and Truth* (London and New York: Routledge, 1986), p. 37.

[6] Michael Polanyi, *Personal Knowledge: Towards a Post-Critical Philosophy* (1958; 2nd edition, London: Routledge, 1962).

against the defence of the indefensible, in particular the rigid
form that predestinarian Calvinist orthodoxy had taken in the
centuries after Calvin. His disapproval of the acceptance of
theological formulas for their own sake, especially when they
bore no relation to salvation, was surely justified. Moreover,
Erskine's theology, even on Newman's rather unsympathetic
account, breathes a concern to humanise theology, to stress the
grace made real in Christ against attempts to frighten into belief.
And yet Newman is justified in many of the charges he makes
against both Erskine and Abbott. The burden of his complaint is
that both of his opponents, and particularly the latter, evacuate
the faith of essential content by their rationalistic treatment of
the given dogmas of the tradition. What Newman means by the
rationalising of Christianity can be analysed into a number of
features, the following salient among them. First, there is the
tendency to anthropocentrism: 'Our private judgement is made
everything to us, – is contemplated, recognised, and consulted
as the arbiter of all questions, and as independent of everything
external to us' (p. 34). Here Newman anticipates what has in
recent years become a commonplace among those who see in
the elevation of subjective judgement which began with
Descartes and took particularly rigid form in Kant the foe of a
due assessment of human limits and fallibility.

Newman expresses the opposition to the deification of human
individual judgement in rather one-sidedly theocentric form:
'The Rationalist makes himself his own centre, not his Maker; he
does not go to God, but he implies that God must come to him'
(pp. 33–4). And yet even there he is not out of step with voices
from other fields of human scientific and cultural activity who
have in recent years been heard to insist that without a due
appreciation of the place of authority, community and tradition
there can be no rational activity. Something must be *received* if
anything at all is to be achieved. It is, furthermore, worth noting
that Newman is not simply making a point about the essential
limitedness of the human intellect. In other respects too he
reveals anticipations of more recent concerns. That he could
destroy his credit in high places with a work entitled *On Consult-
ing the Faithful in Matters of Doctrine* is a measure of a genuine
move to a churchly or communal rather than merely clerical
conception of the nature of authority.

A second vice of rationalism is its tendency to hold that unless everything is known, then nothing can be. The 'all or nothing' conception of knowledge is particularly destructive of theology, and is another fruit of the Enlightenment's deification of human judgement. Newman observes acutely the effects of this aspect of the syndrome on Christianity's teaching. Not only is mystery discarded (p. 34), but revelation is explained away or forced prematurely into a system. 'It [Rationalism] considers faith to consist rather in the knowledge of a system or scheme, than of an agent ...' (p. 39). It is not that Newman denies the systematic nature of Christian doctrine. Rather, he operates with what can be called a dialectic of system. Revelation does indeed belong to a 'vast system' (p. 42), but is not such as can be expressed by means of any particular system of words: there is a gulf between the reality and the words which would give that reality rational form. There is therefore a distinction to be drawn between rationalism and faith. 'Rationalism takes the words of Scripture as signs of Ideas; Faith, of Things or Realities' (p. 35). In other words, we may not encompass divine realities by our logic, even though they have their own (unknown) logic in the mystery of eternity.

A similar point is made against those who will not believe anything unless its truth be first demonstrated. According to Erskine, 'doctrines, it seems, are not true, if they are not explicable' (p. 60). One citation from Erskine's work, indeed, reveals him as a classic rationalist: '"I may understand many things which I do not believe; but I cannot believe anything which I do not understand, unless it be something addressed merely to my senses and not to my thinking faculty"' (p. 39). The implied view of knowledge as a function of the relation of clear and distinct ideas links Erskine with both Descartes and Locke, but Newman's reply takes us much further back. It was in similar terms that Athanasius chided the Arians for assuming that nothing could be true unless they understood it. It is clear that we meet here something more than a mere appeal to mystery. Underlying Newman's objections is a general point about the limits of human ability to penetrate the structures of reality and of human language fully to encompass that which it attempts to express.

Yet another feature of rationalism's drive to system is its

tendency to reduce all Christian teaching to a single principle
and so deny the richness of its various doctrines. In traditional
dogmatic Christianity there is a range of doctrines, each of
which stands as a mystery in its own right. Newman gives a list of
what he takes to be the essentials, beginning: 'the Holy Trinity;
the incarnation of the Eternal Son; His atonement and merits;
the Church as His medium and instrument ...' (p. 45). To this
he contrasts the 'popular theology of the day ... that the
Atonement is the chief doctrine of the Gospel' (p. 47). It is not
that he denies the importance of the atonement; as we have
seen, it is high on his list of *credenda*. It is rather that he opposes
any tendency to reduce Christianity to that which is seen and
experienced. The economy of salvation is only a part, and must
be seen to have its basis in eternity. '[I]t is the triumph of
Rationalism to level everything to the lowest and most tangible
form ...' (p. 89). Corresponding, accordingly, to the dialectic of
system which we have already met, there is for Newman a
dialectic of time and eternity which is, as we shall see, the key to
his conception of dogma. Time and eternity are distinct realms
of being which may not be confused.

The third sin of rationalism is manifest in its tendency to
reduce religion to morality or utility. Against such a practice,
Newman urges the priority of truth, the need to accept the faith
for its own sake. One may not conclude from the fact that
Christianity has a bearing on character the 'general proposition, that in a genuine Revelation *all* doctrines revealed must
have a direct bearing upon the moral character enjoined by it'
(p. 56). Newman suspects that some such reduction underlies
Erskine's desire to concentrate on what we know of God's
saving action in Christ, but is certain that it is operative in
Abbott's more radical reduction: 'the virtue of the great sacrifice is, not expiation, atonement in God's sight, but the *moral
effect* of Christ's death on those who believe in it' (p. 85). As
Newman observes, and the claim has been plentifully verified
since, in cases where utility is given preference over truth the
theologian simply becomes the organ of the spirit of the age (p.
91). A Christianity dominated by thoughts of relevance only
advertises its own irrelevance.

III *The problems*

The strength of Newman's assault on rationalism is manifest. He has unerringly indicated the inadequacies in its assumptions about God, the human mind and the nature of Christianity. And yet the Achilles' heel of his position is to be found in the very moments of truth in the positions he assaults, in their reasons for making the assertions that they do. Corresponding to each of the three charges against rationalism there are equivalent complaints to be made against Newman's reconstituted Augustinianism. First comes the matter of anthropocentrism. Why had Newman's opponents succumbed, apparently so easily, to a sub-Christian anthropocentrism? The simple, and only partly true, answer is that they had succumbed to the spirit of the age, to the Enlightenment's divinising of human knowledge and power.

Yet it could also be argued that the Enlightenment itself was a partly justified protest, within the framework of the Augustinian tradition's tendency to subject everything temporal to what have come to be called the constraints of heteronomy. It was thus the assertion of the due rights of time against eternity, of human freedom against divine determinism. If at the same time there was a tendency to elevate humankind to a kind of surrogate divinity in place of the triune God, its moments of truth should still not be denied. Alongside the negative and secularising protest of the modern movement, there was a positive concern, for human freedom and dignity had suffered at the hands of oppressive regimes which either had been those of the Church itself or had been supported by the Church. No glorification of the Middle Ages should have ignored the wars, tortures and burnings that had been perpetrated in the name of the crucified. In such a context, a reassertion of the centrality of the human could be understood as a return to some of the values of the incarnation, of the eternal Son's enfleshment.

There is little doubt that Erskine's theology is contaminated by a strong dose of anthropocentric rationalism. But it must be remembered that he was in justified revolt against a predestinarian Calvinism which, in its concern for the right of God to do exactly as he pleased, at times appeared to ignore the humanity of the incarnation. Erskine contemplated the biblical teaching about salvation, and found it strongly oriented towards human well-being. He was moved in the direction of a doctrine of universal salvation – as had been Paul before him in Romans 11.32 – because what he read spoke to him primarily of the love of God: of his gracious rather than gratuitous action towards his creation. No doubt he did tend to reduce the being of God to his historical manifestation, but he did at least take that manifestation into the heart of his theology. The stress on grace and love was a note which Newman himself might well have both heard and sounded somewhat more strongly.

The second feature of rationalism which Newman rightly observed and rejected was its tendency to be oversystematic. It is, however, also possible to evade the need to be systematic, and so to give the impression of mystery-mongering, or of what could be called dogmatic positivism – a take-it-or-leave-it casting of the pearls of dogma before the swine of humanity. One of the reasons for the apparent disfavour into which trinitarian belief has fallen of late – and it is the only good reason – is the impression it sometimes gives of being the product of airy, almost mathematical, speculation, divorced from the concrete presence of God to the world through Jesus and the Spirit. Some passages in Newman's writings reinforce the impression:

> the Catholic doctrine of the Trinity is a mere juxtaposition of separate truths, which to our minds involves inconsistency, when viewed together; nothing more being attempted by theologians, for nothing more is told us (p. 52).

We shall return to the matter of the Trinity later, but it must be said that in the light of the history of dogma such an assertion is simply false, being justified neither by Augustine's tireless efforts to do what Newman says we may not ('reduce them [the truths] into an intelligible dependence on each other, or harmony with each other' (p. 53)), nor by the more straightforward and concrete treatments of the Cappadocian Fathers.

Another equally instructive example of Newman's refusal to face the challenge to be systematic is found at the heart of his disagreement with Erskine. The two contestants agree, as we have seen, that the doctrine of the atonement is somewhere near the centre of the Christian dispensation. It is also clear that Paul, for example in Romans 3.26, sees the cross as the place where both the forgiveness of God and the requirements of universal justice are realised. The Epistle to the Romans is therefore itself a demonstration of the nature of divine justice, and an invitation to further reflection upon it. Newman, however, appears to render illegitimate such further theological articulation. 'He [Erskine] considers, in common with many other writers of his general way of thinking, that in that most solemn and wonderful event, we have a Manifestation, not only of God's love, but of His justice' (p. 65). We can, to be sure, understand Newman's warning: certain 'how' questions are ruled quite out of court by the character of God's ways towards us, and indeed, 'some "depth" of God's counsels would have been acknowledged and accepted on *faith*' (p. 66). Yet by his insistence that it is too much to claim that we have in the cross a manifestation of both love and justice, Newman would appear to rule out Paul, and certainly calls into question Anselm's classic articulation in the *Cur Deus Homo* of the inner rationality of God's saving action in Christ.

We come, third, to Newman's – again salutary – protest against the reduction of dogma to its moral relevance and utility. Here, too, he shows signs of lurching into the equal and opposite error of a complete divorce of dogma from life. Again referring to the doctrine of the Trinity, Newman asks: 'does not the notion of a Mystery lead to awe and wonder? And are these not moral impressions?' (p. 59). Up to a point; but much depends upon the nature of the mystery, and a doctrine consisting in the 'mere juxtaposition of separate truths' seems scarcely to be adequate.

The nature of the case can be illustrated from the thought of one who was born two years after Newman said his farewell to Oxford. P. T. Forsyth was as pungent and insistent a critic as Newman of the rationalism which had, by his time, made even greater inroads into the Churches. With his insistence on the churchly nature of Christianity, there is little doubt that this Congregationalist from Aberdeen owed something to the Oxford Movement. Yet he showed a greater freedom than Newman in receiving from the 'opposition' a liberation from abstract dogmatism. A trinitarian thinker, with a strongly christocentric emphasis, Forsyth, like Erskine, saw that, to a degree, dogma needed to be moralised: to be filled out with concrete content by reference to the historic saving activity of God. Forsyth had his weaknesses, too, but he does at least show that the choice is not entirely between rationalism and positivist dogmatism. To be fair to Newman, that is not quite the way in which he presents the alternatives. But there is no doubt that his manner of writing brings him rather near.

IV *Shared presuppositions*

It is sometimes claimed that the divided Churches of Christendom are for the most part right in what they affirm, wrong in what they deny. With Newman's assertions about the nature of Christian doctrine, the opposite could be argued to be the case, in that he is acute in his criticisms of theological rationalism, but less convincing in what he wishes to put in its place. To understand the basis of his position, we must return to the question of the presuppositions he shares with his opponents. In this respect, something has already been said of the Western dialectic, shared by Newman, of time and eternity, reason and faith. Time and eternity tend, on his account, to be conceived as utterly distinct realms, the one treated by human reason, the other unknown, but accepted through revelation on faith and by authority.[7] His own expression of the matter leaves no doubt that such is the case: 'the Church Catholic has ever taught ... that there are facts revealed to us, not of this world, not of time, but of eternity, and that absolutely and independently ...' (p. 69). The impression is consequently given that what happens in time, including even the economy of salvation, remains in an utterly different order from eternity, from God himself, so that the two orders can be related only by appeal to authority. By implication, as we have seen, even such explorations of the rationality of faith as Anselm's are made to appear questionable.

It may be objected that Newman, in a kind of reflex emphasis-

---

[7] There are some clear echoes of Locke to be heard in Newman here. '*Faith* ... is the assent to any proposition, not thus made out by the deductions of reason, but upon the credit of the proposer, as coming from God in some extraordinary way of communication. This way of discovering truths to men we call *revelation*.' Locke, *An Essay concerning Human Understanding*, IV. xviii. 2.

ing of the eternal and mysterious, exaggerates the *diastasis* between time and eternity because of the strength of his opposition to the rationalist's stress on reason and temporality. There is without doubt something in that. But that such a one-sidedness is characteristic of Newman's position as a whole is revealed by features of his thought which are not to be accounted for solely in terms of such a reaction. A brief examination of two instances of his treatment of central Christian dogmas will indicate something of the deep-seatedness of the gulf.

The first is one we have already met, the doctrine of the Trinity. In order to do more than repeat the allusions to his treatment of that subject in Tract Seventy-Three, we turn to what he makes of it in the *Grammar of Assent*. The argument of that work, it will be remembered, centres on the distinction between 'real' – by which is chiefly meant concerned with the concrete and particular – and 'notional' apprehension and assent – that of the abstract and theoretical. Newman illustrates the distinction by references to the doctrine of the Trinity. First, he affirms that the Catholic dogma of the Trinity is that 'this essential characteristic of His Nature (sc. as personal) is reiterated in three distinct ways or modes; so that the Almighty God ... has Three Personalities ... a Divine Three ...'. As such, the dogma is 'notional', a revelation to be accepted on faith as the eternal truth of God.[8] It is notional as belonging to the eternal world, as, so to speak, coming down directly from heaven, and is therefore not the object of rational exploration. Rather, it takes logical form only 'as it is a number of propositions, taken one by one', so that it is not possible to assent rationally to the whole, 'because, though we can image the separate propositions, we cannot image them altogether'.[9] (That last sentence is itself a revealing and surprisingly rationalist conception of what it is to conceive and assent to a proposition. How far must we be able to 'image' something if we are to find it *conceivable*?)

Second, and on the other hand, Newman argues that it can be shown that particular elements of the set of propositions that go to make up the dogma of the Trinity are 'really' apprehensible. 'That systematised whole is the object of

[8] Newman, *Grammar*, p. 85.
[9] Newman, *Grammar*, p. 88.

notional assent, and its propositions, one by one, are the objects of real.'[10] In spelling out what he means by these objects of real apprehension, Newman appeals largely to the particularities of Scripture, to the economy of salvation. Thus in this work too there emerges the dialectic between time and eternity. It is not that Newman fails entirely to relate the two. His thought is far more subtle than to posit an absolute gulf between the two sides of his dialectic. Rather, his tendency is to make the relations between the two more opaque than need be: to use the concept of ecclesiastical authority as the means of crossing an otherwise unbridgeable epistemological divide.

The other illustration of Newman's problematic treatment of the relation of eternity and time is to be found in his christology. One effect of the form the dialectic has taken has taken in Western theology is to be found in a recurring feature of much traditional christology, in which such stress is placed on the divinity of Christ that his humanity, although asserted, appears to be overwhelmed and effectively to play no substantive part in the drama of salvation. It is this which gives the moments of truth to the arguments of Newman's rationalist opponents, under whose impetus the 'quest of the historical Jesus' took place. It must be acknowledged that Newman's fundamental rejection of the shape the modernist quest took has been amply justified by history. 'Mr Abbott, starting with the earthly existence of our Lord, does but enlarge upon the doctrine that a man is God' (p. 75). A typical nineteenth-century christology is indeed one of Jesus as a divinised man, in which some conception of divinity is reached by magnifying or stressing certain human characteristics of Jesus. Nevertheless, it must also be acknowledged that Newman's own christology justifies suspicions that the traditional form of the doctrine endangers the teaching of the full humanity of the saviour. In his rebuttals of Abbott, Newman uses many phrases which can be taken in an orthodox manner, but which do appear to make the humanity of Jesus a cipher, a passive instrument of the eternal Word: 'His personality is in His Godhead' (p. 86); 'The Son of God made flesh, though a man, is beyond comparison with other men; His person is not human ...' (p. 87).

---

[10] Newman, *Grammar*, p. 91.

Thus it is that, while Newman rightly suspects his opponents of limiting revelation to its temporal manifestations, they could in their turn rightly suspect him of evading the implications of the historical events in which God makes himself known. The presupposition that the two share, accordingly, is that, because time and eternity are incompatible realms of being, a measure of choice is required between them. For the rationalist, the eternal may be known only as being in some way a function of temporal things; for the traditional Augustinian, eternity can be apprehended, if at all, only the other side of or outside of the temporal. Of Newman, as of Augustine, it must be asked whether his thought is truly incarnational, truly able to conceive God as involved in time and space, and consequently to conceive of time and space as patient of taking the shape of the eternal. One, apparently almost chance, statement of Newman's in his *Apologia* suggests that there is in this respect a real parallel between him and Augustine. Speaking of his 1838 pamphlet on the real presence, Newman comments: 'The fundamental idea is consonant to that to which I had been so long attached; it is the denial of the existence of space except as a subjective idea of our minds.'[11] If we compare here Augustine's wondering in the *Confessions*,[12] 'whether it [time] is an extension of the mind itself', we shall find the weak spot of all Augustinian thought. If time and space are projections of our minds, rather than qualifications of the objective or real world, how may we affirm that the temporal and spatial Jesus of Nazareth is the real presence of God to the world? It is from such a point of view that rationalism and dogmatism appear to be but two sides of the one coin, the one opting for time and reason, the other for eternity and faith. Both tend to assume that it is finally necessary to come down on one side or the other of the dialectical divide.

V   *Conclusion*

As the modernist fashion takes its course, Newman's protests

[11] J. H. Newman, *Apologia pro Vita Sua*, edited by M. J. Svaglic (Oxford: Oxford University Press, 1967), p. 74.
[12] Augustine, *Confessions*, xi. 26.

against rationalism appear more and more justified. With the benefit of another century of debate, however, it is also apparent that the mere assertion of dogma is an inadequate response to the crisis. But such a consideration raises a question. Is it not anachronistic to criticise a theologian with such benefit of hindsight? Is Newman, a nineteenth-century Catholic, being belaboured with weapons forged in later disputes and partly with his assistance? There are undoubtedly elements of truth in the objection. But a question is thereby raised about Newman's place in the history of theology.

The fact is that Newman was not alone, nor was he the first to engage in intellectual struggle with the forces of the Enlightenment. As we have seen in the previous chapter, a generation before Samuel Taylor Coleridge had done work whose sympathetic appropriation would have enabled Newman to sharpen his perception of what was at stake. In the area of the relation of faith and reason, and in his elaboration of an approach to the trinitarian basis of all thought and reality, Coleridge had engaged with the very topics which Newman was later to treat as if he were beginning anew. But, as we have also seen, he early wrote Coleridge out of his life.[13] Once again, we witness Newman's tendency to so strong an opposition to rationalism that the elements of truth in the modern protest against the past are ignored.

One major difference between Coleridge and Newman, as we have seen, was in Coleridge's attempt to think things whole, to relate what could be related. Without doubt, this did at times lead him into trouble. But now that the question of the nature of reason is being raised again, his more open conception of the relation of faith and reason may be of more benefit than Newman's rather rigid divide. While Newman would have been glad to see the pretensions of modern rationalism called into question by what is called postmodernism, he would have disliked its glorying in flux and difference. While he would have liked its apparent granting of rights to particularity, he would not have been comfortable with its relativising of the truth of Christian dogma. What is needed to engage with the challenge of the end of modernism, if it is the end, is a combination of

---

[13] Above, pp. 8f.

Newman's firm hold on the tradition with Coleridge's willingness to engage with any thought that came his way. As things turned out, Newman was less able than Coleridge to take into his system the best elements of modernity. In that respect, it must be said that he represents a step backwards. In other respects, however, as we have seen, he was an acute observer of the fact that the modernist denial of tradition and dogma is finally a denial of Christianity, as well as the author of a move in the direction of a conception of personal knowledge whose development is the responsibility of later generations.

We move to the topic of the next chapter with another major difference between the two, which was their assessment of the Reformation. Coleridge, for whom Luther was a major spiritual guide, was able to incorporate the thought of the Reformers into a broadly orthodox Anglican position. He was therefore able to take a more synoptic view of the influences that formed English Christianity, and a more balanced approach to the tradition as a whole. Some of the major influences upon Newman, on the other hand, saw in the Reformation simply another form of the modernist enemy. But that is a mistake, though one that is often made.[14] When we come to the matter of the development of doctrine, which Newman made distinctively his own, we shall find that an adequate account of Christian doctrinal history cannot be essayed without giving fairer attention to the Reformers than the Oxford Movement was able to give.

---

[14] We shall see in chapter 8 something of the unique contribution that the Reformers had to make to theology.

CHAPTER 3

THE DEVELOPMENT OF CHRISTIAN DOCTRINE

Karl Barth's understanding of the theological task[1]

I *The idea of development*

The notion of the development of doctrine has a dubious history. Developed by Newman in part to justify his stance in a confessional dispute, to use it is to run the danger of imposing the needs of the moment on one's conception of the theological task. Worse, it is too close for comfort to the modern, and now almost everywhere discredited, idea of progress. It appears to assimilate theology either to an old-fashioned view of science as a discipline whose history shows a steady improvement, or to ideas of the evolution of societies into something necessarily better for the passage of time and liberal social engineering. The wars and tyrannies of the twentieth century should certainly make us beware of that, while it is not necessarily to theology's benefit to be too closely assimilated to science, for various reasons, among them the fact that, although it must speak in the context of the culture of the day, it has not always profited the discipline when it has borrowed uncritically from it.

And yet, it seems impossible to conceive of theology without some notion of progress. Christian theologians are related to at least some of those who have preceded them, and must necessarily do things differently, perhaps in a way betokening a deeper engagement with the subject-matter. If that does take place, it is a deepening made possible by the work of their

[1] First published in the *Scottish Journal of Theology* 25 (1972), 171–80. Revised, chiefly by the addition of opening paragraphs and concluding section.

predecessors, on whose shoulders they stand – to use a hackneyed but indispensable metaphor. While there must be a real sense in which theologians can only seek to do the same thing in a different context, it is surely sometimes justifiable to believe that they can say something better than some of their predecessors, whether this is conceived as saying the same things more intelligibly and authoritatively, or saying something that has not been said before. In what sense there might be conceived to be development will concern us at the end of the chapter. In the mean time, interest must centre not only on whether a theologian believes development to be possible, but also and chiefly on his conception of the character of that development. There may be a model of some kind in mind, or possibly a number of models, more or less successfully integrated. Whatever they are, they will be aids to writers' understanding of their place in history, of their relation to those events that they take to be significant for their place, and of the reasons for the significance of those events.

That this is more than simply a question of the modern idea of progress becomes clear when we remember that Karl Barth's view of the theologian's task reaches its developed form in conversation with Anselm of Canterbury.[2] In view of his repeated assertions of the importance of his book on Anselm in the development of his theology,[3] it can be assumed that he is at least inclined to make his own many of the things he says about Anselm. 'We are ... justified in ascribing to Anselm the explicit notion of progress in theology ...'.[4] Of interest is his careful emphasis on the fact that it is not automatic progress: 'That the perfectibility of theology implies for Anselm both stop and start cannot be ignored.'[5] Much of the Anselmian material would allow for an understanding of the development of doctrine which sees it as the articulation of a fixed and unchanging deposit of faith. But the warning against automatic progress

---

[2] Karl Barth, *Anselm: Fides Quaerens Intellectum. Anselm's Proof of the Existence of God in the Context of his Theological Scheme*, translated by Ian W. Robertson (London: SCM Press, 1960).

[3] For example, Barth, *Anselm*, p. 11 and *Church Dogmatics*, translation edited by G. W. Bromiley and T. F. Torrance (Edinburgh: T. & T. Clark, 1957–69), 2/1, p. 4.

[4] Barth, *Anselm*, p. 32; cf. p. 31.

[5] Barth, *Anselm*, p. 32.

would prepare us to beware of some of the implications of evolutionary or organic models, at least in so far as they suggest progress built into the very activity of the Church's thinking. Further, there are theological reasons for anticipating that Barth would have very little sympathy with the view that theology is concerned with the development or articulation of a deposit of doctrine. For a deposit theory is appropriate chiefly in terms of God understood in substantial, albeit analogously substantial, terms, who communicates a fixed substance of teaching to the Church, while Barth's analogy of event rules out any such conception. 'To its very deepest depths, God's Godhead consists in the fact that it is an event ... the event of his action ... ',[6] so that theology can be conceived only as the event of interpretation that responds to the event of revelation. It may, however, be true that he has failed to carry through the radical reshaping of the doctrine of God suggested in his exposition of the doctrine of the Trinity in *Church Dogmatics* 1/1, and this will be argued to have affected his understanding of the development of doctrine.[7] For it is at least prima facie reasonable to suggest that our view of the nature of God will have close relations with our understanding of the possibilities for the development of doctrine.

II   *Barth, dogmatics and development*

In the opening pages of the *Church Dogmatics* there is indeed a criticism of the deposit theory. 'The task of dogmatics is ... not merely the combination, repetition, and transcription of a number of already present "truths of revelation", once and for all expressed and authentically defined as to wording and meaning.' Barth proceeds to attack the Roman Catholic view as he finds it in Diekamp, because 'by "truth of revelation" we are here to understand the "Apostolic deposit" infallibly set forth

[6] Barth, *Church Dogmatics* 2/1, p. 263; cf. 2/1, pp. 339–83 and 406–23; R. W. Jenson, *God After God: The God of the Past and of the Future as Seen in the Work of Karl Barth* (Indianapolis and New York: Bobbs Merrill, 1969), pp. 95–113; and E. Jüngel, *Gottes Sein ist im Werden* (Tübingen: J. C. B. Mohr, 1966).

[7] Especially important is Jenson's argument (*God After God*, pp. 168–75) that Barth's trinitarian formulation is directed towards the past, and that its goal in the Holy Spirit 'remains an occasional assertion' (p. 173).

by the Church's living teaching staff ... This "deposit" is thus identical with a sum of sacred texts. Dogmatics is faced with the task of "mediating a fuller understanding of these truths by inferences" (Diekamp).' Barth's claim is that this doctrine presupposes that 'in this task of "understanding" there can be no question of anything more than a transcription in a somewhat higher sense'.[8] The theologian can say the same things better, but no more. The objection to this is theological.

> The concept 'truths of revelation', in the sense of Latin propositions given and sealed once and for all by divine authority in wording and meaning, is theologically impossible, if it be the case that revelation has its truth in the free decision of God, made once for all in Jesus Christ, and for that very reason and in that way strictly future for us ... Truth of revelation is the freely acting God, himself and quite alone.[9]

That is to say, the deposit theory of the development of doctrine is ruled out by the character of God as event. Of course, the deposit would still be possible if there were only one event, and that in the past. But this freedom of God is triune and has an eschatological orientation – note especially the phrase 'strictly future for us' – and this appears again in criticisms of an idea associated with the deposit theory of development. This is the notion of an objective principle of knowledge, held to be found 'in the form of Holy Scripture, Church tradition, and the living teaching apostolate of the Church' to which there corresponds the subjective principle of knowledge, 'found in the form of the *fides catholica*, which receives the revelation ...' These, he says, 'take for granted that the essence of the Church, Jesus Christ, no longer the free Lord of their existence ... is finally limited and conditioned by definite concrete formulations of man's understanding of his revelation and of the faith that grasps it'.[10]

Another associated view is the conception of theology as a system of axioms, and that too is attacked, in similar terms.[11] It

[8] Barth, *Church Dogmatics* 1/1, p. 15.
[9] Barth, *Church Dogmatics* 1/1, p. 16.
[10] Barth, *Church Dogmatics* 1/1, p. 43.
[11] Barth, *Church Dogmatics* 1/1, pp. 304–5.

may appear that this is to labour the point, but this further reference is justified by the fact that discussion is brought explicitly into an eschatological context. For an understanding of the nature of dogmatics as a system of axioms is to bring an end to enquiry, to foreclose the freedom of God to say more about himself. 'If inquiry ceased, if instead of dogmas and dogmatic propositions dogma itself took the boards ... dogmatics would be at an end and the Kingdom of God would have dawned.' And he comments, 'To that extent ... one may term dogma an "eschatological concept".'[12] The final truth belongs to the future: because of this we are not freed from further enquiry, and that for Barth means from the question as to the truth and the obedience of the Church's thinking.[13]

How, then, do we stand in relation to the past? What do we do with it? 'Starting from the question how men spoke about God in the Church yesterday, dogmatics asks how this should be done tomorrow.'[14] The assumption is that we may be able to say something that has not been said before:

> Scientific dogmatics has to busy itself with the criticism and revision of Church proclamation, not merely with a repetitive exposition of it. Dogmatics cannot merely be an historical report on the classical expression of the faith proclaimed at this or that past period of the Church ... Its scientific quality consists not so much in confirming as rather in disturbing Church proclamation ... The real Church is waiting for something else than certification.[15]

So far, then, there is little more than a clear view of what the dogmatician is *not* doing. He is not tied to the past, at least not in the way in which the deposit theory believes him to be. What I believe to be lying hidden in the words of Barth, waiting to jump out but never quite able to do so, is the view that the theologian is tied not to the past – or perhaps we should say, not only to the past – but to the future. The question to be asked is whether there emerges from the pages of the *Church Dogmatics* a picture of the Church's thinking moving forward,

[12] Barth, *Church Dogmatics* 1/1, pp. 308–9.
[13] Barth, *Church Dogmatics* 1/1, p. 315.
[14] Barth, *Church Dogmatics* 1/1, p. 86.
[15] Barth, *Church Dogmatics* 1/1, pp. 322–3.

under the impact of the promises of God, or whether the picture remains obscure because of an equivocation in thought between a static-model – if not a deposit, then something like it – and the eschatological model which is trying to break out. 'We are inquiring into the presence of the Word of God between the times ... '.[16] But does Barth take the latter of the two times seriously enough, or does he so fail to carry through his programme that he is left not with a deposit theory but with a doctrine of the recurring present that leaves the theologian's task and position very much the same as that he criticises – the repetition of the old in new words? In the sentence previous to the one just cited he makes an observation in which the problem is clearly revealed. He is speaking of the concrete revelation of God – that is, for Barth, the event God is – and in that we have to do 'with the very concrete bracket which encloses ... a definite past, to wit the epiphany of Jesus Christ, and with equal regularity a definite future, to wit, the recurring moment in which men shall hear the Word of God'.[17]

Here the discussion is best continued with the help of two comments from very different sources on the character of Barth's theology. The first is from Jürgen Moltmann,[18] and concerns Barth's concept of revelation. Moltmann cites an important passage from the *Church Dogmatics* (2/1, p. 635, part of the discussion of God's attribute of eternity), in which Barth criticises his own non-eschatological understanding of time in the *Commentary on Romans*. But Moltmann wonders whether Barth had really carried through his revision when he formulated his mature understanding of revelation: 'Can the impression be allowed to stand that "self-revelation of God" means "the pure presence of God", and "eternal presence of God in time", a "present without any future"?'[19] In our context the point is of enormous significance. If revelation is understood as certain timeless acts of God – though I think this is far from being the whole of what Barth has to say[20] – is not the view of

---

[16] Barth, *Church Dogmatics* 1/1, p. 334.

[17] Ibid.

[18] Jürgen Moltmann, *Theology of Hope*, translated by James W. Leitch (London: SCM Press, 1967), pp. 45ff.

[19] Moltmann, *Theology*, pp. 57f.

[20] See Barth, *Church Dogmatics* 1/1, pp. 373ff., for a stress on concrete historicity.

the dogmatician's work little removed from a deposit model? The deposit is different, but it remains a deposit: a series of events, with the Jesus event the paradigm case and epistemological key, about which we can learn more and more, not so much by deduction, as in the old model, but this time by induction – certainly an improvement, but scarcely revolutionary in its implications. The treasure is, as it were, scattered about the biblical field: we know what to look for, and there is always the chance that we may unearth another piece of the well-known coin. But it is another piece of the same or very similar coin, rather than anything new.

The second comment is equally revealing, and is made by Hans Küng.[21] Barth, he says, '... in Volume 1/2 – despite all his attempts at disengagement – ... comes dangerously close to the Catholic conception when he defines the relationship between Scripture and tradition'. Barth is, not surprisingly, insistent that 'authority in the Church is restricted to an indirect and relative and formal authority' beside the authority of Scripture, which founds that secondary authority.[22] For his part, Küng would interpret Trent in a similar manner, though it may be suspected that he is not himself altogether free of ambiguity.[23] And it must be noted that for Barth there does not appear to be a difference *in principle* between this authority and others: '... Holy Scripture may have a singular authority in the Church but that authority is still mediate, relative and formal'.[24] It is still human, and so not in itself divine, whatever its possibilities for *becoming* revelation. And it can become this because of its character as witness.[25] It is because it points to revelation – that is, to those events that can be described as God – that Scripture is granted authority by the theologian.

The crucial question then is, what happens when those events are taken up into the Church's tradition of learning? Barth's account of what should *not* happen is directly analogous to his strictures on the deposit theory of doctrinal progress. The

[21] Hans Küng, *Justification: The Doctrine of Karl Barth and a Catholic Reflection*, translated by T. Collins et al. (London: Burns & Oates, 1964), p. 107.
[22] Barth, *Church Dogmatics* 1/2, p. 538.
[23] Barth, *Church Dogmatics* 1/2, pp. 108ff. On p. 109, for example, he says that tradition 'revolves around, in fact gravitates towards, Sacred Scripture ...'.
[24] Barth, *Church Dogmatics* 1/2, p. 540.
[25] Barth, *Church Dogmatics* 1/2, p. 541.

Church should not attempt to take revelation – that is, the free God – into her possession and treat it as a piece of property. On this understanding of the process, 'Divine revelation must be an original possession of the Church enabling it to declare with certainty where and what revelation is and therefore where and what the witness of revelation is.'[26] If this happens, revelation is limited to the past, and cannot be taken seriously as a present event. 'There will then be possible a cultus and theology of the revelation which, according to the sacred books, once took place long ago, a revelation which at bottom does not affect us because it cannot be revelation to us, but which always surprises and claims and solemnises us from afar . . .'.[27]

And so Barth's objection to what he takes to be the Roman Catholic view of the place of tradition alongside Scripture must then be seen not as an arbitrary biblicism but as arising from the belief that once any human person or Church (and he includes Liberal Protestantism in his strictures) claims control of Scripture they bind and tame the God to whom Scripture points, placing him securely in the past where he cannot disturb the peace. But, 'the grace directed to the Church cannot be transformed into a possession and glory of the Church'.[28] Again, the analogy to the rejection of the deposit theory is unmistakable. But then Barth asks: is this not to resist what God has in fact given to the Church? Does it not amount to a refusal to accept the grace of God? (And it is interesting that Küng misses 'the final obedient and faithful commitment' in Barth in this very context.)[29]

In reply to his own questions, Barth appeals to Scripture, but in a way reminiscent of the earlier references to the freedom of God: 'His Word . . . is given to the Church in such a way that it is always his Word as against its word . . . It stands over against the authority of the Church.'[30] But how can this be justified? Barth appeals to the unique position of the apostles and prophets:[31] to revert to the metaphor, it is with them that the pieces of

[26] Barth, *Church Dogmatics* 1/2, p. 542.
[27] Barth, *Church Dogmatics* 1/2, p. 545.
[28] Barth, *Church Dogmatics* 1/2, p. 577.
[29] Barth, *Church Dogmatics* 1/2, p. 115.
[30] Barth, *Church Dogmatics* 1/2, p. 579.
[31] Barth, *Church Dogmatics* 1/2, p. 544.

treasure have been deposited, and from them that new pieces may be found. It is here that we can begin to see why Küng can allege the dangerous proximity of the two views. For Barth's 'men of the Old and New Testaments' read 'the apostolic succession' or 'the papacy' and the following passage is equally intelligible:

> They and they alone in the Church can have direct and absolute and material authority, the authority of the sign which is given with the revelation itself. And they do not need to claim it ... They have it. For without them there would be no Church. Their existence is the concrete form of the existence of Jesus Christ himself in which the Church has the foundation of its being.[32]

From one point of view, we are faced with a clear choice between the two conceptions of authority that have divided the Church since the Reformation. And yet, when it comes to a discussion of the relation between the two authorities, the gap begins to narrow, as the very possibility of Küng's exegesis of Trent reveals. While Küng interprets Trent in such a way as to minimise Protestant offence, Barth for his part is careful to avoid anti-traditionalism. He points to the authority of Athanasius and Augustine for the Reformers,[33] and observes that 'what is certain is that the authority of the Reformers in the Evangelical Church is analogous to that of the "Church Fathers" ... in Roman Catholicism'.[34]

The question to be asked, accordingly, is whether both the view Barth attacks and his suggested revision equally necessitate an excessively backwards-looking view of the development of doctrine, the one entertaining the possibility of an ever greater knowledge of an eternally fixed mathematical quantity, the other an ever greater knowledge of repeated events of revelation, understood as Moltmann suggests. Whatever the advantages of the latter model, the difference appears to be one of degree rather than principle. In each case everything significant has happened already. There can be no expectation of new knowledge conceived as coming, to use the modern

[32] Barth, *Church Dogmatics* 1/2, p. 580.
[33] Barth, *Church Dogmatics* 1/2, p. 614.
[34] Barth, *Church Dogmatics* 1/2, p. 606.

jargon, from God's open future. And therefore it is hardly
surprising that their views on the place of tradition are difficult
to separate.

III   *Pneumatological considerations*

But this is in some tension with what the New Testament leads
us to expect, particularly if we refer to its teaching on the Holy
Spirit. R. W. Jenson's argument that in Barth the Holy Spirit
tends to get squeezed out of the trinitarian scheme has already
been mentioned, and this must be significant, for it is in
association with the Spirit that we should naturally wish to
understand doctrinal development. John 16.13 brings together
the two themes that have already been suggested, both as being
latent in Barth and as being crucial for a discussion of this
topic: the Holy Spirit and our anticipation, in doctrine, of the
future. 'However, when he comes who is the Spirit of truth, he
will make known to you the things that are coming (τὰ
ἐρχόμενα).' This conception of the Spirit as the one who
enables us to anticipate that which is to come, rather than
merely to learn more about what is past, is present in Paul as
well: see for example his use of the term ἀρραβών in 2
Corinthians 1.22, translated by NEB as 'pledge of what is to
come', and ἀπαρχή in Romans 8.23, in an explicitly eschatological context. And so for the Christian theologian what is to
come is at least as important as the deposit or events of the past
that are repeated in the present, for it is little exaggeration to
say that for the New Testament the interesting events are those
that point to the future.[35] Matthew may appear to be neutral as
between past and future when he says in 13.52 'When ... a
teacher of the law has become a learner in the Kingdom of
Heaven, he is like a householder who can produce from his
store both the new and the old', but he does allow for the new.
And there can be little doubt in view of its closing verses of the

[35] See R. W. Jenson's analysis of the primitive Christian confession, 'Jesus is
Lord'. 'When this sentence is unpacked, it reveals a set of assertions about
Jesus' future acts. That Jesus is "kurios", "Lord", means, in the summary
language of the Creed, that "he shall come again with glory to judge both the
quick and the dead"' (*The Knowledge of Things Hoped For* (New York: Oxford
University Press, 1969), p. 148).

future orientation of the Book of Revelation, a book whose content is revealed to the author when the Spirit whom we are discussing had 'caught [him] up' (1.10), and he is told, 'Write down therefore what you have seen, what is now, and what is hereafter' (1.19).

And it is not only seers of apostolic times who are to receive the Spirit, and to write 'what is hereafter'. The Fourth Gospel is quite explicit that the promise is for the Church, too, and again speaks in a trinitarian context: 'In truth ... I tell you, he who has faith in me will do what I am doing; and he will do greater things still, because I am going to the Father' (14.12). For John, Jesus' going to the Father is the occasion of the coming of the eschatological Spirit. The Christian, and so also the theologian, who is one variety of Christian, obtains his direction from the past – 'faith in me' – but he cannot remain there, just as Jesus cannot remain with the disciples if they are to go on from where they are.[36] It is this Spirit who enables them to anticipate 'the things that are coming', and thus to do 'greater things still' than Jesus has done. The Spirit, then, is the one who moves the Church through history, and it is to be noted that one of the functions of the Spirit in Acts is of enabling the Church to make radical and unexpected innovations in its missionary out-reach.[37] Theologians, then, should be seen as both part of and makers of this history, for it is possible for them, in the Spirit, to anticipate that time when 'my knowledge will be whole, like God's knowledge of me'.[38] But they can only anticipate it by grace, not achieve it or even be sure of their place in that historical movement: even the best anticipations remain pro-visional, and subject to judgement.[39]

In the light of this, I do not see why we cannot make use of both the deposit and the Barthian models in our under-standing of the development of doctrine, so long as they are both put firmly in their place; that is, under the promise of the Spirit and the coming judgement of God. Both the biblical writers and the Church's teachers are then seen as bearers of

---

[36] John 16.7, 'If I do not go ...'. It is *theologically forbidden* that they should remain where they are.

[37] For example, the missions to Samaria, 8.15–17, and to Gentiles, 10.45.

[38] 1 Cor. 13.12. Cf. Barth's point that dogma is an 'eschatological concept'.

[39] Cf. 1 Cor. 3.12ff.

the promises of God, and in their own way anticipations of his future. But why should not pilgrims travelling to a goal carry a certain amount of baggage, just so much as is necessary for them to reach their destination; some items more essential to them than others, some more subject to obsolescence in the light of new findings on the way? It is, after all, precisely on the basis of the tradition he has received (ὅ καὶ παρέλαβον – 1 Cor. 15.3) that Paul refuses to allow the church at Corinth to be content with the wisdom it thought it had attained. That is to say, the past has its place, but the Christian's past is relativised by that to which it points: in Barthian terms, we might say Jesus Christ as both (past) historical and (future) eschatological revelation.

The thesis of this chapter, then, so far as Barth is concerned, is that his stress on the freedom of God has pointed the way to a historical and eschatological understanding of the movement of the Church's teaching about her faith. But the question remains as to whether God is free enough on this understanding, and whether Barth can see the theologian as open to do the kind of things promised in the New Testament passages concerned with the Holy Spirit. To mix the metaphors once more: has he rightly criticised the idea of the theologian as a kind of theological bank manager, jealous guard of his charge, who can at most accumulate a little interest against inflation, only to replace him with a theological archaeologist, burrowing around for something he already knows to be there? In both cases, theology is in danger of being seen primarily as defence of the faith, and God as somehow in need of defence. Once again, this can hardly be the whole truth about Karl Barth, after whom no one doctrine can be the same again, so radically new is his approach to theology and his insight into so many Christian beliefs. But as with much of his theology, the tendency to underplay the part of the eschatological Spirit does affect his theology materially for the worse.

IV *Enrichment*

What conclusions, if any, should be drawn about the possibilities of a conception of the development of doctrine? If we remember that the Spirit is the Spirit of Church and community, we shall beware of too individualistic a treatment of the matter. The notion of development should not be construed individualistically, as if the question to ask concerned whether this individual or that has improved on the performance of a predecessor. What is of interest is whether we can consider that there can be a history of theology of such a kind that *development* can be conceived to have taken place in it. Here, two rival conceptions are possible. One is the modernist, according to which most teaching before the modern age is necessarily out of date, so that progress consists in being critical of it: in saying what can no longer be believed. On such an account, 'progress' is, with much of the modern world, seen as a kind of freeing from past superstition – a view itself highly superstitious in its high regard for modern enlightenment. It necessarily entails a rejection of much of the history of theology as a mistake.

The second alternative is one that reverses the pattern by treating the modern critical era as an aberration from the main path. It is the one that will be pursued here, because it does allow some understanding of the history of the *whole* Christian tradition as a story with something like a developing history. To elaborate it, we must disregard accounts of theological history which discount important episodes as mere distortion, as happens with a view of the patristic era as a succumbing to Greek philosophical obscuring of the simple gospel, with a modernist view that virtually everything before the seventeenth century is impossibly naive, and with a Tractarian view that the Reformation was a kind of precursor of rationalism. Put these aside, and a kind of process of development can be discerned. In summary, it can be held that it fell to the theologians of the early centuries to hammer out the crucial doctrines of God and Christ, so that they developed doctrines of the Trinity and of the person of Christ which remain foundational for Christian theology, even if their detailed treatment must sometimes come in question. The same degree of systematic attention was not given to the theology of the atonement, because accounts of salvation were not then being subjected to the kind of radical questioning which demanded conceptual clarification. This happened in the Middle Ages, when challenges to the rationality of the faith led to the first attempt to give systematic form to the doctrine, to its overall clarification and enrichment, though not without distortion also. Similarly, it can be argued that the difficulties over the human appropriation of salvation, brought to light by the sale of indulgences, evoked from Luther and Calvin new attention to, and deepening of, the doctrine of justification. In the nineteenth and twentieth centuries the crisis of rationality brought about by modernity has led to attention being given to epistemology, notably in the theologies of Schleiermacher and Barth.

This is not meant to be in any way exhaustive, but to give some examples of the way in which the history of theology can be read in a positive light, as a process in which distortions have occurred, often of such a kind as to evoke deeply considered responses. Heresy is the seed of great theology, as Irenaeus' struggles with the Gnostics make only too clear. But there are warning notes to be heard. The mention of Irenaeus and the Gnostics reminds us that his efforts were designed to *halt* what might have appeared to be the development of doctrine:

> It is fundamental to the logic of Irenaeus' argument that tradition cannot change, or grow or develop. It is not, in this sense, alive ... Bishops and teachers of the Church are not there to develop the tradition, they are there simply to hand it on ... W. Wigan Harvey ... refers pointedly, though anonymously, to John Henry Newman's book [twelve years after it was published]. 'At least here [in Irenaeus] ... there is no reserve made in favour of any theory of development ... A tradition with the potential to develop would ideally suit the gnostic cause, and be utterly fatal for Irenaeus.'[40]

The same is true of some developments which today serve the theology of modernism, which is in many of its manifestations chiefly another name for the Gnostic claim to know better than the tradition.

A more judicious expression of the position, especially in the light of the texts from the Fourth Gospel used earlier in the chapter, is found in some words of Francis Watson, written in the light of the same texts:

---

[40] Denis Minns, OP, *Irenaeus* (London: Geoffrey Chapman, 1994), p. 119.

It is, in fact, crucially important to achieve a correct balance between the assertion that the disclosure of truth lies in the future and the assertion that it lies in the past. What lies in the future is a true apprehension of what has already happened in the past; and revelation is thereby tied irrevocably to the historicity and particularity of human existence within the world and prevented from drifting away into gnostic fantasy. Conversely, however, the meaning of what happened in the past cannot simply be read out of that past, conveyed by means of an authoritative tradition.[41]

The point about Irenaeus, surely, is that his development of the tradition came about by his attempting to penetrate into its truth, not by his trying to develop or improve it. 'In the process of theological knowledge ... *new* can only mean something like *better* knowledge of that which is already given.'[42]

For this reason, in place of a concept of development, I want to suggest an alternative: that of enrichment. Development suggests a relatively unproblematic, continuing process. The fact is, however, that the history of doctrine is replete with examples of distortions and falling away from the possibilities represented by earlier teaching. The doctrine of creation suffered by losing the trinitarian thrust imparted to it by Irenaeus; the doctrine of election by contamination with mathematical ideas; and the doctrines of the person and work of Christ by lack of weight given to the saviour's humanity. But, it can be argued, and will be argued in chapters 8 to 10, that many of these doctrines have been enriched by contributions made by the theologians there expounded, particularly when they struggle to come to terms with the deficiencies they inherit. The encounter with shortcomings, whether deserving of the name of heresy or not, is the seed of renewal. We should seek to enrich the theological tradition as it passes through our hands; but whether what we do is enrichment or distortion – or a bit of

[41] Francis Watson, *Text, Church and World* (Edinburgh: T. & T. Clark, 1994), pp. 260–1.
[42] Eberhard Jüngel, *Theological Essays II*, edited by J. B. Webster (Edinburgh: T. & T. Clark, 1995), p. 43. The essay from which this sentence is taken is full of insights about 'development'.

both – is for the future to decide. But before we approach discussions of central dogmatic loci, four chapters are devoted to the knowledge and being of God as they are explored by Barth and others.

CHAPTER 4

THE KNOWLEDGE OF GOD
'No other Foundation' – one Englishman's reading of *Church Dogmatics* Chapter v[1]

I *The shaking of the foundations*

For the most part and despite exceptions, the English find it difficult to come to terms with the theology of Karl Barth. A recent paper by Daniel Hardy identifies the strongly naturalistic bent of English thought as the chief culprit:

> The English norms [sc. of knowledge] involve the use of naturalistic human knowledge as determinative of what can be believed. Employing these norms in interpreting Schleiermacher and Barth, however, makes them – and indeed most important theology – seem ... either to conflict with or to stretch the bounds of what is considered possible.[2]

Naturalism's predominance brings it about that where Barth is concerned a frequent English reaction is one of puzzlement that someone should commit intellectual suicide in so spectacular a fashion. It is indeed difficult to take seriously one who appears to be hell-bent on intellectual self-destruction. But it is also true that English naturalism is a variation, albeit a particularly dismal one, on a common Western tradition of rationalism. The dominance of ways of thinking created by the Enlightenment in recent times has made the appropria-

---

[1] First published in *Reckoning with Barth. Essays in Commemoration of the Centenary of Karl Barth's Birth*, edited by Nigel Biggar (London: Mowbray, 1988), pp. 61–79.
[2] Daniel W. Hardy, 'The English Tradition of Interpretation and the Reception of Schleiermacher and Barth in England', *Barth and Schleiermacher. Beyond the Impasse*, edited by J. Duke and R. Streetman (Minneapolis: Augsburg Fortress, 1988), p. 147.

tion of the work of a theologian like Barth doubly difficult, and the American Baptist theologian Bernard Ramm is surely right in seeing a major feature of Barth's programme to be an attempt to out-think that movement.[3] This chapter takes its orientation from Ramm's suggestion. A first task, accordingly, is to examine the particular Enlightenment themes which provide the background for Barth's thought; against that background we shall then move to examine some of the features he shares with others who seek to develop alternative directions.

The first general feature of the Enlightenment tradition is its individualism. The model thinker is Descartes, the one who sits alone, attempting to decide in solitude what may and may not be dignified with the name of knowledge. One of Descartes' working assumptions was that his route to knowledge would be more secure if he threw off all that he had obtained from his teachers and accepted only that which commended itself to his naked intellect. Since his time that has been the norm: what I as an individual can or cannot demonstrate, albeit with the use of the appropriate rational methods and criteria. Today individualism is one of the things that all right-thinking people reject, but it is important to be aware that influential representatives of non-individualistic epistemology remain rare: we are not sure if we know what it really involves. That is particularly true of recent theology, marked as it is by the oft-lamented absence of ecclesiology. Alluding again to English lack of comprehension of Schleiermacher and Barth, Hardy comments that 'While both conceive their primary focus of attention as the church's faith, the English understand this as *individual* faith found in members of the church.'[4]

The second feature is the Enlightenment's characteristic view of the relation of mind and reality. It is an epistemology of spatial distance, and has been depicted variously by its critics. For Rorty, it is characterised by its view of the mind as a kind of mirror reflecting only those parts or aspects of the world it is fitted to reflect, our 'Glassy Essence', deriving ultimately from

---

[3] Bernard Ramm, *After Fundamentalism. The Future of Evangelical Theology* (New York: Harper & Row, 1983), pp. 46f.
[4] Hardy, 'The English Tradition', p. 153.

Plato's *theoria*.[5] For Polanyi it is the idea of the godlike, disembodied spectator – a visual image again – with a bird's-eye view of what is happening 'below', rather like Aquinas' view of God's knowledge as the view of a landscape from a mountain.[6] This particular picture is associated with the way in which the subject of knowledge is related to the object: mind and thing confront each other statically, at a spatial distance from each other. The achievement of Berkeley – another thinker the English tend to misunderstand – was to attempt to replace that picture with another which attempts to make more sense of the relation of knower and known than that between inanimate object and intellectual subjects.[7]

The third feature of the modern tradition to which I want to allude is its foundationalism. This is the doctrine, which Ronald Thiemann's recent study has shown to be deeply ingrained in recent theological thought, that there are certain fundamental truths, concepts or axioms, known intuitively, which must be shown to underlie any putative expression of 'objective' knowledge.[8] *Knowledge* is that which is built on the foundations; anything else is not 'real' knowledge. The quest for foundations is an almost universal feature of post-Enlightenment Western thought, with the result that it is very difficult for us to disentangle ourselves from it. There is a deep-seated belief in the existence of an *intuitively* intellectual basis for all thought. There are differences from thinker to thinker in the conception of what the foundations are – such as in the differences between the philosophies labelled rationalist and empiricist – but foundationalism was, until very recent times, all-pervasive nevertheless. There is a theological critique in Ronald Thiemann's recent work, in which it was argued that foundationalism vitiates the thought of three such diverse theologians as Locke, Schleiermacher and Torrance. Whether or not Thie-

---

[5] Richard Rorty, *Philosophy and the Mirror of Nature* (Oxford: Blackwell, 1980), especially pp. 38ff.

[6] Michael Polanyi, *Personal Knowledge. Towards a Post-Critical Philosophy* (London: Routledge & Kegan Paul, 2nd edition 1962), pp. 139f. The reference is to Aquinas, *Summa Theologiae* I.14.3.

[7] Colin E. Gunton, *Enlightenment and Alienation. An Essay Towards a Trinitarian Theology* (Basingstoke: Marshall, Morgan & Scott, 1985), pp. 26ff.

[8] Ronald F. Thiemann, *Revelation and Theology. The Gospel as Narrated Promise* (Notre Dame, Indiana: University of Notre Dame Press, 1985), chapter 2.

mann is justified in all that he says, his book is another indication of the all-pervasiveness of the phenomenon.

In sum, it can be concluded that according to what was until very recently the almost unquestioned mainstream doctrine, knowledge is something (1) possessed by an *individual*, who (2) stands over against something which is conceived to be spatially distant. The spatial distance is bridged by bringing either the mind into conformity with the world ('realism') or the world into conformity with the mind ('idealism'). In either case, (3) the intellectual bridge between the two is provided by the foundational axioms which are conceived to link the mind with the world. In the next section, we shall begin an exploration of whether and how far it is right to understand Barth as a theologian who shared in the process of questioning the Enlightenment approach.

II   *Towards an alternative foundation*

In the remainder of this chapter two theses will be argued. The first is that Barth's theology is in part a conscious attempt to replace the Enlightenment project with something different. It was not altogether successful, for there are many remnants of the old syndrome, so that the achievement is something of a *tour de force*, plucked from the intellectual air by an act of intuitive genius and giving rise to half-baked accusations like that of Bonhoeffer that Barth's is a 'positivism of revelation'. The second is that the Enlightenment project has failed, because it does not register with the way we actually go about the world cognitively, and that therefore Barth's theology is to an extent justified by its fruits. The defence of the first thesis depends in part upon some borrowings from the thought of Michael Polanyi. There has developed in recent years something of a Polanyi cult, accompanied, as is often the case with cults, by an equally disdainful refusal on the part of those who do not share in it to take him seriously. I do not wish to share in that cult, but rather to draw from him certain aids to reflection, and in particular, to begin with, a broad contrast between two fundamentally different approaches to knowledge, which can be called the critical and the post-critical. The former, as we have seen, has among its distinguishing features that it is an epistemology of spatial distance. In such an epistemology, the essence of knowledge is the proposition, in which the distant object is described in words which attempt to mirror what is there. The emphasis is on 'knowledge that' rather than knowledge by acquaintance.

In the Polanyian approach the reverse is the case. The central metaphor here is that of 'indwelling'. The knower knows the world by indwelling body, tools, concepts and the like, which, by being known tacitly, become the bridge by which other parts of the world can be known. It is tempting to speculate that the origin of the metaphor – and it must be remembered that it is a metaphor, so that the limits of its explanatory power are recognised – is ultimately in the Fourth Gospel, where we find an extended use of the notion of knowledge by indwelling.[9] (It is when this fact is overlooked that there is talk of a 'Gnostic' bias in that gospel.) The Father and Son know each other by mutual and asymmetrical indwelling. Briefly to look forward to Barth, we can already here discern a theme emerging: for Barth, the fundamental reality of our being is our indwelling in Christ. But, to leave that on one side, the point for our purposes is that in place of an ontology of spatial distance, we find one of acquaintance. Knowledge is a relation of knower and known before it is propositional. Here there is a link to be seen with the famous Polanyian slogan: we know more than we can tell. Knowledge is something achieved by personal beings with the flexibility to adapt themselves to the world around and to express part – but only a part – of the relationship conceptually.

The crucial presupposition of such a conception of knowledge is that the relationship is prior to any conceptual expression of it. It is therefore not possible to justify the relationship a priori. You cannot prove that you have it before you come to speak about it. According to Polanyi, all knowing is a form of faith seeking understanding: faith in his case meaning a committed orientation to and indwelling within the world and our

---

[9] I have realised since first writing this paper that I owe the point to Professor T. F. Torrance.

language. There is no other route to knowledge. It must be stressed that what is being attempted here is not a proof of the position being taken, although there is surprising support for something of the kind in recent philosophy.[10] Rather, a framework is being constructed with the help of which Barth's distinctive theological epistemology can be approached.

The concept of knowledge as a relationship of indwelling in a specific subject-matter has a number of important consequences. In the first place, it is subversive of all epistemologies of spatial distance because it presupposes that the world is not distant. We live in it, and in our words and concepts as part of it. Second, it is subversive of the choice between realism and idealism as the Enlightenment tradition presents and attempts to compel it, because it presupposes on the one hand that the world is the kind of reality that can be known (that is to say, related to); and on the other that we are the kind of beings that indwell the world rationally. Again, to indicate in advance that such a consideration is not irrelevant to the interpretation of Barth it is only sufficient to refer to his important paper from 1929, the time when he was developing his mature theological method, 'Schicksal und Idee in der Theologie'.[11] Here Barth is quite explicit that theology must take elements of truth from both realism and idealism if it is to come to terms with the actual relation of the knower to God.

Third, the Polanyian conception of knowledge in terms of indwelling presupposes at once the actuality and limits of propositional knowledge. Knowledge is not as such propositional; but propositions are a way in which to express the articulate level of our knowledge. By contrast, the Enlightenment has hoodwinked us into believing that there are two classes of proposition, those adequate to the world – because they are justified according to the canons of the foundational axioms – and everything else. In face of this increasingly discredited view, a Polanyian theory claims both the success and

---

[10] See especially Richard J. Bernstein, *Beyond Objectivism and Realism. Science, Hermeneutics and Praxis* (Philadelphia: University of Pennsylvania Press, 1985) and R. W. Newell, *Objectivity, Empiricism and Truth* (London: Routledge & Kegan Paul, 1986).

[11] Karl Barth, 'Schicksal und Idee in der Theologie', *Theologische Fragen und Antworten* (Evangelischer Verlag A G Zollikon, 1957), pp. 54–72.

the relative inadequacy of all conceptual expression. Fourth, and as a development of the third point, a post-critical conception of knowledge liberates us for an appreciation of the diversity of possible forms of knowledge which derive from the diversity and variety of forms of relationship. Not all relationships are the same, and therefore different ones generate different forms of articulate expression. (That is, of course, another anti-foundationalist point.)

Some of the differences can be brought to mind if we consider the different measures of reciprocity to be found in human cognitive activity. At one extreme, we find relationships in which there is minimal reciprocity, for instance a laboratory experiment upon a chemical. Even that, however, does not reduce the object of knowledge to pure passivity if it is to create conditions in which nature can, so to speak, give up her secrets to the enquiring mind. In other words, there is rarely if ever a time when the knower is purely active, the object entirely passive. There is a measure of reciprocity even there, and we can, without mere anthropomorphism, speak of asking questions of nature.[12] A good way further along the spectrum, in the case of our knowledge of other people, a greater, perhaps a complete, reciprocity, is required. People, unlike some things, cannot be compelled to give up knowledge of themselves, at least so long as we treat them as persons and not things. Moreover, we are often alienated from our neighbours by suspicion, fear, guilt, pride and the rest, so that we sometimes cannot know them at all, repentance and forgiveness apart. The knowledge of our neighbour is a gift, to be given and received freely and in full reciprocity if it is to be worthy of the name. The implications of this for theology are immense if we conceive it as taking shape in personal relations or sets of relations, and here Polanyi is notoriously weak, for he failed to extend to theological knowing the insights he had developed elsewhere. But there is still one more lesson we can learn from him.

[12] 'Einstein used to say that nature says "no" to most of the questions it is asked, and occasionally "perhaps". The scientist does not do as he pleases, and he cannot force nature to say only what he wants to hear.' Ilya Prigogine and Isabelle Stengers, *Order out of Chaos. Man's New Dialogue with Nature* (London: Fontana, 1985), p. 43.

Something has already been made of the fact that a major feature of Enlightenment thought is its individualism. What alternative does the post-critical thesis have to offer? It is the doctrine that without a community – its traditions, its language, its structures of authority – there can be no knowledge. Without, that is to say, other people in our present and past, without a common language, there can be no articulate knowledge. Knowledge is not only personal, but takes form in interpersonal relationships. The fact is demonstrated by Polanyi in the section of *Personal Knowledge* entitled 'Conviviality', but is now increasingly a feature of other writing. The conclusion, then, is that in the absence of intuited intellectual foundations built, so to speak, into the structures of rationality, we have another foundation: the communities, for example, of science or of literary interpretation. It is in and through communities of persons that knowledge becomes possible and takes form. The community is in that respect the only foundation, because it is the matrix within which, as a matter of fact, our cognitive enterprises become possible.

III *Karl Barth* – Coram Deo

On the face of it, and sometimes somewhat deeper, Barth's epistemology is but a repetition of the modern syndrome which was charted in the first section of the chapter. Ronald Thiemann rightly sees that the epistemology of the *Commentary on Romans* bears the marks of the modern tradition. First, there is the imagery of spatial *distance*: 'God is transcendent insofar as he stands outside of or on the boundary of ordinary human existence.'[13] Second, this spatial transcendence carries with it a particular epistemology:

> A position which stresses both God's sovereign transcendence and his knowability is hard pressed to give an account of how we can come to know such a God. Barth's solution ... is to grant to God's Spirit the mediating power to bring divine object and human subject together. The Spirit of God dwells

---

[13] Thiemann, *Revelation and Theology*, p. 47.

within the believing interpreter and bestows the capacity to know the unknowable.[14]

The epistemology of the *Commentary on Romans* is an epistemology of spatial distance: to know God is to be enabled, by means of a timeless theophany and the agency of the Spirit as *deus ex machina*, to cross from ignorance to knowledge.

If we are to understand the programme of Barth's mature work we must realise that, whether or not his later account of the matter uses the benefit of hindsight, the concept of transcendence was at this early stage programmatic or therapeutic rather than theoretical, an attempt 'to turn the rudder to an angle of exactly 180 degrees'.[15] As Steven Smith has written, 'Had the "Wholly Other" been a doctrine of God, rather than a device for placing theology in the right position before God, Barth could not have looked back on his *Romans* more than thirty years later with so much approval.' Similarly, it would be wrong to view 'Barth's theology as a philosophy in disguise, as a preoccupation with the abstract transcendence beyond man's power of knowing ...'.[16] The development from the dialectics of the early Barth to the conception in the book on Anselm of theology as faith seeking understanding has often been charted.[17] Accordingly, if the Anselm book really was as important as Barth repeatedly says it was for his understanding of theological method, we must expect to find after it an emerging conception which builds upon and transcends the therapeutic dialectics of the 1920s. Something of what it became will become clear if, in the light of the discussion of personal knowledge in the previous section, we examine some of the elements of the treatment of the knowledge of God in *Church Dogmatics* 2/1.

For Barth, despite the frequent assertions or at least suggestions to the contrary in the secondary literature, human knowl-

---

[14] Thiemann, *Revelation and Theology*, p. 42.

[15] Karl Barth, *The Humanity of God* (London: Fontana, 1967), p. 40.

[16] Steven G. Smith, *The Argument to the Other. Reason Beyond Reason in the Thought of Karl Barth and Emmanuel Levinas* (Chico, California: Scholars' Press, 1983), pp. 48, 49.

[17] Bruce L. McCormack, *Barth's Critically Realist Dialectical Theology. Its Genesis and Development, 1909–1936* (Oxford: Clarendon Press, 1995), has shown that this is the wrong way to describe the development. But it does not affect the main thesis of this chapter about the *Church Dogmatics*.

edge of God is not the conditioned reflex of the automaton. It is free personal action in relation, deriving from an indwelling in Christ and taking the form of thanksgiving, awe and the ordered employment of human concepts. Let me begin with some of the evidence that he sees theological knowledge as a genuinely human action. He speaks, for example, of 'the movement, the human action which we call the knowledge of God'[18] (p. 204); in it 'we are definitely active as the receivers of images and creators of counter-images' (p. 182). The stress is on the action rather than the results or some completed body of propositions: something very like what we have seen to be, in a Polanyian epistemology, the limits of our conceptual articulations of knowledge. 'Our viewing and conceiving of God and our speaking of Him will never be a completed work showing definitive results ...' (p. 208). In this respect, Barth uses language which is quite startling in its claims for the extent of the human side of the enterprise: 'In and by this way man comes to stand before God, in a situation in which he can perceive and consider and conceive God ...' (pp. 31–2, compare p. 194: 'a real human viewing and conceiving').

The passages cited so far are, to be sure, taken out of context, always a dangerous procedure and particularly dangerous in this case. But they serve to set the scene as well as to overturn some misconceptions. Barth intends to set before us a conception of the knowledge of a personal God by free and thinking persons. The talk is of active human knowledge in the context of a relationship, one indeed in which there is a measure of reciprocity. 'There is ... a reciprocity of relationship between [God] and these objects. Man ... can therefore perceive and consider and conceive God ...' (p. 58). Again, the words are carefully extracted, but they make the point that here is personal knowledge, knowledge taking shape in a particular relationship: 'the event between God and man which we call the knowledge of God' (p. 179).

But, inevitably, it is an asymmetrical reciprocity. How could it be otherwise? We have seen that there can be no true knowledge of people if they choose to hide themselves from us or if

---

[18] *Church Dogmatics* 2/1, p. 204. Further references to this volume will be page references in parentheses in the text.

we are alienated from them. Unless you reveal yourself to me, I shall not know you. Without revelation, there is no knowledge, not only of God but, I believe, of anything at all. Yet to introduce the topic of revelation in a discussion of Barth can hide more than it reveals. There are a number of reasons for this. The first is that concentration on the undoubtedly high noetic content of Barth's theology can obscure other important features, without whose inclusion we shall not see the whole. Even in the part volume with some claim to be the one most dominated by noetic considerations (*Church Dogmatics* 4/3), Barth is insistent that, even when speaking of the knowledge of God, we are in the realm of personal relationships rather than being concerned with the conveying of information. We recall that, in personal knowledge, knowledge by acquaintance is primary, propositional expression secondary:

> We cannot impress upon ourselves too strongly that in the language of the Bible knowledge ... does not mean the acquisition of neutral information, which can be expressed in statements, principles and systems, concerning a being which confronts man, nor does it mean entry into passive contemplation of a being which exists beyond the phenomenal world. What it really means is the process or history in which man, certainly observing and thinking, using his senses, intelligence and imagination, but also his will, action and 'heart', and therefore as whole man, becomes aware of another history ...[19]

The second reason for wanting to give minimal attention to Barth's numerous appeals to revelation is that we shall be tempted to take as the whole what it undoubtedly is in part, an attempt to cross an otherwise uncrossable epistemological gulf, what Thiemann has called 'the epistemological bridging of a spatial gap'.[20] If we are to understand Barth's theology, and in particular its movement beyond familiar epistemologies, it will profit us to pay attention to the features of his thought which revise the theology of the *Commentary on Romans*.

In order to know God, we must be where he makes himself known. For Barth, that is in Jesus Christ according to the

---

[19] *Church Dogmatics* 4/3, p. 183.
[20] Thiemann, *Revelation and Theology*, p. 48.

witness of the prophets and apostles. The eternal God's presence to the world in time is what makes knowledge of him actual. Again, we must be careful. As Robert Jenson long ago pointed out, there is in Barth a tendency to conceive Jesus Christ as a timeless metaphysical idea.[21] The interesting features of Barth's thought, however, are those which transcend this relic of Augustine's Neoplatonism. First, there is the claim that the form of knowledge corresponds to the personal relationship in which it takes shape. As I have suggested, our knowledge of each other depends on the way in which we are or are not able and prepared to make ourselves known. Barth rightly sees that the shape of our knowledge of God must correspond to the covenantal relationship in which we stand. We are, as a matter of fact, those who are elect in Christ for fellowship with God but wilfully deny our election. The knowledge of God, then, can become actual only as that fellowship with God is realised and restored by atonement. This consideration is a real if rather underplayed feature of Chapter v of the *Church Dogmatics*. But the fact that there is too much stress on revelation, too little on reconciliation, does not invalidate the general point:

> Because God forgives us our sins we know that we need forgiveness, and that we are sinners. And because God views and conceives Himself in His Word we know that He is not viewable and conceivable in any other way ... (p. 192).

Knowledge must take shape in the actual relationship.

Similarly, it has been almost a truism for Christian theology that relationship with God, especially for the sinner, comes as the free gift of the Holy Spirit. If knowledge is one aspect of the actual relationship with God, then knowledge too must be the gift of the Spirit, as the theologies of both Paul and John abundantly illustrate. Again that is a prominent, if also in some ways underplayed, feature of Barth's argument: 'it is the work of the Holy Spirit that the eternal presence of the reconciliation in Jesus Christ has in us this temporal form, the form of

---

[21] Robert W. Jenson, *Alpha and Omega. A Study in the Theology of Karl Barth* (New York: Thomas Nelson & Sons, 1963), p. 168.

faith, which believes this truth' (p. 159, cf. p. 200). For Barth, as for Kierkegaard, faith is the appropriate word to use in giving expression to the kind of relationship we have with God. Unlike Kierkegaard – on some interpretations – however, he did not wish to deny that it is also knowledge. As for Polanyi, so for Barth faith is a kind of knowledge, the only form that this particular kind of knowledge can take. But although, given the fact that this is the knowledge of the creating, reconciling and redeeming God, it is a unique kind of knowledge, it is not without continuity with other forms of human knowing. Barth is insistent on that also: the Spirit does not override but perfects nature. Not only does this relationship make legitimate the use of human words in theology (see, for example, pp. 223ff.), but also, 'The fact that it has God not only for its object but also as its origin ... does not mean either the abrogation, abolition or alteration of human cognition as such, and therefore of its formal and technical characteristics as human cognition' (p. 181). The knowledge of God, then, and the theological method flowing from it, is understood by Barth to be a form of personal relation, that between the creator and his erring but forgiven creatures. It is 'a positive relationship, i.e., one in which there exists a real fellowship between the knower and his knowing on the one hand and the known on the other' (p. 224). It is the kind of personal knowledge legitimated by this particular relationship.

A second feature of Barth's treatment is that he takes some, though again a somewhat underplayed, account of the communal matrix in which theology takes form. In one respect, he by no means underplays the matter, for there can be few theologians who have taken so seriously the requirement to listen carefully to other voices in the tradition, and to include in the conversation many of the unbelieving voices that recent centuries have witnessed. One way of reading Barth's theology is as a conversation, albeit at times rather one-sided, with a broad tradition of thought of many kinds:

> ... we cannot be in the Church without taking as much responsibility for the theology of the past as for the theology of our present. Augustine, Thomas Aquinas, Luther, Schleiermacher and all the rest are not dead, but living.

They still speak and demand a hearing as living voices, as surely as we know that they and we belong together in the Church.[22]

We may instructively refer again, in contrast, to Daniel Hardy's characterisation of the typical English approach to theology. 'In England, singular figures from the past do not – as persons – normally have a "lasting" influence on their successors, in the sense that they can be considered to have an importance beyond their time.' Despite some exceptions, 'the more common attitude is neatly summarised, Who do these dead men think they are?'[23]

Similarly, it is part of Barth's genius to have realised that in an era of the shaking of the foundations, Christian theology can take place only as the theology of a community. The movement from *Christian* to *Church* dogmatics signals the movement from the epistemology of the *Commentary on Romans* to that which we are now exploring. The notion that theology is based in the community is present in our chapter, though in rather muted form. 'All speaking and hearing in the Church of Jesus Christ entirely rests upon and is connected with the fact that God is known in the Church of Jesus Christ; that is to say, that this Subject is objectively present to the speakers and hearers, so that man in the Church really stands before God' (p. 3). Barth's conception of theology as serving the proclamation of the Church, for all its inadequacies, must first be seen as a step forward if its significance is to be appreciated. When John Howard Yoder writes that 'The church precedes the world epistemologically',[24] he is making not a Barthian remark so much as one made possible because Barth has been.

But that leads to a problem, and to a third area of discussion. How, on such an account, do we avoid the charge of arbitrariness, of sheer assertion? To a certain extent, the objection has been met already: if the language is the language of a community, extended in both time and space, then that is the only

[22] Karl Barth, *Protestant Theology in the Nineteenth Century. Its Background and History*, translated by Brian Cozens and John Bowden (London: SCM Press, 1972), p. 17.
[23] Hardy, 'The English Tradition', p. 144.
[24] John Howard Yoder, *The Priestly Kingdom. Social Ethics as Gospel* (Notre Dame, Indiana: University of Notre Dame Press, 1984), p. 11.

a priori justification it requires. What other foundation should there be than that laid by the prophets and apostles? And yet it is necessary to face the question from the other end also. Given that the language is the speech of a community, is there no way of providing some account of why we think we are talking about something rather than simply projecting from uncertain experience? Barth rightly rejects appeals to anything outside the theological circle as a ground for that circle. That would be to return to foundationalism. If that is not required in other disciplines, why should it be necessary here? (That is not, of course, the way Barth put or would want to put the matter.) Moreover, if this knowledge takes the form of faith, what right have we to ask for guarantees deriving from outside faith (pp. 247ff.)? Despite this, however, it is right also to ask for a measure of a posteriori justification. A theology must be judged by its content, if not by appeal to foundations outside it.

At this stage, I want to take from Thiemann another point, that in theology there can be a posteriori assessment of a cumulative or holistic kind wherein appeal is made to different but overlapping considerations.[25] Similarly, 'the theologian asks', writes Barth, paraphrasing Anselm, 'to what extent is reality as the Christian believes it to be?'[26] There are many possible ways in which that question and the matter of the holistic assessment of a theology may be approached. It may be thought that Barth has employed too few forms of argument in support of his contentions, while most modern theology in its desperation seeks too many. But there are two areas where his theology is matchless in its depth and richness.

To approach the first, we must keep before our eyes the fact that Barth is a disciple of Anselm, and it is as a relentless quest for the *perfection* of God that his positive contribution to theological epistemology must be assessed. Both the intellectual brilliance and the difficulty of Barth's theology derive from the way in which concept is piled upon concept in an attempt to allow the truth, goodness and beauty of God to take form in rational human language. There is no coming to terms with

---

[25] Thiemann, *Revelation and Theology*, pp. 71ff.

[26] Karl Barth, *Anselm: Fides Quaerens Intellectum. Anselm's Proof of the Existence of God in the Context of his Theological Scheme*, translation of 2nd edition by Ian W. Robertson (London: SCM Press, 1960), p. 27.

Barth's theology without the taking of immense pains to 'think after' it.

There is in Chapter v of the *Church Dogmatics* a number of places where Barth's development of concepts can be illustrated. One is the way in which the concept of the hiddenness of God is treated. For Barth this is not, as it has often been in the tradition, a mere limiting concept, that which emerges when we project onto God our inability to know him. Because God is actually known in the community, our conceptuality must be controlled by our knowledge, and not made a projection of human inability to know God. For this reason, Barth builds upon a hint of Anselm's that the task of theology is *rationabiliter comprehendere (Deum) incomprehensible esse*[27] to argue that God's hiddenness is not a function of his *distance* from us – for that would be to return to precisely that concept of spatial transcendence which he has been trying to avoid – but must be understood ontologically in terms of his judgement and grace (pp. 191–2). It is then the ontological rather than spatial otherness of God which comes to expression in our awareness of the asymmetrical personal relationship between creator and creature.[28] It is not being claimed that Barth is necessarily right in all he says here: the point is that he does enable us to examine the arguments and the conversation with the tradition and so to make some kind of assessment of whether his is an appropriate development of the content of Christian talk of God.

The second way in which Barth offers to us his theology for an a posteriori assessment of its content is found in his concern to give responsible conceptual expression to the object of theology: to give reasons why it is God that we know and not some idol or idea of our own constructing. We have seen that in the dialectics of the *Commentary on Romans* the Holy Spirit tended to be treated as the means of crossing theologically an otherwise unbridgeable epistemological gulf. We have seen also that for Barth God is known only through the Spirit. What has changed? Much in every way. There, it was a means to claim a

---

[27] 'To comprehend rationality that God is incomprehensible', Anselm, *Monologion* 64, cited in *Church Dogmatics* 2/1, p. 185.
[28] For a discussion of Barth's conception of transcendence, see Colin Gunton, 'Transcendence, Metaphor and the Knowability of God', *Journal of Theological Studies* 31 (1980), 503–16.

kind of knowledge of the intrinsically unknowable; here it is the opposite, a means to knowledge of him who is knowable in himself. Some account has been given in the secondary literature, particularly by Jüngel,[29] of the way in which Barth's trinitarian doctrine is a means of giving appropriate expression to the personal being of God, developing a conceptuality which will allow him to be at once objectively real while truly free and personal. Barth is himself aware that he is seeking to avoid both the Scylla and Charybdis of contemporary epistemology: 'We do not say all that so as to commend some sort of realism or objectivism' (p. 13). Rather, the programme is to give a basis in God's trinitarian objectivity to himself for his personal knowability by us. It is because God is knowable in and to himself in the life of the Trinity that he can become object to us, though object only in the ways so carefully delimited in the way we have charted. There is therefore a direct parallel between the personal knowledge of the world which was outlined in section II of this chapter and the personal knowledge of God which is the theme of the *Church Dogmatics*. Both of them attempt to transcend realism and objectivism in the received sense, because their programmes are both designed to transcend the old dualisms. This means that in Barth's theology it is not the intention that the Holy Spirit should function as the means to cross an otherwise unbridgeable epistemological gulf, though there is as a matter of fact a personal gulf which cannot be crossed without him. That gulf, however, has already been crossed in Christ, and, indeed, in God's eternal election of all humankind. The Holy Spirit gives what is there to be given because God becomes 'an object ... in such a way that in His objectivity He bestows ... by the Holy Spirit the light of the clarity that He is God ...' (p. 12).

IV *Some assessments*

It is when we examine the trinitarian dimensions of Barth's theology that we find at once his greatest strengths and

[29] Eberhard Jüngel, *Gottes Sein ist im Werden* (Tübingen: J. C. B. Mohr, 2nd edition, 1967); translated as: *The Doctrine of the Trinity: God's Being is in his Becoming*, by Horton Harris (Edinburgh and London: Scottish Academic Press, 1976).

weaknesses. They are the key to his theology as a whole. Here, however, we shall centre attention on them as they bear upon the epistemological stance that Barth has taken. In it there are, on the one hand, the features I have already reviewed: a brilliant awareness of the requirements of a theological epistemology and an accompanying movement out of the shadow of the Enlightenment. In place of the static, propositionalist, individualist and foundationalist, we have a conception of knowledge which seeks to be dynamic, personal and communal. On the other hand, it cannot be denied that some of the development does have an air of unargued assertion. There are two main reasons for this, and, therefore, two main places where there are questions to be asked. The first is to be found in the contrast Barth makes between the knowledge of God and of other objects. Here he is strangely Kantian. 'We have all other objects as they are determined by the pre-arranged disposition and pre-arranged mode of our own existence' (p. 21). But do we? The wider the gulf is made between theological and non-theological knowing, the more will theology appear, especially under modern conditions, to be no more than a tilting at epistemological windmills. Can one be an anti-Kantian in theology and a Kantian elsewhere without intellectual schizophrenia and an appearance of theological special pleading? It would be a mistake to build too much on that one perhaps careless statement, particularly in view of the fact that the later Barth appears to have been more careful.[30] But the question remains whether Barth would have profited more if he had spent less time polemicising against positions he believed to be invalid, more on considering in greater depth the mutual light thrown by theological and non-theological epistemology on each other. The very strength of Barth's theology, its singlemindedly theological character, can become its greatest weakness.

The second problem is to be found in the doctrine of God itself. Much has been made in recent discussion, especially by

[30] I owe to John Macken, *The Autonomy Theme in the Church Dogmatics: Karl Barth and his Critics* (Cambridge: Cambridge University Press, 1984), a reference to *Church Dogmatics* 4/3, p. 141: 'we may now make the further point that the world created by God does not merely exist but also speaks to one at least of its creatures, i.e., to man, giving itself to be perceived by him'.

Moltmann and Pannenberg,[31] of the modalist tendencies of Barth's Trinity. While their accounts are badly one-sided because they fail to take due account of Barth's critical revisions of Western trinitarianism, it does sometimes appear as though Barth is suggesting that God is more of a thrice-repeated I than one whose being is constituted by the communion of Father, Son and Spirit. Furthermore, there are times when the Holy Spirit appears to exist as no more than the means of the Father's and Son's knowledge of each other, or even to drop out of the transaction:

> In and for Himself He is I, the eternal, original and incomparable I ... God is object in Himself and for Himself: in the indivisible unity of the knowledge of the Father by the Son and the Son by the Father, and therefore in his eternal and irrevocable subjectivity (p. 57).[32]

I do not wish to join the speculation on the Hegelian or other provenance of this modalist tendency, so much as to remark briefly on its impact on our topic. A God whose being consists in the communion of the three persons – and here readers of John Zizioulas' *Being as Communion*[33] will recognise the basis of what is here being developed – will provide a foundation for a conception of theology which is truly the work of a community. There is very little actual pneumatological or ecclesiological content in Barth's major treatment of theological epistemology, and that must remain a serious weakness. Individualism is not entirely vanquished. There is, moreover, an element of the theological virtuoso about Barth, despite his warnings about the danger in the case of Schleiermacher.[34]

However, that is not the note on which to end. What we have

---

[31] For example, Wolfhart Pannenberg, 'Die Subjectivität Gottes und die Trinitätslehre. Ein Beitrag zur Beziehen zwischen Karl Barth und die Philosophie Hegels', *Grundfragen Systematischer Theologie. Gesammelte Aufsätze 2* (Göttingen, 1980), pp. 96–111.

[32] For a discussion of the weakness of Barth's trinitarian theology in this respect, see Thomas A. Smail, 'The Doctrine of the Holy Spirit', *Theology Beyond Christendom. Essays on the Centenary of the Birth of Karl Barth, May 10, 1886*, edited by John Thompson (Allison Park, Pennsylvania: Pickwick Publication, 1986), pp. 87–110.

[33] John D. Zizioulas, *Being as Communion. Essays on Personhood and the Church* (London: Darton, Longman & Todd, 1985).

[34] Barth, *Protestant Theology*, p. 446.

seen in the parts of Barth's work which have been called upon is the great distance he travelled in the direction of a theological epistemology with which to break the stranglehold of the Enlightenment on modern culture. In face of the division of the intellectual world into 'reason' and 'faith', and of the playing of the one against the other, he has begun to develop a post-critical epistemology of faith seeking understanding, learned from Anselm but shaped for modern theological conditions. The original title I considered for this chapter was something like 'A Move in the Right Direction'. I hope that I have shown that to use such a title would be greatly to underestimate the distance which was travelled by one who has done so much to enable the Church to develop the kind of theology that is needed now that Christendom is no more.

CHAPTER 5

THE BEING AND ATTRIBUTES OF GOD

Eberhard Jüngel's dispute with the classical
philosophical tradition[1]

I Eberhard Jüngel: philosophical theologian?

Almost alone among the leading German theologians of the
generation after Barth, Eberhard Jüngel appears to have felt no
need to define his position in opposition to or major qualification of that of the master. This is particularly true in the case of
his philosophical theology. In view, however, of the fact that
Barth is widely believed, certainly in the Anglo-Saxon world,
not to have a philosophical theology at all, we are immediately
faced with a difficulty. Can one expound the philosophical
theology of a theologian who does not have one? One
approach would be that famously adopted by Barth in his
Gifford Lectures, that the theologian required to lecture on
natural theology can remain true to the rubrics by speaking
against natural theology's possibility or propriety.[2] In that
sense, we can say that Barth, and any who operate largely within
his methodological penumbra, are negative philosophical theologians, but philosophical theologians of a kind none the
less.

But, so far as Jüngel is concerned, there is a far better
solution, and it is twofold. On the one hand, it is the case that

---

[1] First published in *The Possibilities of Theology. Studies in the Theology of
Eberhard Jüngel*, edited by John Webster (Edinburgh: T. & T. Clark, 1994), pp.
7–22.

[2] Karl Barth, *The Knowledge of God and the Service of God According to the
Teaching of the Reformation*, translated by J. L. M. Haire and Ian Henderson
(London: Hodder & Stoughton, 1938), pp. 6–7.

he is, in some respects, more of a philosopher than Barth affected to be or succeeded in being. On the other hand, it is worth observing that in any case Barth's work took him into the world of philosophical theology in a more than simply negative way. We shall take the latter point before moving to a discussion of Jüngel's own development. Nowhere is it more true of Barth that he is a kind of philosophical theologian than in his treatment of the divine attributes. In his exposition of the attributes, or what he preferred to call the perfections, of God, Barth gave priority to what can be called the more clearly personal of them, in preference to those more abstractly metaphysical. The whole of the set he chose to expound were those understood as characterisations of the divine love and freedom.[3] But in treating them, and especially the latter, Barth was unable to avoid interaction with many of the attributes traditionally associated with the classical tradition of natural theology.

As Christoph Schwoebel has shown, there are two apparently conflicting sources for the divine attributes. First there is a complex of attributes closely bound up with the idea of God as 'necessary, immutable, uncaused, omnipotent, eternal, omnipresent, omniscient and in every respect perfect', which comes from the philosophical tradition.[4] We could say that it derives from the tradition of Platonic and Aristotelian thought which forms the framework – the *foundation* – of so much Christian theology, especially in the West. It features in the work of Jüngel in frequent references to the metaphysical or classical tradition and in discussions of such divine attributes as impassibility, absoluteness, necessity and self-groundedness. Alongside this there is in the Christian theological tradition a complex of attributes which are derived from the conception of God as a personal agent. 'In the context of reflection on the divine attributes it is clear that the so-called moral, or better, personal attributes of God, his love, his mercy, righteousness, faithfulness, etc., presuppose [the] conception of divine action which

---

[3] Barth, *Church Dogmatics*, translation edited by G. W. Bromiley and T. F. Torrance (Edinburgh: T. & T. Clark, 1957–69), 2/1, §29.

[4] Christoph Schwoebel, *God: Action and Revelation* (Kampen: Kok Pharos, 1992), p. 50.

is expressed in the biblical traditions and in the discourse of the church.'[5]

Professor Schwoebel proceeds to argue that one cannot, without some form of intellectual evasion, simply make an absolute choice between the two approaches.[6] Indeed, we could add the point, and this brings us to a consideration which will be seen to be important for Jüngel's thought, that the historical context within which modern systematic theology must operate requires some interaction with both sources of talk of God in the West. Rational engagement with the question of God inevitably involves some kind of discussion of the metaphysically derived attributes of God, and in view of the fact that he engages in such discussion, we can say that Barth is a philosophical theologian. That is to say, in so far as he is concerned, in his treatment of the divine perfections, to interpret such language as he accepts from the philosophical tradition in the light of an action-led theory of the attributes, he is involved in a kind of philosophical theology.

Paradigmatic in all this, especially as a background to Jüngel, is Barth's discussion of the doctrine of impassibility. The doctrine of the impassibility of God has a far more complex history than its more naive opponents are these days liable to acknowledge. Plato's argument that God, being perfect, cannot change at all is not simply based upon a belief in 'static' perfection, but upon perfectly respectable arguments against the anthropomorphic characterisations of the gods of Olympus. If the gods succumb to unruly passions, then they are scarcely worthy of the worship that deity demands. In that respect, God must be impassible if he is to be morally credible. But there is a Christian relevance also. If the suffering of Jesus on the cross represents, as it appears to represent in some of the arguments of Moltmann, the subjection of God to some kind of external necessity, there follow two consequences which are subversive of the Christian gospel. The first is that the cross

---

[5] Ibid., p. 51. Compare Jüngel: 'The *substantia quaedam infinita, independens, summe intelligens, summe potens* was completely incapable of tolerating any deficiency. Can something like that be alive?' Jüngel, *Gott als Geheimnis der Welt*, 3rd revised edition (Tübingen: J. C. B. Mohr (Paul Siebeck), 1978), p. 264. (Hereafter abbreviated as GG.)

[6] Schwoebel, *God*, p. 54.

is not necessarily a victory, whose final outcome is assured, over the powers of evil. Rather, its outcome depends upon the completion, by other agents, of what it began. The second consequence is that – and it is the same point made from a different angle – the actual lord of things is not God but history. Just as Irenaeus argued in support of the doctrine of creation out of nothing that anything which limited God's power is to all intents and purposes God, so it is here. If God's passibility implies his subjection to necessity, he is no longer God.[7] As Henry Chadwick once said, the point of the patristic doctrine of impassibility is that it shows that God cannot be pushed about. Many modern critics of impassibility appear to formulate their positions in such a way as to suggest that he can. As we shall see, Jüngel himself does not fall into this trap, though he sometimes treads very near to it.

None the less, there is little doubt that the tradition did require radical critique. There are limits beyond which the Christian doctrine of God does indeed become the prisoner of a priori metaphysical commitments, and it is frequently argued that they were passed in much of the theology of previous eras, for example in the 'impassibility axiom'. This is a form of the concept which made it so difficult for theologians of the first few centuries to formulate a truly orthodox christology,[8] and generates the tendency of mediaeval philosophical theology and deist rationalism alike to imprison God in his eternity. It is on behalf of the freedom of God that Barth characteristically protests against certain forms of the doctrine:

> ... the personal God has a heart. He can feel, and be affected. He is not impassible. He cannot be moved from outside by an extraneous power. But this does not mean that He is not capable of moving Himself. No, God is moved and stirred ...[9]

That revision of the philosophical tradition was made largely on the basis of trinitarian revelation, but later in the *Church Dogmatics* Barth adds a characteristically christological dimen-

[7] There is an argument for a form of another metaphysical attribute, omnipotence, here also.

[8] Werner Elert, *Der Ausgang der altkirchlichen Christologie* (Berlin: Lutherisches Verlagshaus, 1957).

[9] Barth, *Church Dogmatics* 2/1, p. 370.

sion. This is worth mentioning, because it anticipates what Jüngel is himself to develop. 'It is not at all the case that God has no part in the suffering of Jesus Christ even in His mode of being as the Father. No, there is a *particula veri* in the teaching of the early Patripassians.'[10] Perhaps more telling still is a later passage, in which Barth speaks of the way in which the Christian God is distinguished from 'all the general notions and concepts of divinity invented and projected by man'. Speaking of the crucifixion, he writes:

> As the Doer of this act He is the one true God. He is this, therefore, in the death of the man Jesus Christ. In the death of this man, in Him the Crucified He reveals not only the work done, but in and with this Himself, His divine person, His divine essence ...[11]

The echoes of Feuerbach in the third of the above citations from Barth and the raising of the question of the relation between crucifixion and divinity in the fourth show something of the background to Eberhard Jüngel's own distinctive philosophical theology.

II   *Ontology without metaphysics*

As has already been made clear, Jüngel is not a slavish follower of Barth, and it must be said that he is also somewhat more sophisticated a philosopher, as well as being aware of the necessity for philosophical seriousness.

> In theology, God must indeed be *thought*. He must be thought for the reason that nothing can be achieved against the 'God of the philosophers' by renouncing the thinkability of God. Christian theology must rather, in working through the concept of God, carry through its business of thinking its concept of God far more rigorously than philosophy has done. Taking leave of the 'God of the philosophers' is quite another matter than taking leave of the responsibility to think God.[12]

[10] Barth, *Church Dogmatics* 4/2, p. 357.
[11] Barth, *Church Dogmatics* 4/3, p. 412.
[12] Jüngel, GG, p. 269.

Jüngel's engagement with the classical metaphysical tradition is rightly oriented towards its very beginnings in the philosophy of Greece. In *Gottes Sein ist im Werden*, which has established itself as one of the major introductions to Barth's doctrine of God, he shows how Barth's attempt to replace the analogy of being with categories derived from revelation trinitarianly conceived brings him into relation with the very roots of systematic theological thought in pre-Socratic philosophy. This is true at the level of hermeneutics, for Barth's view that revelation must commandeer the language rather than the reverse is understood to be a repudiation of what Jüngel calls a *Signifikationshermeneutik* – a theory according to which the meaning of words prescribes the meaning of things – which has its roots in Parmenides.[13]

But Barth's trinitarianism is shown in this book to be in direct confrontation with Hellenic theories of being as well as of meaning. The problem is this. Theology, certainly as it takes shape in the dispute about Barth's theology in which Jüngel was there engaging, appears to require the affirmation of the independent being of God. But if the concept of God is bound to traditional theories of substance a dilemma is presented. Aristotelian first substances are by definition non-relational beings, while relational forms of being require reciprocity and so cannot be first substances. The outcome is that one cannot, within the conceptual framework provided by ancient metaphysics, develop a genuinely relational theology without implying the mutual necessity of God and the world:

> Thus if one were to conceive God's being as such under the category of relational being, and if one were to have to regard man as the other to which God as God is related, then God could not be conceived as being God without man; as, conversely, God would also always have to come to speech as part of the meaning of the concept of man.[14]

As we shall see when we come to discuss his later work, the contingency of the relation of God and the world is important for Jüngel for some very good reasons. At this stage, however,

---

[13] Jüngel, *Gottes Sein ist im Werden* (Tübingen: J. C. B. Mohr (Paul Siebeck), 2nd edition, 1966), pp. 18–19. (Hereafter abbreviated as GS.)

[14] GS, p. 104.

he is concerned to show that Barth's trinitarianism makes it possible to conceive both the relational character of God's ('inner') being *and* that God's relations to the world are real and unnecessitated. 'The grace of God's being-for-us must *be able* to image (*abbilden*) the freedom of God's being-for-himself, so that this freedom as the "original" (*Urbild*) of that grace becomes perceivable (*anschaulich*) in that grace as the "image" (*Abbild*) of this freedom.'[15] Gracious personal action presupposes and requires a preceding inner (immanent) freedom of God.

The overall concern of Jüngel's interpretation of Barth is thus to show that an understanding of the relation of God to the world derived from divine revelation can generate not only a critique of, but also a genuine alternative to, a philosophical theology that appears to imprison God in eternity. 'The *substantia quaedam infinita, independens, summe intelligens, summe potens* was completely unready to suffer any kind of need. Can such a being be alive?'[16] What Jüngel thus seeks to show is that there can be an ontology without metaphysics: that is, an articulated account of who God is that neither is determined by a priori philosophical decisions and linguistic structures nor generates some timeless theory of being which rules out the forms of divine action from which Christian theology takes its orientation. '[T]his first makes it fully intelligible that God's being is not only able to bear historical predicates ... but also demands them.'[17] That is to say, theological ontology must be driven by the second set of divine attributes, those derived from a conception of God as personal agent. Yet it must also be an ontology whose content should be developed only through a continuous confrontation with classical metaphysics and its various historical consequences and inversions.

III   *Christology, Hegel and the divine attributes*

While Jüngel's interpretation of Barth took the classical philosophical tradition as its backcloth, his later work raises the

[15] GS, p. 108.
[16] GG, p. 264.
[17] GS, p. 109.

spectre[18] of Hegel. Barth some time ago famously asked why it did not come about that Hegel was accepted as the Protestant Aquinas,[19] but a quarter of a century after he wrote there is some reason to suppose that as a matter of fact the great unintelligible is beginning to claim the status of being *the* provider of philosophical theology to large parts of the Protestant and, in these ecumenical days, Catholic theological worlds.[20] Hegel, however, is a many-sided figure, as our subject has himself shown in one of the most interesting of his chapters,[21] and offers different gifts to different successors. For example, and this is directly relevant to an understanding of the place of Eberhard Jüngel on the modern intellectual map, he is often alleged to have provided Barth with a concept of God as absolute and unitary subject. We have already seen something of how Jüngel would qualify this interpretation of Barth, but for the latter's critics it is the use of particular Hegelian conceptuality that places Barth in the camp of the classical enemy. That is to say, Barth is supposed not to have criticised sufficiently sharply the classical metaphysic according to which God and the world were supposed to be two opposed entities, standing in some relation of contradiction to one another. Thus his theology has an authoritarian air, the stamp of the unhappy consciousness, and, seemingly paradoxically but only apparently so, the Hegelian borrowings reinforce rather than mitigate it.

Barth's critics and successors have used Hegel to somewhat different effect, and here we must say something of the influence of Hegel the Lutheran, the one who 'at bottom ... remained throughout his life a loyal son of the Tübingen seminary'.[22] Christology is the key to the new Protestant philosophical theology, for Hegel's is a philosophical theology which is based on a kind of christology. For him, christology becomes a principle of immanence which affects the basic structures of

[18] *Geist?*

[19] Barth, *Protestant Theology in the Nineteenth Century: Its Background and History*, translated by B. Cozens and J. Bowden (London: SCM Press, 1972), p. 384.

[20] 'It was only in the course of centuries that Thomas Aquinas acquired the position at present accorded him in the Roman Catholic world' (Barth, *Protestant Theology*, p. 390).

[21] GG, §7.2.

[22] Barth, *Protestant Theology*, p. 396.

the thought of much theology that comes under his influence. But what kind of christology is it? To understand the influence of Hegel, something needs to be said about the difference between Lutheran and Reformed tendencies in christology. It is sometimes remarked that whereas Calvin's christology is closer to that of Antioch, Luther's orientation is towards Alexandria. That is to say, while Calvin tends to call attention to the distinction of the divine and human in the person of Christ, Luther is more interested in their union. The latter appeals in particular to a version of the patristic teaching of the communication of attributes, according to which anything attributable to the divinity of Christ must be also attributable to his humanity, and the reverse. It is thence, of course, that he derives his famous and problematic teaching of the ubiquity of the humanity of Christ, and hence of his capacity to be present in the eucharistic elements.

By the time it has been transmogrified in Hegel's tender hands – 'the divine nature is the same as the human . . .'[23] – this teaching becomes a general principle of immanence. The divine involvement in Christ becomes in different ways generalised, so that the locus of divine *being* as well as of action comes to be centred on forms of divine presence to and in the world. This tendency makes its mark on Barth in his theology of the humanity of God, and even more so in the trinitarian theology of one of Barth's Lutheran interpreters, Robert Jenson.[24] It is in some such way that a christologically determined philosophical theology comes in its turn to shape modern treatments of the doctrine of God. The influence is particularly marked in the theologies of Moltmann and Pannenberg, whose concern to identify God from his historical immanence has, in the view of some commentators, not been without problems. While Moltmann consciously uses the principle of immanence to cast doubt upon the propriety of speaking of an immanent Trinity at all, preferring to speak of 'the trinitarian history of God',

[23] G. W. F. Hegel, *The Phenomenology of Mind*, translated by J. B. Baillie (London: George Allen & Unwin, 1949), p. 760.

[24] See Colin E. Gunton, *The Promise of Trinitarian Theology* (Edinburgh: T. & T. Clark, 1991), pp. 134–8. It always surprises me that Barth is so often held to be a theologian of transcendence. The fact is rather that his thought is pervaded, if not controlled, by a very strong christological immanence.

Pannenberg appears, particularly to Anglo-Saxon readers impatient of apparent ambiguity, to want to say both that there is a sense in which the world constitutes or shapes the being of God and that God is eternally the one on whom all things depend.[25]

Let us pause to examine the use that Moltmann makes of theological immanence in *The Crucified God*. This is, of course, an over-used example, but it will prove to be important in showing the rather different use which Jüngel makes of a similar thesis. It is important to note that there is in Moltmann no unrelieved immanence. Jesus' death is not the death of God, but death in God.[26] But the relief from immanentism is far from adequate, so that Moltmann comes very near to making the cross of Jesus a general principle of immanence. '[T]he Trinity means the Christ event in the eschatological interpretation of faith.'[27] While that may be unclear in its meaning and implications, others of Moltmann's expressions are more obviously problematic. 'In the death of Jesus, the deity of his God and Father is at stake.'[28] Perhaps most significant for our purposes is a turn of phrase which brings Moltmann into direct disagreement with Jüngel. 'The abandonment on the cross which separates the Son from the Father is something which takes place within God himself; it is *stasis* within God . . .'[29] Readers of Jüngel's first book on Barth will know that he has set himself against drawing such conclusions. The notion of stasis within God is a denial of the reality of grace and the unity of God. Although, says Jüngel, Barth comes near to presenting a 'contradiction and conflict' within God himself, he will not

---

[25] This is less the case in the more traditionally articulated theology of creation in Wolfhart Pannenberg, *Systematic Theology*, volume 2, translated by Geoffrey W. Bromiley (Edinburgh: T. & T. Clark, 1994).

[26] Jürgen Moltmann, *The Crucified God. The Cross of Christ as the Foundation and Criticism of Christian Theology*, translated by R. A. Wilson and J. Bowden (London: SCM Press, 1974), p. 207.

[27] Moltmann, *The Crucified God*, p. 255.

[28] Moltmann, *The Crucified God*, p. 151.

[29] Moltmann, *The Crucified God*, pp. 151–2. The question here arises of whether Moltmann is projecting on to the cross the now much criticised Lutheran tendency to distinguish between the *deus revelatus* and *deus absconditus*. Whether or not that is fair, Jüngel interestingly speaks of it as follows: 'the distinction (*Unterscheidung*) between God and God can never be understood as a contradiction in God' (GG, p. 474).

cross the boundary. However: 'The rejection of this consequence leads in Barth not to a blunting of the doctrine of
God's suffering, but on the contrary, to a criticism of the
traditional metaphysical concept of God, according to which
God cannot suffer without running into contradiction with his
being.'[30]

The point of all this is that the tendency of Hegelian
philosophical theology is to bind too closely the being of God
with that of the world. It is used, in the thought of some of its
proponents, to obviate the objectionable features of the classical philosophical tradition, in which God was in some way
opposed to the world. But as a principle of immanence, it
cannot, and here we return to features of the previous section,
avoid suggestions of necessitarianism. The version of necessitarianism particularly in evidence is that which makes the existence and flourishing of the world in some way necessary to the
being of God. God has, it is sometimes argued or at least
suggested, bound himself up so closely with the world that he
has tied his future to that of the creation. The distinctive
contribution of Jüngel in this respect is to draw upon the
Hegelian theology in order to sift its wheat from its chaff, and
so to build upon it in offering an alternative doctrine of God to
that of the classical tradition. Our chief object now will be to
expound something of what he says, and to ask how far he
succeeds.

Our subject's engagement with this topic takes him from the
classical philosophers and Barth to the modern problem of
atheism, which he argues to be in part the product of the
Western tradition of philosophical theology. His discussion of
the problem set by the tradition centres on this very matter of
necessity. The contention is that the enterprise, initiated in the
modern era by Descartes, to demonstrate the necessity of God
for the being of the world, generated by a kind of reflex the
atheism that demanded to be free from such a binding deity.[31]
Alongside this, the philosophical tradition, which conceived
the omnipotence of God as prior to his love, led not only to a
desire to stress the non-necessity of God, but also to an active

[30] Jüngel, GS, p. 98.
[31] GG, p. 23.

demand to deny God in the name of freedom.[32] It is because they liberate from bad theology that the criticisms of opponents of Christian theology should be accepted as making contributions to the process. Feuerbach's and Nietzsche's critiques should be heard. 'Is not Feuerbach right to suspect that theology is more interested in the *potentia dei absoluta* and a *deus absconditus* than in the truth that God *is* love?'[33]

Underlying the modern rebellion is the tradition's tendency so to stress the necessity of God that the importance of the contingent was undermined. What is therefore needed is a concept of God not tied to the kind of necessity which calls the being of the world in question; that is to say, an idea of God as something '*mehr als notwendig*'. Such necessity, however, should not be quantitatively construed so as to make God metaphysically necessary to the world,[34] but should imply an understanding of God as one who through the miracle of revelation is recognised in gratitude as the one who rescues from nothingness. This is a kind of necessity, for the one who is revealed as being beyond being and non-being is one who is *grundlos*.[35] He thus shares the classical attributes of necessity and aseity, but in his own distinctive way. God's is not a necessity detracting from gracious and free action, but one that is grounded in a conception of the being of God as love. Thus the traditional attributes of self-determination, omnipotence and transcendence are now construed on the basis of a theology of gracious personal action rather than on metaphysical necessity, and are accordingly transformed in their meaning.

What then is the difference? The mistake of the metaphysical tradition was to understand the divine self-groundedness in a non-trinitarian way, that is to say, apart from the man who died on the cross.[36] Here we engage with that which marks Jüngel's distinctive development of the Barthian position, for his appeal at the next stage of his argument is to Luther and his successors. He concedes that in certain respects Luther himself was too close to the metaphysical tradition, suggesting nominalistic

[32] GG, pp. 25–6.
[33] GG, p. 432.
[34] GG, p. 30.
[35] GG, p. 41.
[36] GG, p. 46.

conceptions of divine absoluteness in his understanding of
freedom and justification.[37] But his affirmation of the real
involvement of God in the death of Christ is of crucial importance. By virtue of his understanding of the *communicatio
idiomatum,* he shows the way to a proper understanding of the
notion of the death of God.[38] It is at this stage that Jüngel
engages with the Hegelian tradition which, as we have seen, has
tended to introduce a new metaphysic, a philosophical christology of immanence which is the mirror image of that philosophical theology with which so many moderns are deeply
dissatisfied.

Hegel's principle of the death of God, Jüngel argues, should
not simply be understood as a philosophy of culture, as it has
tended to become after Nietzsche – that is, as merely giving an
account of what has happened in human cultural experience –
but as having genuinely Christian theological content also.
Christianly understood, the theology of the death of God frees
theology from metaphysics.[39] In Bonhoeffer's discussion, for
example, the false assumption of the worldly necessity of God is
set aside, while Hegel uses the principle in the interest of the
Reformed emphasis on faith alone.[40] Hegel's particular interpretation of the death of God, however, must be resisted as a
threat to a proper distinction of God and man.[41] The principle
should not be taken as far as Hegel took it, to suggest that
through the incarnation and death of Christ there was a
transformation into a general unity of God with human nature.
But that raises a question: how are the genuine identification of
God with the world and a proper critique of divine impassibility
to be affirmed alongside a similarly proper conception of the
continuing distinction of God from the world? Jüngel's answer
is to be found in his distinctive use of the concept of divine
mystery and its trinitarian construal.

Much, in the first instance, hangs upon a conception of

[37] GG, pp. 52–4.
[38] Jüngel takes from Luther the claim that 'God cannot die in his nature, but
now that God and man are united in one person, it is right to speak, when the
man who is one thing or one person with God dies, of the death of God' (GG,
p. 126).
[39] GG, p. 62.
[40] GG, pp. 78, 94.
[41] GG, p. 127.

divine action in and towards the world. The fact that God is the mystery of the world as he comes to the world[42] implies a capacity to cross that which seems to us to be a boundary and was institutionalised in the classical tradition as a barrier.

> In place of the God who is in heaven *because* he cannot be on earth there comes the Father who is in heaven in such a way that his heavenly kingdom can *come into the world*, that is, a God who is in heaven in *such a way* that he can *identify himself* with the poverty of the man Jesus, with the existence of one brought from life to death on the cross.[43]

Such a conception of divine action calls in question traditional construals of omnipotence and impassibility. On Paul's account of the cross, '[w]eakness is not ... understood as a contradiction of God's power'.[44] But the critique of the tradition is more radical than that. The cross of Jesus entails a major revision of the classical doctrine, with its axioms of absoluteness, impassibility and immutability.[45] But it is a *revision* which is involved, not the kind of inversion to be found in Process thought and perhaps in Moltmann. God's suffering by involving himself in nothingness *affects* without *overcoming* the being of God. On the one hand, therefore, 'the *being* (*Wesen*) of God can no longer be placed outside of this struggle'; on the other, 'God is the one who can and does bear, can and does suffer, in his being the annihilating power of nothingness ... without being annihilated by it.'[46]

Is, then, the divine action in the world to be understood as a revelation of the being of God, or, more radically, as a determination of it? If it is the former, is there not, then, a place for some version of the doctrine of the immutability of God? The question is important, for any theology which implied that the cross determined the being of God would suggest either a destruction of divine freedom, or a lack of confidence that some other, more determinative, historical event might not determine the being of God in another direction. (In either

---

[42] 'Als Geheimnis der Welt ist God insofern begreifen, als er zur Welt *kommt*' (GG, p. 518).
[43] GG, p. 284.
[44] GG, pp. 279–80.
[45] GG, p. 511.
[46] GG, pp. 295, 298.

case, some form of trinitarian modalism would result or be implied.) That is to say, if the death of God on the cross in some way determines or constitutes the being of God, is it not conceivable that, if we have no reason for believing in some form of divine immutability, a further divine act could truly be the death *of* God? That Jüngel wishes to affirm *some form* of revelation of the eternal – and therefore immutable – being of God is clear from his criticism of Aquinas' negative theology which implies, he holds, that God is a mystery because we are unable to know him adequately, not because he is full of mystery in his being.[47] Similarly, he is clear that the trinitarian distinction implied by the cross must not be understood as an 'enforced opposition' (*aufgenötigter Gegensatz*),[48] nor is it an 'alien fate' (*fremdes Schicksal*).[49]

But it must be said that Jüngel's formulation of the trinitarian basis of the matter is not in every way transparent. His argument appears to operate with a kind of dialectic of self-love and other-love according to which the identification of God with the crucified Jesus is in some way in correspondence with the inner-trinitarian love of Father and Son.[50] God the Spirit is the key to this correspondence between the eternal self-relatedness of God and his relations outward with the world, particularly in the cross of Jesus. The Spirit's role in the economy of salvation is to maintain the oneness of God in the differentiation of Father and Son that is revealed in the event of God's coming to the world. God the Spirit is the one who 'allows the Father and the Son to be one in real distinction, but also face to face with one another, in the death of Jesus'.[51] He is thus, and Jüngel uses the Augustinian expression, the *vinculum caritatis*, the bond of love, between the two. That expression serves also to place the Spirit in the being of the immanent Trinity, where he is the focus of a kind of immutability, albeit of a dynamic kind: 'a third divine relation, the relation between the relations of the Father and the Son, and thus far an *eternally* new relation of God and God'.[52]

[47] GG, p. 334.
[48] GG, p. 498.
[49] GG, p. 532.
[50] GG, p. 506.
[51] GG, p. 504.
[52] GG, p. 512, my emphasis.

Accordingly, in his treatment of the divine attributes, it would appear that Jüngel has not simply rejected the tradition, but revised it in the light of the trinitarian dialectic of action-in-difference. In sum, in his theology of the being and attributes of God, the coming of God to the world in Christ is made the basis of a doctrine of the immanent Trinity which both writes the historical action of God into the being of God and maintains a proper distinction between God and the world. God is 'more than necessary', as the dynamically eternal triune being whose action towards and for us corresponds to his eternal being in himself, so that the metaphysical attributes are given radically Christian meaning in the light of a theology of personal divine action in Christ.

IV Some trinitarian questions

What is to be said of all this? The chief point is that it is infinitely preferable to its less nuanced, though sometimes more fashionable, contemporary alternatives. Unless the real otherness of God and the world is maintained by some form of the doctrine of the immanent Trinity, forms of necessitarianism which will deny to God the right to be truly God and the world the right to be truly worldly will find their way into the system. One way in which the otherness can be maintained is christological, for it is through the person of Christ that we are able to understand and conceptualise the otherness-in-relation, the free but real relatedness, of God and that which he has made. However, as we have seen, there is christology and christology – that which does and that which does not degenerate into being a philosophical theology and so a general principle of immanence. One way of maintaining the former is the way that Jüngel has himself chosen, and that is by a kind of dialectic, the mystery in which God is and is not identical with his presence in Jesus.

But is the concept of mystery strong enough to do what is required of it? Is it, that is to say, different enough from the negative theology which Jüngel has rejected to serve as a way of conceiving the otherness-in-relation of God and the world which he sees to be so necessary for his case? I believe that there are problems, and they are closely associated with the main thesis of this chapter. We shall realise something of the point if we begin from where our exposition of Jüngel's theology left off. The Achilles' heel of Western theology, as is often enough repeated, is the under-determination of the person of the Holy Spirit in almost all areas of dogmatics. This has had at least two effects. The first is to make it difficult to give adequate dogmatic weighting to the humanity of Christ. It is God the Spirit as the focus of the relationship of Jesus and the Father whose office it is to maintain attention on the particular Jewish human being, Jesus of Nazareth, as the one mediator between God and the world. Such an emphasis, by its focus on the particular, will always resist the turning of christology into a general principle of immanence; correspondingly, its inadequate weighting will let in the Hegelian threat to the distinction between God and the world. Here a question to Jüngel will be similar to one asked of Moltmann. Has the Lutheran christological tradition on which he has drawn made so much of the cross as the act of the crucified *God*, that attention is taken away from the action of the *human* Jesus? That is one way in which christology can slip into becoming a principle of immanence.

The second effect of an under-determined pneumatology is an inadequate theology of the immanent Trinity. When the Spirit functions chiefly as a bond between Father and Son, as tends to be the case in the tradition of Augustine, the way is opened for the kind of philosophical theology against which the modern theological tradition is in almost unanimous rebellion. What happened in the tradition is that the one God, defined chiefly with the aid of concepts derived from the monistic theological traditions of Greek philosophy, comes to operate as a dialectical counter over against the claims of incarnational christology, which, by virtue of its orientation to notions of free agency, appears to entail rather opposite characteristics of the God it implies. It is in this context that we can see the point of T. F. Torrance's claim that Karl Barth's theology represents an attempt to bring together the being and act of God, by integrating them in a theology of the Trinity.[53] As

---

[53] T. F. Torrance, *Karl Barth. An Introduction to his Early Theology, 1910–1931* (London: SCM Press, 1962).

we have seen, it is in this revisionary tradition that Jüngel also stands (*Gottes Sein ist im Werden*).

As we have also seen, however, Barth's theology at times comes perilously close to replacing the monist philosophy of the tradition with a monist christological principle, and it is little surprise that many of those influenced by him have come to do just that. That is the (Lutheran) Hegelian danger. Eberhard Jüngel's attention to the part played by the immanent Trinity in maintaining a non-necessary relation between God and the world has saved him from submission to the shibboleths of modern immanentism. But there must still be a question of the under-determination of the place of the Spirit, and therefore a weakness in conceiving the manner of the presence of God to the world. It must be doubted whether Jüngel's conception of the Spirit in the Trinity is strong enough to prevent a possible ambivalence from creeping into his thought at this crucial juncture. Another way of focusing that question would be to ask: is the Spirit a relation or a person, and what difference does an answer to the question make? Whatever be the response to those queries, we can be sure that our theologian has not made his last contribution to the doctrine of the being and attributes of God, and we shall eagerly anticipate future writings on this most central of questions.

CHAPTER 6

THE DOCTRINE OF GOD

Karl Barth's doctrine of election as part of his doctrine of God[1]

I *Introduction*

The term 'neo-orthodox' is often used as a label for the theology of Karl Barth, particularly by its opponents.[2] The contention of this chapter is that, while a final judgement on its orthodoxy must wait a greater distancing in time, there can be no doubt of the radical newness of what has been said, and nowhere is this better illustrated than in the five hundred or so pages devoted to the doctrine of election in the *Church Dogmatics*.[3] It is demonstrated both by the placing of the doctrine in the doctrine of God – so far as Barth knows, he is the first dogmatician to do this (p. 76) – and by the fact that many critics have failed to understand what Barth is doing despite, or perhaps because of, his usual determination to make himself utterly clear.[4] Dr Hartwell has seen the point: 'It is no exaggeration to say that the heart of Barth's theology beats in this doctrine in which he radically departs from all past and present teaching on predestination, above all from Calvin's doctrine of

---

[1] First published in the *Journal of Theological Studies* 25 (1974), 381–92. Revised, chiefly by the addition of a new conclusion.

[2] The misleading use of the expression is well criticised by Bruce McCormack, *Karl Barth's Critically Realistic Dialectical Theology* (Oxford: Clarendon Press, 1995), pp. 23–6.

[3] Karl Barth, *Church Dogmatics* 2/2, translation edited by G. W. Bromiley and T. F. Torrance (Edinburgh: T. & T. Clark, 1957), pp. 3–506. All further references to this part volume will take the form of page references in parentheses in the text.

[4] For an account of criticisms based on misunderstanding, see J. D. Bettis, 'Is Karl Barth a Universalist?', *Scottish Journal of Theology* 20 (1967), 423–36.

predestination.'[5] The first part of this judgement is abundantly confirmed by Barth himself, when he says, 'The election of grace (*die Gnadenwahl*) is the sum of the Gospel – we must put it as pointedly as that. But more, the election of grace is the whole of the Gospel, the Gospel *in nuce*. It is the very essence of all good news' (pp. 13–14). And from the opening words of the book: 'of all words that can be said or heard it is the best: that God elects man; that God is for man too the One who loves in freedom' (p. 3).

As to Hartwell's second point, from the warmth with which the topic is introduced the reader may be justified in assuming that Barth is not writing without glances over the shoulder. If he is concerned with avoiding all possible misunderstanding in this area, it is unlikely that he had in mind those who foolishly and ignorantly assume that election or predestination is synonymous with moral determinism, though the point would be well made. Rather the object of any such concern is the great Calvin, whose doctrine of the *decretum absolutum* that lies hidden behind what God actually does in Jesus Christ is the very reverse of what Barth wants to say. The point against Calvin here is made by J. K. S. Reid, for whom a chance phrase in the *Institutes* represents the whole weakness of the Reformer's position. Calvin there says: *gratiam istam Dei praecedit electio.* 'Who, then', asks Reid, 'is this God who determines men's election before grace becomes operative?'[6] For Barth, as we shall see, a God who is not gracious from the very first is not the God who reveals himself in Jesus Christ.

Of course, Calvin's doctrine, too, was for him part of the good news. That is not Barth's complaint, but rather that God's Yes to man in election came to be overwhelmed by his No in reprobation (pp. 39–41). It is worth observing that according to Wendel the doctrine of election gained a relatively late prominence in Calvin's theology 'under the sway of ecclesio-

---

[5] H. Hartwell, *The Theology of Karl Barth: An Introduction* (London: Duckworth, 1964), p. 105.

[6] J. K. S. Reid, 'The Office of Christ in Predestination', *Scottish Journal of Theology* 1 (1948), 5–19 and 166–83 (12). A careful reading of Calvin's words in their context will reveal that Reid has misread him badly. Calvin is in fact saying the opposite. But the point remains that for Barth Calvin's doctrine is inadequately christological.

logical and pastoral preoccupations'.[7] Furthermore, in the 1559 edition of the *Institutes* Calvin rejected as 'inopportune' the treatment of predestination in relation to the doctrine of God (p. 268),[8] and preferred to treat it in Book III, which is concerned with the believer's appropriation of the grace of Jesus Christ. This emphasis not only makes the assurance of his status a matter for the believer's experience, but, when placed alongside a conception of a hidden God who is something apart from his grace, completely nullifies the gospel character of the doctrine. 'If he (sc. the Christian believer) is elect, what else can he do to be assured of the fact except to reach back to a *sentire* quite apart from faith, to enter on the way of an "examination of conscience" with its resultant self-righteousness?' (pp. 338–9).

But that, for Barth, is a secondary matter. If he rejects the path taken by Calvin, it is for reasons different from the practical ones that at least bulked large in Calvin's own mind. His refusal to have anything to do with an experiential criterion and his determination to reject Calvin's hidden decree follow from the character of his theology, as does the positive side of his change of direction, the placing of this topic in the doctrine of God. For Barth, doctrines that are not theologically grounded are not Christian theology. That is to say, a doctrine of election that does not have its grounds in the God whom we know in Jesus Christ, in the known rather than the unknown God, is not the Christian Gospel. R. W. Jenson summarises: 'What can be the basis of this doctrine? It can be neither tradition, nor pastoral utility, nor the experience that some seem to be saved and others not, nor a deduction from the doctrine of God's omnipotence. All such approaches to the doctrine of election deal with God-in-general and man-in-general. But this is neither the God nor the man of whom Scripture speaks.'[9]

This statement of the gospel character of the doctrine and of the consequent rejection of approaches to election that

---

[7] F. Wendel, *Calvin: The Origins and Development of his Religious Thought*, translated by Philip Mairet (London: Fontana, 1965), p. 264.

[8] The reference is to Calvin, *Institutes*, I.15.8.

[9] R. W. Jenson, *Alpha and Omega: A Study in the Theology of Karl Barth* (New York: Nelson, 1963), p. 143.

obscure or destroy that character sets the scene for a threefold task. First, we must ask what it is about God that makes the doctrine of election to be part of the doctrine of God; second, we must examine the rational basis of the account in the very roots of Barth's theology; and third, we must investigate the place of the doctrine of election in the wider context of the structure of Barth's theology as a whole. When that is done, we shall be able to see how the doctrine is both part of the doctrine of God and a locus of theological interest in its own right, without its having its shape imposed upon it by a concept of God developed in abstraction from it.

II *Election as grace*

There are two, converse, emphases to be made in any exposition of election as part of Barth's doctrine of God. The first is that when theology develops a doctrine of election it is saying something about God, and, moreover, about who God really is. Before it speaks about man or his experience, whether Christian or otherwise, it speaks about God. Second, it is not possible to say what the Christian means by God without at the same time saying that he is the electing God. It is indissolubly part of the very being and essence of God that he elects. This cannot be put too strongly. The Christian God is one who elects. To be the Christian God *is* to be the one who elects, chooses, predestines.

This central insight can be elucidated under a number of headings. First, by what it denies: it denies that election is an *also* in the will of God, that God is really something else, but also happens to be the one who elects man into relationship with himself. Thus: 'According to this conception God is everything in the way of aseity, simplicity, immutability, infinity, etc., but He is not the living God, that is to say, He is not the God who lives in concrete decision. God lives in this sense only figuratively. It is not something which belongs to his proper and essential life, but only to his relationship with the world' (p. 79). Quite the reverse. For Barth, God's decision of election is part of what it means to be God.

Second, the central statement can be elucidated by means of

what it implies about God's eternal being, about what God always is: ' ... in Himself, in the primal and basic decision (*Ur- und Grundentscheidung*) in which He wills to be and actually is God ... God is none other than the One who in His Son or Word elects Himself, and in and with Himself elects His people' (p. 76). Thus election has priority over all the acts of God. 'Priority' of course is ambiguous, and can refer either to something preceding in time or to a pre-eminence in being. The latter meaning is clearly present. All the other things that God does – creation, reconciliation, redemption – are, he says, 'grounded and determined in the fact that God is the God of the eternal election of His grace' (p. 14). The God who creates, etc., is the one who is the electing God. There are even overtones of a temporal priority as well, though they must be carefully qualified. The point being made is that God's electing grace is not an afterthought, hastily improvised after the catastrophe that overtook the first and independent order of creation. God, as essentially the electing God, makes the universe in order that it may be the arena on which his gracious purposes may come to pass. It is therefore the presupposition (*Voraussetzung*) of all God's works. 'It is because of this that we put the doctrine of election ... at the very beginning, and indeed before the beginning, of what we have to say concerning God's dealings with His creation' (p. 89).

The third important feature of election is that it is first of all, before being the election of man, something that God does in, with and to himself. It is God's self-ordaining (p. 89), his self-determination (p. 91), his self-giving (p. 121). Therefore, even though it entails a commitment of himself, it is free because God is its sole author. But it is also and at the same time gracious. For it is not a game played in the privacy of the Godhead, nor does the theologian speak in this way to satisfy his own intellectual curiosity about the inner being of God. There is a double movement, or, better, a single movement with two aspects, both 'inside' the being of God and 'outside', and they belong inseparably together. What happens in what may be called the privacy of the Trinity is done therefore *in order that* God may be gracious also to what is not God. But he would still be gracious had he not decided to elect man also, or had he chosen to elect him in an altogether different way.

Grace of election is only grace if it is free.[10] Once, however, this inner grace and freedom are established, the outer movement can be seen to belong inseparably to it as the binding by God of himself to what is not God – that is, to man, in and with Jesus Christ. The outcome is that God's 'self-determination is *identical* with the decree of His movement towards man ... The reality and revelation of this movement is Jesus Christ himself' (pp. 91–2, italics added). 'It is self-giving. And that is how the inner glory of God overflows' (p. 121). 'Under the concept of predestination ... we say that in freedom (its affirmation and not its loss) God tied Himself to the universe' (p. 155). 'In this primal decision God did not remain satisfied with His own being in Himself. He reached out to something beyond ...' (p. 168). And so we have been brought irresistibly to the fourth characteristic of election, that it is exercised by God in himself, but also in relation to that which is not God.

Fifth, the twofold movement of the grace of God both comes to expression in and *is* the history of Jesus Christ. He is both the subject and the object of election, the electing God (p. 103) and the elect man (p. 116), for he is at the same time the God who elects graciously and the man who is the recipient of grace. For our purposes, all that needs to be said here is that in this statement we come to the heart of Barth's radical restructuring of the doctrine of election. If the history of this man is the electing action of God, then we need look neither at our own experience nor for a God different from or lying behind this story. The assertion that Jesus is the electing God 'crowds out and replaces the idea of a *decretum absolutum*' (p. 103).[11]

III   *The event of election*

Here it is essential that we stand back and view what is

---

[10] It is failure to understand that election is about God that has led to fruitless arguments about Barth's alleged universalism. So argues Bettis, 'Is Karl Barth a Universalist?' For the criticisms of Barth on this score, see E. Brunner, *Dogmatics Vol I: The Christian Doctrine of God*, translated by Olive Wyon (London: Lutterworth, 1949), pp. 346–52; and G. C. Berkouwer, *The Triumph of Grace in the Theology of Karl Barth*, translated by H. R. Boer (London: Paternoster, 1956), pp. 287–96.

[11] It is interesting that in saying this Barth goes behind Calvin, Aquinas and Augustine to Athanasius for support. See pp. 106ff.

happening. For two quite fundamental questions arise directly
from what has been said so far, and they are related to one
another. First, what licenses all this talk about primal decision
(p. 168), self-ordination, etc.; indeed, any language at all about
God in eternity? The language is all highly personal, and
undoubtedly characterises God not as somebody or some
substance-like entity who does things, but as someone who
takes place. God, on this account, *is* his electing will, or, in
Barth's own words, '. . . predestination is the divine act of will
itself and not an abstraction from or fixed and static result of it'
(p. 181, cf. p. 187). It necessarily follows from the oft-repeated
assertion that there is no other God behind the acts of election
that God *is* a kind of personal decision-event taking place both
in eternity and on the plane of history. The second question is
equally serious and also concerns the difficult notion that God
is eternal event. We have, in the recent exposition, gently and
apparently without justification, slid happily from eternity into
time; from the eternal God, in his self-determination to be
gracious, to Jesus of Nazareth, that grace in historical action.
How do we hold together such diverse statements as that God is
eternally and essentially the one who graciously elects himself
and his people and that Jesus Christ, a man, *is* this eternal
electing God?

The beginnings of an answer to both questions lie in the brief
sentence that Barth has characteristically woven into his exposition of the doctrine of election. 'God is the self-revealing God,
and as such He is the electing God. The eternal will of God
which is before time is the same as the eternal will of God which
is above time, and which reveals itself as such and operates as
such in time' (p. 156). Here we come, inevitably, to Barth's
conception of revelation. As should be well known, this is not for
him religious experience or even religious experience connected with the person of Jesus. It is something that happens. 'God
reveals Himself as the Lord' is the thrice-repeated refrain of one
of the most important passages in the *Church Dogmatics*,[12] and
means that something happens in history that by its very nature

---

[12] *Church Dogmatics* 1/1, pp. 349–83. This passage should be read alongside
Barth, *Anselm: Fides Quaerens Intellectum. Anselm's Proof of the Existence of God in
the Context of his Theological Scheme*, translated by I. W. Robertson (London:
SCM Press, 1960), especially pp. 11–72.

authenticates itself to certain observers of that event as being unavoidably describable in sentences containing the word 'God'. It is Barth's application to the history of Jesus of Nazareth of what he learned from Anselm: that God authenticates his reality by what he does here. Something happens. It is God; it happens at the initiative of God; it communicates its reality to people of a certain time and place. It is threefold, and in each of its three aspects it is wholly the event that is God. The doctrine of the Trinity therefore is theology's attempt to conceptualise the threefold divine event: to say what God essentially is if this kind of thing happens.

The conception of God as triune has direct relevance to the discussion of election, some aspects of which can be pointed out immediately. For example, if the events that are the life, death and resurrection of Jesus *are* the presence of God on earth, we have no need to look behind them for another God or, specifically, for an election that is something different from them. They *are* election taking place. Further, and by precisely the same logic, if these events are God, then God is something that happens. But he is not anything that happens, nor any kind of triune happening. He is the God who happens as he reaches out to his creation by becoming part of it without being any less himself. In particular, he becomes man. It is immediately clear how close already is this language to that used in the doctrine of election proper. To cite at length a passage already used, '... that is how the inner glory of God overflows. From all eternity it purports and wills its own impartation to the creature, the closest possible union with it, a fellowship which is not to its own advantage but to that of the creature' (p. 121). It is a short step from the exposition of the Trinity as such to saying that election is one of the most characteristic acts, perhaps the characteristic act, of the triune God.

Still, however, there remains the question of how the revelation of God in time licenses us to speak of an eternal Trinity. The move is made by Barth by means of an ontological principle which, in the memorable words of R. W. Jenson, 'may seem to hover between obfuscation and utter triviality',[13] but

---

[13] R. W. Jenson, *God After God: The God of the Past and the God of the Future as Seen in the Work of Karl Barth* (Indianapolis and New York: Bobbs Merrill, 1969), p. 103.

which in fact contains within it a vital key to Barth's theology. If God has indeed revealed himself, then he must, in himself, be such that he *can* reveal himself. What God does, he can do.[14] Actuality implies possibility and, particularly, the freedom to become what he is not, to become man. God is gracious in becoming man: *therefore* in his innermost being he is the kind of God to whom it is not unnatural to become what he is not. Barth's move, therefore, in the process of his argument, is from time to eternity, and not the reverse. But once the move is made, it is clear that priority in being belongs to the eternal God. History is a sure guide to what God really is; but it is what God really is that makes the temporal history possible at all. Grace is possible because God is gracious.

The link is then established between God's revelation and his triune reality. But in order that we may see more clearly the bearing of this on election, and particularly on the conception of God as personal electing event, more must be said of what we mean when we say that God is triune. The conception of God entailed by Barth's understanding of revelation as event has been spelled out by Eberhard Jüngel in his book significantly entitled *Gottes Sein ist im Werden*, God's being consists in his becoming.[15] Because revelation is the event in which God happens among us it must, Jüngel argues, be understood as God's self-interpretation of himself to us. This self-interpretation brings with it a threefold distinction within the unity of the one revelation and the doctrine of the Trinity follows as *our* interpretation of God's self-interpretation.[16] But because this really is God's self-interpretation we cannot posit a gulf between what God does in revelation and what he is in himself, and we must draw two conclusions. First, God's being, as being, is *reines Ereignis*, pure event.[17] Second, it is a being that is relationally structured,[18] in the sense that God is what he is in the relations of Father, Son and Holy Spirit. God is what happens as Father, Son and Holy Spirit. Therefore, 'God's

---

[14] *Church Dogmatics* 1/1, p. 363.

[15] E. Jüngel, *Gottes Sein ist im Werden* (Tübingen: J. C. B. Mohr, 2nd edition, 1967). See also Jenson, *God After God*, especially Part Three, 'God Who Happens', pp. 95–135.

[16] Jüngel, *Gottes Sein*, pp. 27–9.

[17] Jüngel, *Gottes Sein*, p. 39.

[18] Jüngel, *Gottes Sein*, p. 37.

being is thus as the being of God, Father, Son, and Holy Spirit, a *being in becoming*.' This means that God is already, in himself, 'no other than he who he is in his revelation. He is thus in this his being already in advance *der Unsrige, our God . . .*'.[19]

In simple summary, it might be said that that the Word became flesh is our justification for saying that before all time God decided freely to be our God. The doctrine of election is then the rational exposition of the characteristic[20] triune event. Jüngel refers in this context to Barth's characterisation of God's eternal election as God's '*Urentscheidung . . .* in which *God* irrevocably determined his being in act. This self-determining of God is an act of his *Selbstverhältnisses* as Father, Son, and Holy Spirit. But it is *at the same time* a relating of God to men . . .'.[21] Once again we come upon what has previously been described as the double movement within the Trinity and *ad extra*, which is yet one single movement. And there is one more term to which Jüngel draws our attention. Barth speaks of the *Urgeschichte* (pp. 7–9), a word which, as Jüngel notes, here means something different from what it meant in the *Commentary on Romans*, where it was equivalent to that which precisely is *not* historical.[22] Now, the primal history is not the negation of the temporal story but its ground, and is therefore understood in the latter's light as that 'God determines himself . . . to be our God as one of us.'[23] God *is* the event of triune love, the decision taken before all time to be a God of electing grace. That is what we mean when we use the word *God*.

IV   *Election and the structure of the* Church Dogmatics

We have now seen that election is the characteristic act by which God is what he is. And yet the doctrine of election is not

---

[19] Jüngel, *Gottes Sein*, p. 77, Jüngel's italics.

[20] I avoid the word 'archetypal' because although Barth sometimes uses language of this kind, the usage reflects a problematic side of his thinking about time and eternity. See Jenson, *God After God*, pp. 154f. and 172–5, and R. Prenter, 'Karl Barths Umbildung der traditionellen Zweinaturlehre in lutherischer Beleuchtung', *Studia Theologica* 2 (1957), 1–88.

[21] Jüngel, *Gottes Sein*, pp. 83–4.

[22] Jüngel, *Gottes Sein*, p. 88, n. 57.

[23] Jüngel, *Gottes Sein*, p. 89.

part of the doctrine of the Trinity. How are the two related? The first point to be made is that Barth is not a systematic theologian in the sense that he has a system. His theology does not form a close-knit circle, in which all the parts are related by logical implication as, for example, is the case with the metaphysics of Spinoza or, possibly, the theology of Paul Tillich. He explicitly rejects the image of a circle as a model for the theologian's structure or rather, it would be more accurate to say, uses the analogy of the circle in an altogether different way. '[T]he unfolding and presentation of the content of the Word of God must take place fundamentally in such a way that the Word of God is understood as the centre and foundation of dogmatics and of Church proclamation, like a circle whose periphery forms the starting point for a limited number of lines which in dogmatics are to be drawn to a certain distance in all directions.'[24] That is to say, in the exposition of the Trinity Barth has expounded the place from which those who would speak of the activity of God towards and in the world must set out. Thus this topic is treated not as an afterthought to the discussion of who God is, but as part of the prolegomena to dogmatics, that is to say, prolegomena to the unfolding of what is the Word of God for man.[25] It is on the periphery of this circle that the doctrine of God begins, and is then free to develop its own themes as centres of interest in themselves. The very freedom of the triune God precludes system-building or a theology of the closed circle.

But this is all very metaphorical. What is the logical relation between the doctrine of election, as part of the doctrine of God, and the doctrine of the Trinity which forms its rational base? Once again it is to Jüngel that we must go for illumination, and he refers us to Barth's use of the patristic devices of perichoresis (or *circuminsessio* for those more familiar with the Latin) and appropriation. What do these doctrines say? Perichoresis, in the words of Barth, 'asserts that the divine modes of existence condition and permeate one another mutually with

[24] Karl Barth, *Church Dogmatics* 1/2, p. 869.
[25] Thus it takes the place traditionally filled by so-called natural theology. It should be clear from all that has been said so far that this is not an arbitrary or irrational step, but part of an attempt radically to rethink what rational theology is.

such perfection, that one is as invariably in the other two as the other two are in the one'.[26] The purpose of the doctrine is to preserve the unity of God in his acts. Election is the act not of God the Father, but of the whole Trinity. Perichoresis avoids any suggestion of tritheism by expressing the interrelationship of Father, Son and Spirit in the event of election. Thus the Son assents to the will of the Father in the freedom of the Spirit,[27] and this is the 'harmony of the three-in-one God'.[28] We recall that Jüngel has characterised the being of God as relational, and here we have an expression of it, what he calls an '*Entsprechung*, in which the Son *bejaht* – says yes to – the will of the Father in the freedom of the Spirit ...'.[29] And this is far from being simply a theoretical matter, or a desire for a merely verbal orthodoxy. It has direct relevance to the point already made, that Barth rejects an unknown electing God behind his acts in Jesus. 'God is what he does among us. All the complicated subtleties of Barth's developed doctrine of the Trinity say this one thing at all the different places where it might be forgotten.'[30]

But it is the doctrine of appropriation, which in trinitarian theology performs the function of balancing the doctrine of perichoresis, that brings us to the answer to our question about structure. Appropriation teaches us that, despite the very proper safeguards in perichoresis against tritheism, it is none the less *appropriate* to attribute some acts to God the Father, some to God the Son, and some to God the Holy Spirit, because in revelation we are given a 'hint' (*Hinweis*) that this is the case.[31] '*Per appropriationem* now this act, now that attribute in respect of this or that mode of existence *must* be brought to the forefront, to make it possible to designate it as such at all. But it is only *per appropriationem* that this may be done ...'[32] Jüngel makes two observations about Barth's use of this doctrine, both highly suggestive. First, he remarks that appropriation is *ein hermeneutischer Vorgang*, a hermeneutical enterprise. 'Appropria-

[26] Barth, *Church Dogmatics* 1/1, p. 425.
[27] Jüngel, *Gottes Sein*, p. 86.
[28] Jüngel, *Gottes Sein*, citing Barth, *Church Dogmatics* 2/2, p. 105.
[29] Jüngel, *Gottes Sein*, citing Barth, *Church Dogmatics* 2/2, p. 105.
[30] R. W. Jenson, *God After God*, p. 113.
[31] Barth, *Church Dogmatics* 1/1, p. 428.
[32] Barth, *Church Dogmatics* 1/1, p. 430.

tion is thus what makes it possible to bring God to speech, for example *as Father.*'[33] Second, it provides a key to Barth's whole dogmatic enterprise, and he believes it possible to show that 'appropriation and thus the understanding of God as concrete event fundamentally determines Barth's whole dogmatic, and in particular his doctrine of election ...'.[34]

If this is so, we can see that each of the great themes of Barth's theology is an exposition of a particular appropriation of the different modes of being of the one triune God, and each is possible because what happened in Jesus Christ empowers us (simply because it is God's concrete presence among us) to speak in that way.[35] To revert to the geometrical metaphor, the lines going outward from the theological circle are related to it in that they are all about the triune God, but about him in all the richness, diversity and freedom of his love to the world. The appropriations are about what he does to and in his world (rather differently from the received opinion of Barth's theology that it is unconcerned with the world) but show that what God does in his world is ontologically based in what he really is. Thus, in Volume Three of the *Church Dogmatics* there is appropriated to the Father, by which is meant, among other things, the one who raised Jesus from the dead,[36] the function of creating. Volume Four articulates the reconciliation accomplished by God the Son, and the projected fifth volume was to have been about the redemption achieved by God the Holy Spirit. After the exposition of the Trinity, and before the volumes just mentioned, comes the doctrine of God, which contains election as one of its four major themes. It is clearly an appropriation of God the Father but, more than that, and more than any of the themes of the doctrine of God, it forms a bridge between the Prolegomena and the later volumes. First, it speaks massively of the reality of the triune God as one who goes outward, whose whole being is his concrete taking to himself of the creatures he has made. In that function it goes forward from the Prolegomena. Second, and here it looks forward to creation, reconcilia-

---

[33] Jüngel, *Gottes Sein,* p. 49: '... die Möglichkeit, Gott z. B. *als Vater* zur Sprache zu bringen'.
[34] Jüngel, *Gottes Sein,* p. 53.
[35] Here the hermeneutical function is also observed.
[36] See Barth, *Church Dogmatics* 1/1, p. 445.

tion and redemption, it makes it plain that everything else that Barth will say about God is said of the one who is gracious from all eternity, who just is his grace. The God who creates, reconciles and redeems, the God of the later volumes, is first and foremost the one who elects: that is, who loves and chooses the other to be his own, before the other knows it, before he shares in it, indeed, when he resists it, before, even, he is created. The doctrine of election as part of the doctrine of God is that which teaches us that all we are and receive is of grace, and it is therefore the sum of the gospel.

V Election and the structure of Barth's theology

'In Christ he chose us before the world was founded ...' (Eph. 1.4). Behind that verse lies the belief, almost unanimous in the New Testament, that Jesus Christ is at the heart of God's good pleasure, both for man and for the universe in which he lives.[37] Add to this Barth's attention to the concrete reality of God's action in Christ, something else that is not without biblical support, and it becomes clear that in his doctrine of election Barth has given rational expression to the distinctive character of the Christian God that is possibly without equal in power, comprehensiveness and originality. But there has been much criticism of the place of the doctrine of election in the structure of Barth's theology. A major aspect of this is that it is held to function in such a way as to decide the whole of history in advance. While there is something in that, such a conclusion seems not to follow necessarily from Barth's location of divine election in some pre-temporal sphere. Much of the scriptural testimony to election, the affirmation of the Letter to the Ephesians among it, requires that at least some weight be given to this factor. That God has destined all for reconciliation with himself need not preclude the eschatological space – that is to say, the time and freedom – for the way in which this pre-destiny works itself out. We might say, for example, that in creating a world God the Father destines it for completion in time and through the perfecting work of God the Spirit, who

---

[37] Of relevance to this theme is J. G. Gibbs, *Creation and Redemption. A Study in Pauline Theology.* Supplement to *Novum Testamentum* 26 (Leiden: Brill, 1971).

enables the world to achieve its end in Christ. Such a statement does not foreclose the various ways in which the particularities of the outworking in time may be conceived to take shape.

The characteristic difficulties with Barth's doctrine are not there, but are to be found where its great achievement is also, in its being linked with the doctrine of God. As in the case of Barth's theology of revelation, this locus raises in interesting form the way in which inferences may be drawn to eternity from the economy of divine action in and towards the order of space and time. How far may it be argued that, because God makes himself present to the world as God in the event of revelation, he is in some way or other event in himself? Once prepared to accept the validity of the argument, I am increasingly unhappy with the replacement of 'substance' with 'event' language in the ontology of God. Neither is *in itself* personal, and that is surely the heart of the matter of divine being. In our context, the question becomes, how far may it be argued that because God, in Christ, elects Israel and the Church to be his people, it follows that there is a sense in which he elects himself in eternity? There are a number of questions to be elucidated here.

The central one is whether in his description of God as a kind of primal decision, in the way so well articulated in Jüngel's book, Barth is still not beholden to the existentialist conceptuality he struggled so hard during his formative years to throw off. The achievement of the movement from the *Commentary on Romans* to the *Church Dogmatics* is the remarkable movement to a conception of the relation between the knower and the known which avoided making human existential choice in some way determinative for faith and theology. But the existentialist conceptuality appears to remain in the discussion of the reality of God. Let us begin an examination of this question with Barth's treatment of the divine attributes or perfections. It can be argued, for example, that the polarity of love and freedom in Barth's doctrine of creation in the second part of *Church Dogmatics* 2/1 has great potentiality for a move from revelation to the eternal being of God. Because God shows in revelation that he loves in freedom, Barth rightly concludes that he is loving and free in himself. But how is the love-in-freedom to be conceived?

The problem with Barth's employment of the concept is not

that he appears to wish to use the concept of freedom analogously, that is to say, to speak in a related but different way of divine and human freedom. There must be a sense in which human freedom is different from divine freedom, because it is only properly understood in terms of our relation to God, while God's freedom is self-grounded. Similarly, if the doctrine of creation is to give the world the distinct reality it needs to be truly creation, it must be the case that God was not bound to create. Because God is love, in himself and in advance, he does not need to create, so that in the theology of creation an element of voluntarism is essential. If the world is not to be in some way a mere emanation of the infinite God rather than truly the finite world, its being must be freely willed. But how are we to construe the inner-divine freedom? In Barth, as we have seen, there is a strongly christological determination of the concept. 'God is none other than the One who in His Son or Word elects Himself, and in and with Himself elects His people' (p. 76). But Barth suggests that this willed electing is what makes God to be God. One difficulty with this is succinctly expressed by Pannenberg, in saying that 'the act of election is part and parcel of the freedom of God's relation to the world, so that its content cannot be constitutive for the eternal identity of this essence'.[38] To put the matter another way, it is perhaps no accident that many commentators have suggested that the shape of Barth's doctrine of election, in appearing to define God in terms of an eternal decision of a particular kind, does detract from both divine and human freedom. That is not to deny the propriety of speaking of an eternal decision, in which creation and redemption are properly spoken of as acts whose basis is in the eternal being of God, but it is to question whether that is constitutive for the being of God.

If we are to avoid an element of apparently arbitrary voluntarism – though that is a very one-sided way to put the matter – we have to ask whether a more adequately trinitarian account of divine freedom should not postpone its generalising until there has been a little broader engagement with the relations of Father, Son and Spirit as they are made known in the economy

[38] Wolfhart Pannenberg, *Systematic Theology Volume 2*, translated by G. W. Bromiley (Edinburgh: T. & T. Clark, 1994), p. 368.

of creation, reconciliation and redemption. In the following chapter, an attempt will be made to understand the place of the Spirit in the Trinity in terms of his being the one who frees God to be for the other. In such a theology, the polarity of love and freedom ceases to be quite so dialectical a relationship as it is in Barth's treatment of election, because God loves in freedom as the three persons are mutually constituted in eternity. They are, accordingly, free only as they are eternally constituted by their mutual relationships of perichoresis. That is to say, God's inner freedom is not read off one privileged dimension of the economy, whether that be election or anything else, but is taken to be an implication of all the divine acts 'outwards'.

An account of how this might be conceived has been given by Robert Jenson in conversation with Martin Luther. Suppose that Luther is right in saying that freedom is a gift that we are given without, however, the overriding of our human reality: 'to have "liberum arbitrium" is to be rapt into freedom without dependence on alien freedom'. Such an account, which is scarcely one that comes from our 'natural' belief that we are free simply in ourselves, clearly derives from the gospel of justification of the sinner, who is given freedom by God. But what kind of analogous freedom does this imply God to have? Jenson states the matter as follows: 'God is freedom antecedent to himself as determinate free will. He can intelligibly be said to be this if the Father is the source of the Son and both are freed in the Spirit. God is rapt by another without dependence on an other than God.'[39] The expression of the doctrine below is not quite in these terms, but the point is the same. God's freedom, the freedom that is prior to but revealed in all his acts outwards, is the personal freedom of the mutually constituting love of Father, Son and Spirit. In that sense, God is the one who loves in freedom. The doctrine of election is thus the expression of his loving freedom, but it derives from his personal being in communion rather than from his being an eternal *decision*. In this way, a 'space' is created between the eternal being of God and all his acts *ad extra*, a space which enables both God and the world to be themselves, in relation but also in distinction.

[39] Robert W. Jenson, 'An Ontology of Freedom in the *De Servo Arbitrio* of Luther', *Modern Theology* 10 (1994), 247–52 (250).

CHAPTER 7

GOD THE HOLY SPIRIT
Augustine and his successors

I Introduction. The task of a systematic theology of the Holy Spirit

The task of a systematic theology of the Holy Spirit is by no means easy to define. If pneumatology is contrasted with christology, one difficulty will be immediately apparent. In the latter, there is one clear and dominating concern: to enquire, in conversation with the tradition and other interested parties, about the humanity and divinity of Christ – their possibility, scriptural justification, interrelation, implications and the rest. In the former, however, there is little debate about the question of the Spirit's divinity. Once the historic battle in the early centuries to establish the full deity of the Spirit had been won, the question was rarely raised again. Where the difficulty really lies is in the identification of the Spirit and the location of his activity, as will be apparent from a glance at some of the ways in which the Spirit has been understood and expressed in recent centuries.

There are three places at least where we find highly varying accounts of the person and work of the Spirit. One is what can be called the mainstream dogmatic tradition, which tends to concentrate on the work of the Spirit as applying to believer and Church the benefits of Christ. Karl Barth is a major modern representative of this classical Western approach, and provides an illustration of its strengths and weaknesses. While there is no suggestion that Barth fails to pay due attention to the doctrine – indeed, one study of his pneumatology invites us to see him as a theologian of the Holy Spirit[1] – it is sometimes

---

[1] Philip J. Rosato, *The Spirit as Lord. The Pneumatology of Karl Barth* (Edinburgh: T. & T. Clark, 1981).

observed that his treatment of pneumatology is far more conventional than his contributions to other dogmatic loci.[2] A further criticism takes us to the heart of our problem, and it is that, by tending to limit the work of the Spirit to the application to the believer of the benefits of Christ, Barth shares the 'tendency to see the Spirit as functionally subordinate to the Son'.[3]

Thomas Smail, rightly in my view, claims that in this Barth reproduces a general weakness of the Western tradition. On such an understanding the Spirit is identified almost exclusively in terms of his function, and as such in relation to the Son who saves us. (That is not to suggest that the person and work of the Spirit should ever be defined in any way independently of the Son. The point of the objection is the limitation of the function to the application of Christ's saving work.) Barth did, to be sure, argue that it was necessary to move from function to being: if God the Spirit performs a distinctive role in the economy of salvation, we are entitled to infer that the Spirit's eternal being in some way corresponds to his historic act. But because the function is defined so narrowly – almost wholly christologically – such a move maintains an effective *ontological* subordination of Spirit to Son and militates against an identification of the Spirit's specific *persona*.[4]

The second source for the modern identification of the Holy Spirit is that amorphous group of phenomena known as the charismatic movement. Its weakness tends to be the opposite of those of the dogmatic tradition against which it is often in reaction, in that it is sometimes in danger not of relating the Spirit and the Son unsatisfactorily, but of separating them from one another. The tendency is to identify the Spirit as the *cause* of particular religious phenomena: speaking with tongues,

[2] 'One is even tempted to think that the incompletion of the *Church Dogmatics*, with the eschatology and doctrine of the Spirit missing, is not merely a matter of chronology.' Robert W. Jenson, *God After God: The God of the Past and the God of the Future as Seen in the Work of Karl Barth* (Indianapolis and New York: Bobbs Merrill, 1969), pp. 173f.

[3] Thomas A. Smail, 'The Doctrine of the Holy Spirit', *Beyond Christendom. Essays on the Centenary of the Birth of Karl Barth, May 10, 1886* (Allison Park, Pennsylvania: Pickwick Publications, 1986), pp. 87–110.

[4] For a defence of Barth against this charge, see John Thompson, *The Holy Spirit in the Theology of Karl Barth* (Allison Park, Pennsylvania: Pickwick Publications, 1991).

conversion experiences and the rest. There is also sometimes a tendency to depersonalise the Spirit, and unguarded character-isations of the Spirit as 'it' are sometimes to be heard. And yet, just as we must take seriously the contentions of the first tendency I have sketched – the identification of the Spirit as the one who applies to the believer the benefits of Christ – so here there are moments of truth that we must not ignore. However much, for example, we may wish to argue that the theology of the Spirit in parts of the Acts of the Apostles represents a relatively primitive development, to be corrected by the more sophisticated analyses of the Fourth Gospel, it would be a mistake to play the one too much against the other. Both Acts and the charismatic movement represent a strand in the Christian tradition that has a place in any theology aiming at comprehensiveness. It is here worth observing that one recent treatise did suggest reasons why it might be appropriate to characterise the Spirit as 'it',[5] and if we are to identify the Spirit as personal or as a person we must be aware of the fact that the attribution is not so obvious as in the case of the other persons of the Trinity. There is something about the action of the Spirit which invites characterisation in terms of such non-personal phenomena as bird, wind and fire.

But, third, there is yet another focus for the modern identi-fication of the Spirit, one which is more broadly cultural than the other influences. Owed to the influence of Hegel above all is a tendency to identify the Spirit with or in particular cultural and historical developments. According to this view, which will be sketched here only crudely, the Spirit is identified as the being or force which operates either (1) within the created order to lead it in a certain direction or to bring about certain developments within it; or (2) within the human person or human culture to direct it in a certain way. The Spirit's operation – and it is here not always easy to distinguish between Spirit and spirit – is conceived to be essentially immanent, and the numerous variations on the theme are witness to the current influence of this trend. (It can be seen to be influential also in certain forms of

---

[5] Alasdair Heron, *The Holy Spirit. The Holy Spirit in the Bible, in the History of Christian Thought and in recent Theology* (London: Marshall, Morgan & Scott, 1983), p. 176.

charismatic theology, especially in so far as they tend to identify the Spirit with certain subjective experiences. That is the religious rather than the secularising variation on the theme.) A recent employment of the non-charismatic version of this approach in Christian theology is that of G. W. H. Lampe, who used the conception of God as immanent Spirit to advocate a Spirit theology in place of the christological-trinitarian approach of the tradition.[6]

It will be noticed that all three of the above tendencies share a common direction: of *internalising* the action of the Spirit, the first two in the believer or the church, the latter in culture or the cosmos in general. To that extent, the tendency, from Hegel onwards, to secularise the action of the Spirit is a proper attempt to give the Spirit a function beyond the merely ecclesiastical or religious–subjective. To that extent it carries forward the Reformation's concern to liberate the Spirit from the control of the ecclesiastical institution. But, and here we reach a point of major importance, it may be that the restriction of the Spirit to forms of immanence, whether in Church, believer or culture, is a symptom of what is wrong with the whole tradition, Catholic, Protestant and secularising alike. Against the widespread assumption that the Holy Spirit is to be understood as the immanence of God – in the believer, the creation or the human being in general – it must be argued that the Spirit is better identified in terms of transcendence than of immanence. The Spirit may be active *within* the world, but he does not become identical with any part of the world. That is the function of the Son, who becomes flesh; and if without more ado we think of the Spirit also as a form of God's immanence, we may be in danger of being unable effectively to distinguish between Son and Spirit. Here again is the root of our problem of identification. And yet there may also be moments of truth in the characterisation of the Spirit as immanent. Is talk of the Spirit's action 'within our hearts' simply loose and inaccurate? Perhaps it will be necessary to distinguish different forms of immanence, certainly if we are to do justice to the apparently immanent character of some

[6] G. W. H. Lampe, *God as Spirit. The Bampton Lectures 1976* (London: SCM Press, 1977).

biblical characterisations of the way in which the Spirit is present and active.

II *The roots of the problem*

Before, however, we move to the positive task of identification, we must seek for some of the reasons why the Western Christian tradition is in the state of confusion that it apparently is. If there is a problem of identification, it may be traceable in part to the fountain-head of Western theology, one who himself notoriously found the identification of the Spirit a great difficulty. Robert Jenson has indicated the symptom. 'For Augustine, the three "persons", over against us, are functionally indistinguishable. Thus Augustine could no longer conceptualise the saving relation between God and creatures by saying that the Father and the Son are transformingly present in the Spirit, as the Greek originators of trinitarianism had done.' Jenson goes on to point out that the outcome – what I have already indicated by referring to the tendency to speak of the Spirit as 'it' – was a tendency to identify the work of the Spirit as a process, as the means of God's causal action upon us, rather than, say, his free personal relation with us.[7]

There are a number of features of Augustine's treatment of the doctrine of the Holy Spirit in the *De Trinitate* which can be said to foreshadow the features we have surveyed. The first has in recent times become notorious, and it concerns Augustine's attempt to identify the *persona* of the Spirit as love and gift. Here it must be said that no objection can be taken to Augustine's programme. We do need concepts with whose help the Spirit can be identified, not only as Spirit but in distinction from Father and Son. Otherwise, we shall be in no position to say who or what the Spirit *is*. The problem is that the concepts that Augustine finds are inadequate, and for two reasons in particular. The first is that they do not distinguish the Spirit adequately from the Son, who might equally, perhaps with more justification, be described as the Father's love and gift to the world. That is undoubtedly the case when we are thinking

---

[7] Robert W. Jenson, 'The Holy Spirit', *Christian Dogmatics*, edited by C. E. Braaten and R. W. Jenson (Philadelphia: Fortress Press, 1984), volume 2, pp. 126f.

of the economy of salvation, as will be evident from the number of times it is said that God 'gives' or 'gives up' his only Son. It does not follow from this that we cannot speak of the Spirit as the gift of God; clearly we can and must. It is rather that such a concept does not serve its purpose of identification, certainly not if part of that purpose is to distinguish the Spirit from the other persons of the Trinity.

The second reason, and it follows directly from the first, is that the lack of adequate support Augustine can find from Scripture – as has been said, he has to employ 'rather desperate exegesis'[8] – effectively introduces a breach between the economic and the immanent Trinity. The Spirit in himself is conceived to be other than he is shown to be in revelation, which, as we shall see, is not primarily as love and gift. Augustine's speculative drive has led him to treat the immanent Trinity in isolation from his work in the economy of creation and salvation. As a result, certain features of the biblical presentation of the Spirit – and particularly the eschatological dimensions of his action – are overridden in the quest for the justification of Augustine's two concepts.

The suspicion must be – and this brings us to a second major feature of Augustine's treatment of the Spirit – that one source of Augustine's theology must be sought elsewhere. It is, of course, his analysis, owing much to Platonism, of the immanent Trinity by analogy with the threefold structure of the human mind. According to this, and it brings us to the third central concept in terms of which Augustine understands the Spirit, the Spirit in the Trinity plays an analogous part to the will in the human mind. The function of the will is to bring the contents of memory – the fount of the mind – into the (conscious) reason. (For Plato, it will be remembered, knowledge consists in the recollection of the Forms known in pre-temporal existence.) It thus relates memory and reason or understanding. Analogously, the function of the Spirit in the Trinity is to relate Father and Son; to close the circle of the trinitarian being. The function is thus essentially unitive, again in neglect of other features of the Spirit's action.[9]

---

[8] Cited from J. H. S. Burleigh, by James Mackey, *The Christian Experience of God as Trinity* (London: SCM Press, 1983), p. 155.

[9] I have presented some of the evidence for this claim in *The Promise of Trinitarian Theology* (Edinburgh: T. & T. Clark, 1991), pp. 48–55.

Many of the features of the mainstream Western theology of the Spirit, as they emerge in the three forms of identification listed in the previous section, can be seen to derive at least in part from Augustine's influence, or, if it is thought dangerous to draw direct lines of historical causality, to echo the kind of things that he says. Augustine's tendency to treat the Spirit as essentially a link between Father and Son – the unitive function – can easily lead to a subordination of the Spirit to the Son, while the treatment of the Trinity on the analogy of the human mind easily slips into the immanentism which finds in either the human consciousness or the human mind – or even the immanent mind of the universe – the place where the activity of the Spirit is located. The analogy with the mind, and especially with its inwardness, can also be understood as the source both of charismatic subjectivism and the idealism that is so marked a feature of modern theologies influenced by Kant and Hegel. Charles Taylor has argued that 'It is hardly an exaggeration to say that it was Augustine who introduced the inwardness of radical reflexivity and bequeathed it to the Western tradition of thought.'[10] The impact on pneumatology can, similarly, scarcely be overstated. Even in theologians who seek a more orthodox solution to the problem of the identification of the Spirit, the temptation to intellectualism, to the use of some essentially mental analogy for the identification of the Spirit, can remain.

But it is not only in the West that problems are to be found, and it can be argued that in the East too there are inadequacies. A frequent charge is that, like the charismatic movement, Eastern Orthodox theology tends to develop an insufficiently christological doctrine of the Spirit, so that, as Barth has suggested, there can be a suggestion of a mystical ascent to the Father without the mediation of the Son.[11] Although it is also true that, as in the West, there are differences of emphasis in Orthodox theology, there is something to be said for John Milbank's recent judgement that:

There appears to be a gulf between the confident proclama-

[10] Charles Taylor, *Sources of the Self. The Making of the Modern Identity* (Cambridge: Cambridge University Press, 1989), p. 131.
[11] Karl Barth, *Church Dogmatics* 1/1, p. 481.

tion of the Spirit as a separate hypostasis, and the lack of an adequate rationale for this separation. Where the Spirit is understood as 'applying' the benefits of Christ, then she seems in danger of being reduced to the power of Christ's person. And the problem is compounded on the level of the immanent Trinity. We can begin to understand the one God who is also difference, who includes relation, and manifold expression. But a second difference? This still smacks of the arbitrary, and the incantatory. It is not surprising that the western tradition has so often described the Spirit as the re-assertion of unity after difference, while eastern tradition since Photius has talked of an absolutely ineffable mystery, which risks reduction to the status of a purely extrinsic datum.[12]

What is to be done? There are a number of requirements. First, any attempt to identify the Spirit must show that there is a way of God's action towards us and his world which is not *separable* from his action in Christ, but not *reducible* to it either. In particular, arguments like those of Lampe for varieties of a single imma-nence of God must be shown to fail to 'save the appearances'. Here, we must return to the economy of divine action in time and space to enquire whether there can be found a more com-prehensive articulation of the Spirit's action than has been cus-tomary in the tradition. That will lead to the second require-ment, which will be to show that on such a basis there can be a legitimate attempt to identify the Spirit both as a trinitarian person and in relation to the other persons of the Godhead.

III   *The Spirit in the economy. Creation and incarnation*

First, then, we treat the action of the Spirit in the economy, and here we shall find that the problems in christology and pneu-matology are parallel rather than distinct. In both cases, it is often argued that there is such a diversity of biblical character-isation that no overall unity of treatment can be found. Against

[12] John Milbank, 'The Second Difference: For a Trinitarianism without Reserve', *Modern Theology* 2 (1986), 211–34 (213).

this, it can be claimed that while there is no uniformity in biblical talk of the Spirit, neither is there such a diversity that it is illegitimate to attempt to isolate a common strand of meaning. It has already been suggested that one difference between the Son and the Spirit, and therefore the beginnings of an identifying characteristic of the Spirit, is the immanence of one in the divine economy, the transcendence of the other over it. The Son *becomes* flesh; the Spirit acts *towards* and *in* the world. Such a distinction enables us to understand the biblical representations of the work of the Spirit, without overriding the differences that are also apparent. Thus the suggestion that can be made on the basis of some of the gospel narratives, and especially the first two chapters of Luke, that Jesus is *given by* the Spirit in no way contradicts, given the different historical perspectives employed by the writers, the Johannine teaching that the crucified, risen and ascended Christ is the mediator of the Spirit to those who believe. The one who, during his earthly incarnation, is the gift from the Father, made the human being he particularly is by the creating and renewing Spirit, becomes after his ascension the mediator of that same Spirit to those who come to the Father through him. It is of course to that latter gospel that we owe two important features of later theology: that there is a distinction in the economy between the gift of the Spirit before and after Christ (see John 7.39, 'for as yet the Spirit had not yet been given, because Jesus was not yet glorified', though compare 1.32); and that there is a clear distinction between Jesus and the 'other paraclete'.

But what of Paul? It sometimes appears that there is for him no real distinction between the risen Christ and the Spirit who is Lord. If so, appearances are deceptive, in that there are in Paul clear characterisations of the distinctive being of the Spirit[13] and, moreover, passages in which there is a clearly threefold conceptualisation of the divine being and activity.[14] Nor should it be an insuperable problem[15] that the attributions

---

[13] Yves Congar, *I Believe in the Holy Spirit. 2. The Holy Spirit in the 'Economy'*, translated by David Smith (London: Geoffrey Chapman, 1983), pp. 29–40.

[14] See, for example, 2 Cor. 1.21f. and R. W. Jenson, *The Triune Identity. God According to the Gospel* (Philadelphia: Fortress Press, 1982), pp. 42f.

[15] Except, on anti-trinitarian or Kantian presuppositions of the kind that underlie much of the discussion of this matter in Mackey, *Christian Experience*.

sometimes overlap or are conflated. We are concerned with the action of the one God, and within that of distinct, but not separate, ways of construing it. We are therefore not seeking absolute delimitations but general attributions whereby the (temporal and historical) creative and redemptive action of God in and towards the world drives us to conceive differences in the way he is in himself, eternally. In treating of the Spirit in the economy, accordingly, what is under consideration is the act and being of the Spirit in relation to Church and world, in distinction from how we may wish to speak of him as he is conceived to be God in himself, apart from worldly involvement. The topic can be approached through two focuses.

(1) Creation and incarnation. 'For it is the Spirit who, everywhere diffused, sustains all things, causes them to grow, and quickens them in heaven and in earth.'[16] The Spirit appears in the Old Testament, classically in Ezekiel 37, as the free, life-giving power of God active in and towards his creation.[17] This is to claim not that there is to be found already in the Old Testament a distinct hypostasis, identifiable alongside Father and Son, but that it is justifiable to interpret the language in the light of later understanding, just as it is right to interpret instances of divine immanence as anticipations of the incarnation. It has sometimes been observed that Luke's pneumatology in the first two chapters is in continuity with this Old Testament tradition: the Spirit's freedom in relation to the creation is expressed paradigmatically in the forming of the Son's body in the womb of Mary. But there is no need to rest a case only on the opening chapters of Luke. The point is that they open our eyes to what is going on elsewhere, also, and enable us to realise that it is in the incarnation and particularly in relation to the humanity of Christ in general that we can discern the activity of the Spirit as the life-giving power of God in and towards his creation. It is in that way that the Spirit particularises: brings it about by his action in relation to the creation that this Jewish humanity is able to be distinctively what it is as the bearer of God's salvation.

[16] John Calvin, *Institutes*, I.13.14.
[17] The anthropological dimensions of the matter are spelled out in H. W. Wolff, *The Anthropology of the Old Testament*, translated by Margaret Kohl (London: SCM Press, 1973), chapter 4.

If we bear this function of the Spirit in mind, we shall be able to make far more of the humanity of Jesus – his existence as a creature – than has often been the case. It has been taught in East and West alike that the Son is sent by the Father and becomes incarnate by the Spirit. In the West, however, and classically in Augustine's contention that Jesus could not have received the Spirit at his baptism because he must have had it already,[18] there has always been a tendency to minimise the particularities, in contrast to assertions of a general presence, of the Spirit's action in relation to Jesus. The outcome has been a stress on the divinity at the expense of the humanity of Christ, along with developments emphasising the virginal – and eventually immaculate – conception of Jesus as the real source of his sinless humanity. Calvin, that 'theologian of the Holy Spirit' (Gordon Rupp), is an at least partial exception: 'For we make Christ free of all stain not just because he was begotten of his mother without copulation with man, but because he was sanctified by the Spirit that the generation might be pure and undefiled as would have been true before Adam's fall.'[19]

Calvin's relatively muted witness was taken up and developed by John Owen[20] and later by Edward Irving. As we shall see in chapter 9, for soteriological reasons Irving insisted, in terms similar to but far more emphatic than Calvin's, on the full and complete humanity of the incarnate. In order to redeem the human will from bondage, the Son must 'take up into Himself the very conditions of a human will ...',[21] which entails that his human *persona* must, like ours, be liable to sin. That it was so without falling was due to the action of the Holy Spirit, whom Irving sees to be 'the author of his bodily life, the quickener of that substance which He took from fallen humanity',[22] and therefore crucially active at crises of the human story, and in particular the temptation. The Spirit, therefore, is conceived not, as appears to be implied by Augustine, as the immanent

---

[18] 'For it is very foolish of us to believe that He received the Holy Spirit when he was already thirty years old ...', Augustine, *On the Trinity*, XV.26.46.

[19] Calvin, *Institutes*, II.13.4.

[20] See Alan Spence, 'Inspiration and Incarnation: John Owen and the Coherence of Christology', *King's Theological Review* 12 (1989), 52–5.

[21] Edward Irving, *The Collected Writings of Edward Irving in Five Volumes*, edited by G. Carlyle (London: Alexander Strahan, 1864), volume 5, p. 23.

[22] Irving, *Collected Writings*, volume 5, p. 126.

possession of Jesus, but as God's free and life-giving activity in and towards the world as he maintains and empowers the human activity of the incarnate Son. The Spirit is thus revealed ('manifested') in 'subduing, restraining, conquering, the evil propensities of the fallen manhood, and making it an apt organ for expressing the will of the Father; a fit and holy substance to enter into personal union with the untempted and untemptable Godhead'.[23] God the Spirit opens, frees, the humanity of the Son so that it may be the vehicle of the Father's will in the world. The Spirit is on such an account not so much an endowment as the one sent from the Father who in personal divine action enables the incarnate Son to be himself. *That is why the Holy Spirit is rightly called a person, a hypostasis. By this is meant at least a centre of action rather than merely a 'substance' – in the usual sense*[24] *– or 'force'.* Overall, what Irving is able to convey through his attention to the work of the Spirit in relation to Christ is the dynamic of his humanity:

> I am unfolding no change in the eternal and essential Divinity of the Son, who is unchangeable, being very God of very God; but I am unfolding certain changes which passed upon the humanity, and by virtue of which the humanity was brought from the likeness of fallen sinful flesh, through various changes unto that immortality and incorruption and sovereign Lordship whereunto it hath now attained, and wherein it shall for ever abide.[25]

In this connection it is possible to discover other continuities with the Old Testament than those found in the opening chapters of Luke's gospel. Jesus' ministry is in continuity with those of the typical figures of the Old Covenant, prophet, priest and king. The link between their anointing and the cognate significance of the word *Christ* has often been noted. Calvin explicitly draws out the links between anointing and endowment with the Spirit:

A visible symbol of this sacred anointing was shown in

---

[23] Irving, *Collected Writings*, volume 5, p. 120.

[24] This is complicated by the fact that *hypostasis* can be translated as 'substance'. In this case it is rightly so translated if substance can mean 'personal substantiality'.

[25] Irving, *Collected Writings*, volume 5, p. 133.

Christ's baptism, when the Spirit hovered over him in the likeness of a dove. It is nothing new . . . that the Spirit and his gifts are designated by the word 'anointing'.[26]

There has been much talk recently of Jesus as the man filled with the Spirit, and justifiably. It is one of the ways in which excessive weight given to his divinity can be counteracted: his teaching, healing and raising from the dead all have antecedents in the work of the prophets and the wise. And it must be remembered that, according to hallowed tradition, the Spirit rests not only on the prophet. There is a tradition also of the kingship of Jesus. By virtue of his endowment with the Spirit, Jesus is the bearer of an authority, of power constitutionally because obediently exercised, which is not that of the great ones of this world, but real and inescapable none the less.[27]

An important development of our theme is owed to Irving, and it shows how attention to the work of the Spirit in connection with Jesus' humanity enables us to explore different dimensions – particularities – of it which would otherwise be neglected. Irving argues that at the baptism of Jesus we see his endowment by the Spirit with the charism of the prophet, not yet of the priest. The priesthood, as the Letter to the Hebrews suggests, is achieved not at the baptism, but after the resurrection and ascension. Because Irving understands the Spirit to be a personal agent rather than some semi-substantial possession, he can understand the Spirit to be present to and with Jesus in different ways at different stages of the ministry. He can thus speak of different 'measures' of the Spirit's being given, but never abstractly, always for soteriological reasons: so that there is a 'third measure of the Spirit which quickened Him in the tomb, with which our bodies also shall be anointed when we shall be quickened in the tomb'.[28] It is only after the quickening from the tomb that the one maintained in obedience by the

---

[26] Calvin, *Institutes*, II.15.5.

[27] See below, chapter 13.

[28] Irving, *Collected Writings*, volume 5, p. 237. While there are reasons to doubt Irving's restriction of the priesthood of Christ, his treatment of it remains an excellent example of the way in which an explicitly pneumatological treatment of christology allows weight to be given to the different episodes of the gospel story. For a qualification of Irving's treatment, see my *Christ and Creation* (Carlisle: Paternoster Press, 1992), pp. 56–7.

Spirit and ordained by the Spirit to the prophet's office becomes the source of the Spirit – as eternal high priest – to believers. In such a way, a pneumatology of the person of Christ enables Irving to do justice to the whole narrative of the incarnation, as well as to its saving dynamic.

We have seen that for Irving the Spirit is, among other things, the agent of the resurrection, as the giver of eschatological life. The Lord, the giver of life, transforms the body of Jesus so that it may partake of the life of the age to come, the first-born of the new creation. A brief return to that theme will enable an anticipation of matters we shall consider under the second aspect of the topic. Reasons have been given in the chapter so far for speaking of the Holy Spirit as 'a person', although one only so by virtue of mutually constitutive relations with the Father and the Son. Despite this, reason has also been given to show why it is not altogether inappropriate sometimes to speak of the Spirit in impersonal or subpersonal terms, as a power or force. The suggestions of mysterious and unpredictable power, the freedom of the Spirit in relation to the created order, make it quite understandable that his work should be described in metaphors suggesting materiality. The Spirit is the Father's agent enabling the created order in all its material concreteness to be and do that for which it was created. By understanding matters thus, and showing something of the universal scope of the Spirit's activity, we are able to avoid suggestions that the incarnation and the resurrection are 'interventions', the work of a *deus ex machina*, unrelated to the whole work of the Spirit in and towards the creation. On the contrary, they are paradigm cases of the way of the Spirit with all created reality. Just as Irving sees the Spirit as the dynamic of the life of Jesus in order that it may be the dynamic of all human life, so such an understanding has implications for the being of matter as a whole. We shall return to this point in (2) below.

But before we move from christology, some resolution must be made of the problem adumbrated at the end of section I. How far can we use those slippery terms, immanence and transcendence, as aids in distinguishing between the action of Son and Spirit? We can see in the above discussion the value of the claim that the Spirit is understood better in terms of God's

free transcendence over the world than of his immanence
within it. In Jesus of Nazareth, we are confronted by the eternal
Son of God, made immanent in fallen matter by the recreating
energies of the Spirit, who as free agent is thus *personally*
transcendent over the matter he forms into the body of Jesus.
But even as immanent, the incarnate Word, as the one who
confronts us, is also transcendent, as our atoning Other; and,
by a corresponding logic, by his involvement in the redemption
of matter, the Spirit is, in a manner of speaking, immanent.
The point here is not to play with words, but to allow the
conceptuality both to serve understanding and to indicate its
own limits.[29] And the outcome here is that although the Son
and the Spirit are distinct, as performing different kinds of
function in relation to the world, they are, as the two hands of
God the Father, also inseparable. There is a perichoresis, an
interanimation of energies, which makes it a mistake to say of
the one, immanence only; and of the other, only transcendence. The incarnation of the Son is, as we have seen, a
transcendent immanence; that of the Spirit, an immanent,
involved, but eschatological transcendence.

IV *The perfecting cause*

(2) A distinctive feature of the New Testament characterisations of the Spirit's action is their thoroughgoing eschatological emphasis. In Paul, the Spirit is the presence now, by
anticipation, of that which belongs to the age to come: hence
he is the ἀρραβών (down-payment, 2 Cor. 1.22), ἀπαρχή (first-
fruits, Rom. 8.23). Similarly, in Acts, the Pentecost event is
portrayed as the fulfilment of Joel's eschatological promise.
Again, the Spirit performs the divine actions of the end time in
the here and now: judgement (John 16.8, cf. Luke 3.16);

---

[29] It is for reasons such as this that I have suggested elsewhere that there
might be gains to be had from replacing the concepts of transcendence and
immanence – which are so easily patient of impersonal or merely spatial
construal – with otherness and relation. That God is other than the world – in
a sense, transcendent – does not preclude his relatedness with it. Quite the
reverse, in fact: by virtue of his triune otherness – ontological difference – God
is able freely to enter into relations with that which is not God. See my *The
Promise of Trinitarian Theology*.

redemption (Rom. 8); love, prophecy, truth (1 Cor. 12–14). Important here is the link Paul makes between the Spirit and freedom: liberation, as some contemporary theologies seem to forget, is an essentially eschatological concept; it is only won – or rather, given – proleptically, by the Spirit. 'Now the Lord is the Spirit, and where the Spirit of the Lord is, there is freedom' (2 Cor. 3.17). The Spirit is God in his freedom to create in the here and now the conditions of the redemption of all things promised for the end. He is the freedom of the Father to create through the Son, to incarnate the Son in the flesh, to raise the mortal body to immortality. He is the freedom of God to choose Israel and the Church, and to enable both of them to be, from time to time, particularisations of the community of the end time.

In this second case-study, then, we are not so much adding another essential focus for understanding the Spirit's characteristic mode of action to what was said in the first case-study and will be said in the related chapter on the Church (chapter 11, below) as bringing them together theologically. Both are attempts to show concretely something of what is meant by saying that the Holy Spirit is the perfecting cause of the creation. The christological discussion in particular has, as was suggested at its end, implications far beyond the merely human. It shows us that the Spirit is the perfecting cause of the whole creation, for the New Testament is clear that Jesus is the incarnation of the Word through whom all things came to be. The Spirit is thus the agent of the Father's determination to bring all things into relation to himself through Christ: the agent of God's perfecting of the creation. Therefore we must say that whenever the created order, in any of its levels or aspects, is able to praise its maker, there is the agency of the Spirit. In this respect, the resurrection of Jesus Christ from the dead serves as a model for the possibilities for the transformation of matter in general.

But it is also a model for particularity and elusiveness. That is the implication of the point made above about the transcendence of the Spirit. The shaping of the body of Jesus, his empowerment for ministry and his being raised from the dead are particular acts, not symbols of a general immanence. The creation holds together in Christ, as the agent of its order: he is its principle of immanence, the *person* through whom all things came to be, in whom they hold together and to whom they are directed. The work of the Spirit is related to the creation's cohesion and destiny in Christ, but his distinct function is at once to restore lost order and bestow eschatological freedom: transformation into the conditions of the age to come. This does not happen in a general way, but takes place as particular parts of the creation are set free through Christ and enabled to be themselves, and so anticipations of the universal redemption in the age to come. The stress on particularities, however, does not prevent us from drawing general conclusions about the work of the Spirit. As the one who perfects the work of creation, we may discern his work in, for example, works of art, as particular samples of the material order are transformed into that which brings praise to God and delight and instruction to his people.[30]

The same kind of point can be made in the light of the theology of the Church. We are so used to a merely personal or social conception of the Church that we are in danger of forgetting that the Church too has a cosmic context and function. The materiality of the sacraments reminds us that the transformation of matter is at the heart of the Church's being. Colossians 1 is witness that it is the cosmic Christ who is the head of the Church, while Ephesians develops the eschatological dimension. It is the function of the Spirit as the perfecting cause 'to unite all things in Christ, things in heaven and things on earth' (Eph. 1.10). As the Church is called to be the community of the last days, so it is commanded to play a central part in the perfecting through Christ of the created order. But such perfecting is the work of the Spirit, as the fourth chapter of Ephesians makes clear. The gifts of the Spirit are given for the building of that community which is called to praise God in worship and life and so achieve in its worship and work anticipations of the reconciliation of all things in Christ. (It is interesting that here, too, the Spirit is concerned with particularities, as the allusion above to Paul's stress upon the diversity of charismata has already suggested.)

In conclusion and summary of this section, we must return to

---

[30] See Jeremy Begbie, *Voicing Creation's Praise* (Edinburgh: T. & T. Clark, 1991).

the christological. It is Christ to whom all creation moves, and therefore to Christ that the Spirit directs his eschatological work. Part of the continuing difficulty of identifying the Spirit lies in the fact that the Spirit takes us to the Father not directly, but only through the mediation of the Son. Unlike the Son, who is identified through Jesus' ministry, death and resurrection, the Spirit's identity is more elusively mediated through that of the Son. So Lossky:

> He comes, not in His own name but in the name of the Son, to bear witness to the Son – as the Son came in the name of the Father, to make known the Father ... The divine Persons do not themselves assert themselves but one bears witness to another ... It follows that the third Hypostasis of the Trinity is the only one not having His image in another Person. The Holy Spirit, as Person, remains unmanifested, hidden, concealing Himself in His very appearing.[31]

This is of extreme importance if we are not to succumb to the temptation to baptise everything of which we happen to approve at the time as the work of the Spirit. 'Progressive' politics and a concern for ecology may well be the work of the Spirit, but unless submitted to christological testing will be simply a reflection of the fashionable trends of the age.

To speak of the Spirit in the economy, in his relation to the world, then, is to speak of a personal agent of the Father's action in and towards the world. The action of the Spirit is distinct but not separate from that of the Son, for he brings the creation to the Father through the Son. Hence, theology often alludes to his essentially self-effacing character (something shared, in a different way, by the Son, incarnate incognito as he is). The Father is the fount of all being: a transcendence of origination. The Son is the mode of God's immanence in the world, in which he is witness not to himself, but to the Father. The Spirit is God's eschatological transcendence, his futurity, as it is sometimes expressed. He is God present to the world as its liberating other, bringing it to the destiny determined by the Father, made actual, realised, in the Son. The 'contribution of the Spirit ... is to liberate the Son and the economy from the

[31] Vladimir Lossky, *The Mystical Theology of the Eastern Church* (Cambridge and London: James Clarke, 1957), pp. 159f.

bondage of history ... The Spirit is the beyond (of) history, and when he acts in history he does so in order to bring into history the last days, the eschaton. Hence the first fundamental particularity of Pneumatology is its eschatological character.'[32] But that is why the identification of the Holy Spirit must remain systematically elusive even while we attempt such identification as is possible. It is in the light of eschatology and elusiveness that we must move to a brief attempt to discuss what we may say of the eternal Spirit in the light of the economy.

V *The eternal Spirit*

What shall we make of all this for a treatment of the place of the Spirit in the immanent Trinity? First, some remarks about method and approach. I shall follow the general approach, although not the specific content, of Karl Barth. Barth's view is that in the order of knowing we may move from what God (economically) shows himself to be to a corresponding conception of what God is in himself. If God is what we are given in the economy, then we may conclude that the economy is a reliable guide to what God is, eternally and in himself. There is, however, an asymmetrical relationship between knowing and being, and we are not obliged to accept the apparent view of Rahner that the thesis 'the Economic Trinity is the Immanent Trinity' is also true 'reciprocally' (*umgekehrt*). Barth's conception of the relation of economic and immanent is similar to that of Zizioulas, who says that the distinction 'is nothing else essentially but a device created by the Greek Fathers to safeguard the absolute transcendence of God without alienating him from the world'.[33]

The chief implication of this methodological dogma is that an exposition of the triune economic and temporal action must form the basis of an appropriate conception of the place of the Spirit in the eternal Trinity. Here there are problems in both Eastern and Western traditions. That of the West is twofold. First is Augustine's move to conceive the Spirit as the link

[32] John Zizioulas, *Being as Communion. Studies in Personhood and the Church* (London: Darton, Longman & Todd, 1985), p. 130.

[33] J. D. Zizioulas, *Credo in Spiritum Sanctum* (Vatican, 1982), pp. 50f.

between Father and Son. We have already seen that in terms of the Platonic schema which provides the matrix for Augustine's discussion the Spirit tends to be conceived as a link in an inward-turned circle. The outcome is that far from being in some respect an implication of the economy – in which, as we saw, the Spirit is understood eschatologically and as the freedom of God's movement outwards – the immanent Trinity is in effect conceived in terms contradictory of the economy. Here, as a recent translator of Augustine acknowledges – though he appears to welcome it – is the root of the distinction, rightly seen by Rahner as a dogmatic disaster, between the treatises *De Deo Uno* and *De Deo Trino*.[34] This breach between economy and theology is of a piece with, and a partial consequence of, the failure of Augustine to give the Spirit adequate weight economically.

The second aspect of the Western weakness is another consequence of the preference for a Platonic over an economic Trinity, and it is Augustine's tendency to intellectualism. In Augustine, the inner-trinitarian love, while not wholly intellectual in character, is very largely so, and is construed partly in terms of self-love.[35] The outcome is that the West has since been dominated by noetic patterns of conceiving the inner-trinitarian relationships. (This is not to deny that among the gifts of the Spirit is knowledge; it is, however, as we have seen in thinking of the Spirit's work in the whole created order, but one of the eschatological gifts.) Here there are many interesting ramifications for East–West relations. John Zizioulas again: 'Pneumatology is weakened whenever the approach to God is dominated primarily by the epistemological concern ... A strong pneumatology, therefore, leads to a stronger sense of the "beyond creation" aspect and thus to the emergence of meta-historical and eschatological tendencies in theology.'[36] That is why John Milbank's interesting attempt to develop a conception of the second difference with the assistance of Hegel's notion of the Spirit as 'the divestment of all immediacy' will not in the end convince. His 'idea of a second positive

---

[34] Stephen McKenna, 'Introduction', *Saint Augustine: the Trinity* (Washington, DC: Catholic University of America Press, 1963), pp. vii–xvi (xiv).

[35] Colin Gunton, *The Promise of Trinitarian Theology*, chapter 3.

[36] J. D. Zizioulas, *Credo*, p. 52.

difference which takes absence as the occasion for rhetorical, and not dialectical unity ...'[37] seems still to be dominated by epistemological rather than eschatological emphases.

There are questions to be asked of the Eastern tradition also. James Mackey has asked one of them by suggesting that in Gregory of Nyssa, for example, 'the distinguishing properties of the Holy Spirit are described in terms which are either wholly negative or remarkably uninformative'.[38] Is not the notion of 'proceeding' rather colourless to provide a ground for some of the economic actions with which we are concerned? It seems to me that we must take Mackey's contention seriously, but not necessarily in the form in which he makes it. Is 'information' that which we seek, or is it not a matter rather of whether we may so conceive the being of God that our theology both grounds our thought about him and enables further thought and action in its light? What is our concern when we seek to characterise the identity of a *person*? Without doubt, we should beware those who come bearing information. Is not the very problem with Augustine's account of the Spirit as 'love' or 'gift' that it seeks too much 'inside information' and helps to constrain the eschatological freedom of the Spirit into being part of a non-eschatological Platonic triad? The advantage of maintaining the defining distinction to be between begotten and proceeding is that it enables us to denote a difference between a person conceived in terms of a genetic metaphor and one conceived to subsist in a distinctively different pattern of relationships. In such a way we are able to locate conceptually but apophatically the fact that there is an immanent distinction corresponding to the distinction in the economy.

But to remain there is to evade the question of the point of making the distinction at all. Why do we distinguish between the Son and the Spirit in the immanent Trinity? One reason is the need to ground what we have learned of the historical and cosmic action of God firmly within a doctrine of his eternal being, in an account of who the God is who works thus among and towards us. That point has emerged already in the course of the argument. But if, as Augustine rightly saw, the doctrine

---

[37] J. Milbank, 'The Second Difference', 231f.
[38] J. Mackey, *Christian Experience*, p. 145.

of the Trinity has much to do with our ability to conceive God as love, there is a further task to be performed. What is the nature of the love of which we speak so much, and how does the doctrine of the eternal Spirit enable us to speak of it? In following up the question, we shall not reject the notion of the Spirit as the one whose distinctive *persona* is to be encapsulated in the notion of 'proceeding', but will expand that notion by spelling out some of the connotations of the dynamic, transcendent, outward-going freedom that we have seen to be the mark of the Spirit in the economy.

The weakness of the traditional Augustinian account of the Spirit is, as we have seen, its failure to conceive the eschatological dimensions of the Spirit's activities. Much of this weakness is not only the result of a failure of attention to the eschatological revelation, but also the cause of further theological weakness. Put simply, it must be said that the lack of eschatological dynamic produces a conception of love as self-involved rather than as oriented outwards. That is the almost unavoidable outcome of any conception that sees the Spirit chiefly as the link between Father and Son. It encourages the conceiving of love in terms of return, of a closing of an eternal circle: love as moving outward to the Son and back to the Father through the Spirit, so that the Spirit has little function except as a link in a love that is a relation between Father and Son alone. This is why Staniloae is right to insist that the Spirit is the agent not only of the unity of the Godhead, but also of the diversity of the persons.[39] We are then bound to ask: what difference does the existence of the Spirit within the Trinity make to the conception of the love of God?

To see something of the conception of love that emerges, we must draw upon Richard of St Victor's crucial insight that love limited to any two persons is intrinsically incomplete. In his writing, the argument is of a rather a priori kind, and is employed to justify the propriety of speaking of a third member

[39] Dumitru Staniloae, *Theology and the Church*, translated by Robert Barringer (New York: St Vladimir's Seminary Press, 1980), p. 67. See also p. 102: 'The Holy Spirit is what unites the Father and the Son, not as essence, but precisely as Person, leaving Father and Son at the same time as free persons. Hence the Spirit is also the one who unites men among themselves, but as a Person himself he leaves other persons free.'

of the Trinity.[40] That kind of argument is no longer necessary if the argument in this chapter from the distinctive functions of Son and Spirit in the economy is correct. But as an insight derived from the doctrine of the Trinity about the nature of love, it is of crucial importance. The perfection of the divine love is revealed by the fact that it is neither self-love nor the merely reciprocal love of two for each other, but a love intrinsically oriented to community. The Holy Spirit is then indeed the dynamic of the divine love, but one that seeks to involve the other in the movement of giving and receiving that is the Trinity: that is, *to perfect the love of Father and Son by moving it beyond itself.* Corresponding to the eschatological movement of the Spirit *ad extra* there is within the divine eternity one who perfects the love of God as love in community. To be God is to be intrinsically related to the other in communion, and the Spirit is the one who enables this communion to be. From this it follows that if the Son is the basis of God's movement out into the creation to bring that which is not God into covenant relation with him, the Spirit is the dynamic of that movement, the one who perfects creation by realising the communion of persons and the transformation of matter. Here, we can indeed speak of 'return'; but of a process by which that which was in the beginning is not so much restored to a former integrity as returned perfected to the Father through the Son and by the Spirit – an eschatological rather than protological return, if we may so speak.

But a problem has to be faced. What is implied for God's relation to the creation if we assert that it is the function of the Spirit to enable us to conceive the intrinsic orientation of the love of God to the other? Here we reach an acknowledgement of the (small) moment of truth in claims, made from Origen onwards, that God is in some way necessarily creator, and so bound to create. The claim must be rejected, because if God *must* create there is a loss of freedom both for God and for the created world, because its being is then bound up with his so closely as to call into question its distinctive reality. Yet if God's love is essentially self-satisfied rather than self-sufficient, an

---

[40] Richard of St Victor, *De Trinitate* 3, xix, *Sources Chrétiennes* 63, ed. G. Salet (Paris: Les Editions du Cerf, 1959).

inward-turning circle, there is to be found within it no reason at all for God's creating and redeeming but arbitrary will.

Both of these extreme positions can be avoided by means of the pneumatological conception of the divine love which has been attempted here. The third person of the Trinity is the one whose function is to make the love of God a love that is opened towards that which is not itself, to perfect it in otherness. Because God is not in himself a closed circle but is essentially the relatedness of community, there is within his eternal being that which freely and in love creates, reconciles and redeems that which is not himself. The relation of God to the creation, which is expressed in creation, reconciliation and redemption, is grounded in the other-related love of the Father, Son and Spirit in eternity. It is the particular being and function of the Spirit to be the dynamic of that love, both in itself and towards the world. We thus come full circle to a revised version of Augustine's position. The Spirit is indeed to be understood as the one who completes the relations of Father and Son. The difference is that the introduction of the eschatological note changes radically the way in which the relationship is understood: not a closed circle, but a self-sufficient community of love freely opened outwards to embrace the other.

CHAPTER 8

THE DOCTRINE OF CREATION

The end of causality? the Reformers and their
predecessors[1]

I *Some presuppositions*

I begin with the articulation of some presuppositions and
working assumptions, prejudices perhaps, and an attempt at
some conceptual clarifications. The first is that a Christian
theology of creation requires articulation through some conception of personal divine agency; that is to say, it attributes the
existence of the world – a word used to refer to all that is not
God – not to chance or mechanism but to some form of
intentional action. I do not wish to suggest that the understanding of the attribution of personal agency to God the
creator is a straightforward matter, but rather that without such
an affirmation we should be no longer in the realm of recognisably Christian doctrine. I shall return to this theme at the end
of the chapter.

The second working assumption is that during its history the
conception of creation deriving from personal agency has
suffered some contamination, not necessarily – though often in
practice – to its detriment, notably by notions of emanation and
causality. The former can be said to mark the thought of both
Plotinus and Hegel, who is in many ways remarkably like the
Neoplatonist. Moltmann is an interesting recent heir of this
tradition.[2] The latter, causality, is, as scarcely needs to be said,

---

[1] A revised version of a paper delivered to a conference of the Research
Institute in Systematic Theology, King's College, London, in September
1994.

[2] Jürgen Moltmann, *Spirit of Life. A Universal Affirmation* (London: SCM
Press, 1992).

characteristic of the Aristotelian forms of expression which still mark theology indelibly.

We shall engage with Aquinas later, but the problem is this. Causality is a polymorphic concept, with one meaning shading over into one another across a wide range. At one end of the range, it can indeed be construed in terms of personal agency, and indeed it is arguable that it was originally a personal notion. When John Zizioulas understands the Father as the αἰτία of the Trinity, or Adam as the cause of humanity, he clearly regards the notion as personal, archetypally so, indeed.[3] Similarly, one person can cause another person to do something in a way that does not impugn the latter's personality and freedom. At the other extreme, causality can be assimilated to logical implication, with Spinoza the clearest case. For him, to cause something is to *entail* it logically. While Spinoza's model is geometry and modern mechanism, there can be little doubt that he was given encouragement by some of his mediaeval predecessors.

It is here worth observing, parenthetically, that there is a case for saying that the critique of the notion of cause by Berkeley, anticipating as it did the work of Hume, is an attempt to retrieve an original and more personal construction. We should not, Berkeley holds, conceive causation as an inner-worldly chain of logical-type relations, because only God can cause in anything like that sense. What we call causality is not a type of logical implication, but observed regularities, regularities whose reliability derives from the fact that God causes them contingently – and so intentionally and voluntarily – to be what they are. Berkeley's attempt to restore a personal conception of causality in face of the threat of deist mechanism can be said to have failed for a number of reasons, but largely because it lacks a conception of mediation. However, that is not what interests us at this stage. What does is that Berkeley's attempt to destroy the notion that there is natural causality, autonomous and independent of divine action, and to replace it with a conception of a world in which everything is in some way

---

[3] John D. Zizioulas, 'On Being a Person. Towards an Ontology of Person-hood', *Persons, Divine and Human. King's College Essays in Theological Anthropology*, edited by Christoph Schwoebel and Colin E. Gunton (Edinburgh: T. & T. Clark, 1992), pp. 33–46, especially pp. 38–40.

caused by the personal God, does indicate where the centre of our question lies. Are things reliably the way that they are by virtue of some impersonal process, understood immanently – that is one of Berkeley's objections to Locke's substance language[4] – or by virtue of the omnipresent agency of God? The background to that question should become more evident as the chapter proceeds, but it is worth noting that the dispute between Berkeley and his materialist opponents is in some sense but the re-run of an earlier development in late scholastic disputation.

The third presupposition of this chapter is that, along with cause, the concept of will is equally important, because its use shapes the way in which personal agency is conceived to operate. The most explicit and detailed dogmatic statement of the doctrine of creation in the New Testament makes direct reference to the will of God. 'Thou hast created all things and by thy will (διὰ τὸ θέλημά σου) they were and were established (ἐκτίσθησαν) ...' (Rev. 4.11). But, like the concept of cause, it too is problematic. What has been made of it in the tradition is far from straightforward, as one case will illustrate. The most relentless exponent (before Ockham, that is) of the notion of creation by the will of God is Augustine of Hippo. His achievement is crucial for the development of the doctrine of creation and, indeed, of modernity.[5] But, like all of Augustine's legacies, it is ambiguous, and its dubious features are well marked by the fact that later generations found it difficult to maintain an adequately personal conception of divine action in and towards the world. The reason is that although will is an essentially personal concept because it is personal agents who will, it is also one that easily collapses into impersonalism. This is because it can encourage the kind of conception of unmediated divine

---

[4] If it was Locke he was opposing. See David Berman, *George Berkeley. Idealism and the Man* (Oxford: Clarendon Press, 1994), pp. 33ff.

[5] See here Michael B. Foster, *The Political Philosophies of Plato and Hegel* (Oxford: Clarendon Press, 1935). 'The failure of Greek ethics to achieve a notion of will was a necessary consequence of Greek metaphysics ...' (p. 131). The converse is that it comes from Christian revelation, and specifically in connection with its doctrine of creation. For example: 'the doctrine of Creation is the source from which the conception of sovereignty is derived. This doctrine is the fundamental doctrine of the Christian revelation ...' (pp. 191f.).

omnicausality that ultimately undermines rather than establishes the being of that which is willed. God can be conceived to will everything in such a way that the reality of the other is in some way or other imperilled – it becomes his 'creature' in the pejorative sense of that term. In this respect, willing and causing appear to have a similar logic, because under certain conditions both encourage a collapse into necessitarianism. Here the position of Plotinus is worth an allusion, in view of the fact that the essentially impersonal emanation of lower forms of being from the One appears to be the result of the One's willing of itself.

But let me illustrate the problem rather from the thought of one who can be said, for all his greatness, to have introduced disturbingly determinist elements into his own Reformed heritage. Jonathan Edwards appears to understand the concept of cause as an analogical one. *Created* causality is not determinist or necessitarian. 'Cause is that, after or upon the existence of which, or the existence of it after such a manner, the existence of another thing follows.'[6] But the causality exercised by God does appear to be understood in a determinist or even necessitarian manner. Along with Berkeley, Edwards wished to replace the theory that sensations were caused by substance with one that they were caused directly by God:

> The reason why it is so exceedingly natural to men to suppose that there is some latent substance, or something that is altogether hid, that upholds the properties of bodies, is because all see at first sight that the properties of bodies are such as need some cause that shall every moment have influence to their continuance, as well as a cause of their first existence. All therefore agree that there is something that is there, and upholds these properties; and it is most true, there undoubtedly is. But men are wont to content themselves in saying that it is something; but that 'something' is he by whom all things consist.[7]

[6] Jonathan Edwards, *Scientific and Philosophical Writings*, *The Works of Jonathan Edwards*, edited by Wallace E. Anderson (New Haven and London: Yale University Press, 1980), volume 6, p. 350.

[7] Edwards, *Scientific and Philosophical Writings* p. 380, cf. p. 339: 'Our perceptions, or ideas that we passively receive by our bodies, are communicated to us immediately by God while our minds are united with our bodies.'

This led Edwards to what a recent commentator has called his doctrine of omnicausality.[8] Michael Jinkins says that 'he wanted to demonstrate that it is reasonable to enlightened people, not only to believe that all things are causally determined, but that all things are causally determined – *by God*'. And he notes the reason: there is otherwise no way of ascending by a chain of causation to prove the existence of God.[9]

The point of all this is that neither the concept of God as cause nor the attribution of creation to his will prevents theology from lapsing into conceptions of impersonal determinism. The reasons for the fact that it has often so lapsed, and the approach to some kind of a solution, will be sought in the theological history of the West. The general contention will be that if either of those concepts are to be used, their use must be controlled by the context in which they are deployed. In the next section, we shall review, fairly summarily, some of the features of the reigning theology of creation in the Middle Ages.

II *Some mediaeval theologies of creation*

The thesis to be argued in this section is that, despite the immense differences between Aquinas and those, like Ockham, who undermined his Aristotelian conception of causality, they remain in certain crucial respects the same in their understanding of the relation of God to the world. What they have in common is reliance on the concept of cause *along with* the almost total absence from their conceptions of the mediation of creation of any trinitarian reference. It is this that makes the achievement of the Reformers, despite all the limitations that we shall observe, so remarkable. It is worth saying here, in anticipation of the outcome of the argument, that the point about trinitarian reference is that it allows a concept of the mediation of the created order that is personal and so does not abolish the space in which the creation can be properly itself.

---

[8] Michael Jinkins, '"The Being of Beings". Jonathan Edwards' Understanding of God as Reflected in his Final Treatises', *Scottish Journal of Theology* 46 (1993), 161–90 (164).

[9] Jinkins, '"The Being of Beings"', pp. 172f., citing *The Freedom of the Will, The Works of Jonathan Edwards*, edited by Paul Ramsey (New Haven and London: Yale University Press, 1957), volume 1, p. 182.

If we begin with Aquinas, we must emphasise that it is not the case that either personal or trinitarianly conceived agency in creation is completely lacking from his thought; he is in the tradition of Augustine in teaching that creation is the outcome of the free, personal willing of the creator. The problem is that the act of willing is rather monistically conceived. The Trinity plays little or no constitutive part in his treatment of the divine realisation of creation, as is evident already in the Question that sets the scene for his treatment of creation, number 44 of the first part of the *Summa Theologiae*: 'the first cause of things'. This question precedes the discussion of creation, which is thus introduced with a chiefly abstract and merely 'monotheistic' treatment of the status of God as first cause.[10] When we come to Question 45, 'Creation', article 7 is reached before there is mention of the trinitarian attributions, and there the distinctive forms of agency in creation are minimised rather than taken fully seriously. What emerges is a fairly strong conception of divine omnicausality.

Among the disturbing symptoms of the discussion is the rejection of Peter Lombard's view that power to create can be delegated to a creature which works *ministerially*, in apparent neglect of the pattern displayed in Genesis 1, where God does precisely that – 'Let the earth bring forth'.[11] There are other problematic features, crucial among them two which threaten to undermine the distinct reality of the creature. First is a denial that God acts to achieve a purpose in creating – 'he intends only to communicate his own completeness';[12] and second is a denial that creation puts a reality into a creature except as a relation ('[Creation] in God is not a real relation, but only conceptual').[13] Both of these detract from the creature's value as creature, for they tie the creature too closely to

---

[10] I am here operating with one recent and pejorative use of the word 'monotheism'. See here Christoph Schwoebel, 'Monotheismus IV. Systematisch-theologisch', *Theologische Realenzyklopädie* XXIII, 1/2, 256–62, for a demonstration of the variety of usage.

[11] Aquinas, *Summa Theologiae*, I.45.5. See Francis Watson, *Text, Church and World. Biblical Interpretation in Theological Perspective* (Edinburgh: T. & T. Clark, 1994), p. 142, for the conception of mediated creation to be found in Genesis 1.

[12] Aquinas, *Summa*, 44.4.

[13] Aquinas, *Summa*, 45.3 ad 1.

God, and so fail to give it space to be. We might say that they detract from the proper substantiality of the creature. Here it should be noted that there are two requirements for a satisfactory construal of the relation of God and the world: adequate conceptions of the continuing relatedness of the world to God and of that world's due reality – we might say due autonomy – in its relation to God. It is not that Aquinas does nothing to ensure the reality of the creature; it is rather that the *contingence* of the creature on God (its dependence) is given more adequate weighting than its *contingency*: its freedom to be itself. 'The whole of what is genuinely real and true virtually exists in God though not in creation.'[14] A similar, and stronger, point could be made against Schleiermacher.

Many of the same ways of putting things reappear in the thought of Duns Scotus, although there are one or two features that might be considered to suggest significant differences. First, the concept of cause is less prominent; and, second, some reference is made to the subordinate authority of Jesus Christ in creation, with allusion to the dialectic in John 5 of Jesus' being able to do nothing of himself, but doing what the Father has given him to do.[15] By contrast, Thomas virtually never appeals to New Testament creation texts, nearly always to the first verse of Genesis alone. His Word tends to mean the Logos asarkos, not the incarnate Jesus Christ.[16] The point of all this is not simply to assert the impropriety of all doctrines of the pre-incarnate Word, but to make the point that much

[14] '... virtualiter in Deo, sed non totum existit in rebus creatis' (Aquinas, *Summa*, I.19.6). Much difference would be made by saying: 'really exists in the Son'. For Thomas' tendency to necessitarianism, see a sentence in the same question: 'An effect cannot possibly escape the order of the universal cause.'

[15] John Duns Scotus, *God and Creatures. The Quodlibetal Questions*, 8.1.17, translated by F. Alluntis and A. B. Wolter (Washington. Catholic University of America Press), p. 211.

[16] There is little or nothing in Thomas' text here to provide support for the editor's assertion that 'St Thomas' doctrine of creation is christocentric and scriptural ... that God created in Wisdom and the "word". This does not appear in the foreground of most of the discussions ... The weight St Thomas attached to a topic cannot be judged by the number of words he devoted to it ... In the present case, unless the doctrine of *Colossians* 1, 15–23 is seen as central to his thought, he is no more than a religious philosopher who is the peer of Avicenna and Maimonides' (St Thomas Aquinas, *Summa Theologiae* (London: Blackfriars/Eyre & Spottiswoode, 1967), volume 8, editorial note, pp. 87f.).

of Western theology has been able to operate with a highly abstract theology of the second person of the Trinity, with the result that the New Testament linking of Jesus Christ and creation ceases to be determinative for the theology of creation.

When we come to the thought of William of Ockham, there are both similarities and differences. So far as the differences are concerned, Ockham is far more interested than Aquinas in the doctrine of creation out of nothing and the distinctive conception of contingency it generates, one very much derived from a stress on the free willing of the creator. It is thus a conception of contingency *from above* rather than one from below of the kind Aquinas, and, as we have seen, Edwards, use as the basis for an argument for the existence of a first cause. We might say that Ockham's scepticism about the latter has enabled him to move to a stress on creation as an act of free and personal divine willing. Ockham is celebrated, in works on the history of science, as one who, by stressing the contingency of creation, helped to lay the ground for that celebration of the distinct reality of the world which did so much to further the advance of modern science.[17] The outcome is that, in this case, will has come to predominate over cause, so that causality's tendency to suggest logical links between God and the world is replaced by one suggesting freely willed personal creation.[18] As Oberman comments in connection with Biel's similar epistemology, a demonstration of the deficiencies of the natural knowledge of God enables an elimination of Anselmian necessity, without losing

---

[17] Harold Nebelsick, *The Renaissance, the Reformation and the Rise of Science* (Edinburgh: T. & T. Clark, 1992), pp. 52–63, and referring to such classics of the history of science as A. C. Crombie, *Augustine to Galileo* (London: Heinemann, 1959), volume 2, pp. 43–5 and 79. For Ockham's conception of the contingency of the divine act of creation, see, for example, William of Ockham, *In Librum Sententiarum* LI. D17. Q1, *Opera Philosophica et Theologica* (New York: St Bonaventure University, 1981), *Opera Theologica* volume 3, pp. 453f.: 'quidquid Deus contingenter creat, potest contingenter illud adnilihare quandocumque placet sibi.' That is voluntarism at its most stark.

[18] Indeed, Ockham's is, as is often enough noted, a highly voluntarist conception of deity, and he holds against Scotus that the divine essence cannot be distinguished from the divine will; 'essentia divina nullo modo distinguiter a voluntate divina sed omni modo identitatis quo essentia est eadem essentiae etiam essentia est eadem voluntati' (*Opera Theologica*, volume 4, p. 663).

the faith seeking understanding.[19] What this enables Ockham to do is to establish, in some contrast to Aquinas, a central place for the doctrine of creation out of nothing.[20]

But, and here the similarities between the two mediaevals present themselves to view, the matter is not so straightforward. I return to the point that certain concepts of will are as problematic as certain concepts of cause. The other desideratum for a doctrine of creation, a satisfactory conception of the continuing relation of creator God to created world, remains lacking. There is contingency, but little account of the stability which derives from a continuing dependence of the world upon God. This is a theme which will recur, but for now the point to make is that Ockham continues to couch his discussion in terms of causality, rather monistically conceived, and so is unable to prevent the emergence of a conception of divine omnicausality, whose final outcome is an inadequate conception of creaturely reality. In that respect, the significant feature of Ockham's discussion of creation is not so much – as is often supposed to be the problem – the introduction of a radical doctrine of *potentia absoluta* as the entirely non-trinitarian treatment of creation, perhaps best exemplified in the fact that he can refer to the opening verses of the gospel of John without noting the part played in its conception of creation by the mediation of the Word.[21]

As we know well, to Ockham goes the credit – if one believes in the legitimacy of modernity – for so cutting off the world from its creator that God eventually disappears from the picture altogether. That is the other, opposite but equal, side of the doctrine of omnicausality. Might things have been otherwise if certain of the things said by the Reformers in this context had been more clearly heard? While one should

[19] H. Oberman, *The Harvest of Medieval Theology* (Cambridge, Mass.: Harvard University Press, 1963), pp. 40f.

[20] 'Creatio est simpliciter de nihilo, ita quod nihil extrinsecum et essentiale rei praedicat; similiter in adnihilatione nihil remanet; igitur si aliquid essentiale rei creabili et adnihilabili praecedat et remanet non adnihilabitur nec creabitur' (Ockham, *In Librum Sententiarum* LI. D2. Q4, *Opera Theologica*, volume 2, p. 116).

[21] *Quodlibetal Questions* 2, Q4. Art. 2. Ockham understands John 1.3 to mean that God made all other things through himself ('omnia alia a Deo per ipsum facta sunt'), *Opera Theologica*, volume 9, p. 215.

probably not speculate about the hypotheticals of history, it remains the case that Luther and Calvin have things to say that are quite remarkable in their historical context – one could almost use that much abused word revolution – even though with them too a certain ambivalence remains.

III *Luther and Calvin*

In view of what we have just noted about the non-trinitarian treatment of creation in the Middle Ages, Luther's claim that he was the only person to have understood the first chapter of Genesis is only slightly exaggerated. The change he brings about is remarkable. Unlike Augustine – of whom it can be said, without much exaggeration, that he was more interested in allegorising the text in the interests of his view that God created all things instantaneously and reading between the lines a Platonic two-order creation – Luther interprets it in trinitarian fashion.[22] It is now fashionable, and perhaps justifiable, to reject as fanciful the traditional interpretation of the 'Let us' in Genesis as referring to a plurality, and therefore a three. What is of interest, in any case, is not the plural so much as the manifoldness of the concept of mediation to be found in the passage, as Francis Watson has shown.[23] Luther is right to read it in the way that he does, especially in the light of a theological understanding of the unity of the Testaments. Both witness the action of the same God, and, if he is indeed triune, then his Old Testament revelation should also be so understood. 'Luther', says Regin Prenter, 'always speaks of creation in terms of the Trinity.'[24]

Of importance here is what this trinitarian reading enables Luther to say. First, he denies Augustine's Neoplatonising view that matter is almost nothing ('I disagree entirely'). To the contrary, the text teaches us 'not about mystical days of

[22] *Luther's Works*, 1, *Lectures on Genesis chapters 1–5*, edited by J. Pelikan (St Louis: Concordia, 1958), p. 9. Luther is contemptuous of Augustine's mystical interpretation of the text, as well of his and Hilary's view that God created instantaneously, pp. 4–5.

[23] Watson, *Text, Church and World*, pp. 140–4.

[24] Regin Prenter, *Spiritus Creator. Luther's Concept of the Holy Spirit* (Philadelphia: Muhlenberg, 1953), pp. 192f.

knowledge among angels and an allegorical world, but about real creatures and a visible world apprehended by the senses'. Second, recognising the concepts of mediation in the chapter, Luther reaffirms that which was scarcely of interest to Aquinas, that God created heaven and earth out of nothing. He can do this because he sees it to take place through the work of the Son, who adorns and separates the crude mass which was brought out of nothing; and the Spirit, who makes alive.[25] (How, he asks, could the word rendered spirit in Genesis 1.2 refer to the wind when the wind did not then exist?) Whatever we are to make of his exegesis, the fact remains that with Luther doctrines to which little more than lip-service had been paid for centuries come again to life. The result is that Luther's theology of creation is one not of absolute so much as of personal dependence: its atmosphere is of grace and gratitude. 'For here we may see how the Father has given Himself to us, with all that he has created, and how abundantly he has cared for us in this life ...'.[26] There are, of course, problems, and it might be said that here too more might have been done for the substantiality of the created world. There is to be seen in Luther's treatment of creation in the *Greater Catechism*[27] a tendency to the reduction of the created world to its instrumental use for us, something which was taken further by Schleiermacher.

Calvin's legacy is similar, and again somewhat ambiguous. As is well known, his theology of creation has an existential orientation similar to Luther's, articulated as it is in a dialectic of the knowledge of God the creator and of the knowledge of ourselves. The characteristic Reformation polemic against scholastic abstraction can be observed in his claim that these two together constitute the sum of wisdom. There is no interest

---

[25] Luther, *Lectures on Genesis*, p. 9.

[26] Luther, *Lectures on Genesis*, p. 98.

[27] *Greater Catechism*, p. 98. Luther's exposition of the creed in the second part of *The Greater Catechism* appropriates creation to God the Father, following the rather modalistic manner of the Apostles' Creed. He also understands creation personally, from the point of view of the believer. Creation means that: 'I understand and believe that I am God's creature, that is, that He gave me and preserves for me continually my body, my soul and life, etc.' Luther is not very interested in the non-personal world for its own sake. Creatures are there to 'serve for my use and the necessities of life' (p. 97). But there is no trace of the causal conception of creation which is so dominant in the thought of his predecessors.

in abstract speculation. But the other side is also apparent in
Calvin's tendency to narrow the scope of a theology of creation
to its anthropological relevance, a narrowing similar to Luther's. Although he affirms the doctrine of creation out of
nothing in his commentary on Genesis,[28] there is surprisingly
little interest in it in the *Institutes*. There is, again in line with
Luther, a new interest in the christological mediation of
creation. Yet what interests Calvin is not speculation, Augustinian or other, about creation out of nothing, so much as the
relevance of conceptions of divine action for the confidence of
the believer in God's government of things.

It should not be denied that some of the implications of
creation out of nothing do appear in Calvin's thought, and are
of crucial importance in that process of freeing the created
order from the Platonic and Aristotelian intermediate quasi-
agencies so essential for the development both of a satisfactory
doctrine of creation and of modern science. The presentation
of the created order as a semiotic system, a system of signs
which as a system pointed beyond itself to its maker, helped to
assure the relative independence of creation from the creator
without which a proper notion of contingency could not
develop. But there is an Achilles' heel, which can be inspected
through a study of Calvin's writings on the continuing relation
of creator with his creation. His real interaction with his
predecessors comes in the extended treatment of providence
that dominates the later chapters of Book 1 of the *Institutes*.

In it we meet a theology of the omnipotent will of God
containing more than a few echoes of the merely monotheistic
treatment which we met in the Schoolmen. Augustine is cited
in support of the claim that there is no higher cause of things
than God's will.[29] Repeatedly it is asserted that there is no such
thing as chance. What may appear to be chance faith recognises
as a secret impulse from God.[30] In what may be a criticism of a
Thomist conception, Calvin refuses to say 'that God is the first
agent because he is the beginning and cause of all motion'.
Quite the reverse: 'believers comfort themselves with the solace

---

[28] John Calvin, *Genesis*, translated by John King (Edinburgh: Banner of
Truth, 1965), p. 70.
[29] John Calvin, *Institutes*, I.14.1.
[30] Calvin, *Institutes*, I.16.2 and 9.

that they suffer nothing except by God's ordinance and command ...'.[31] '[P]rovidence is lodged in the act', not simply in the foreknowledge of God. Elsewhere he appeals to Augustine in defence of a belief that 'nothing is more absurd than that anything should happen without God's ordaining it, because it would then happen without any cause'.[32] What are we to make of all this? There are three main points.

(1) It is sometimes remarked that Calvin is not very interested in the third possible form of knowledge, that of the world in and for itself, though much is made in treatments of his relation to science of the encouragement given to the development of science by his celebration of the glory of God visible in the created world. But the question must remain whether the sum of wisdom includes knowledge of the world also. It has been argued, by T. F. Torrance[33] and Harold Nebelsick in particular, that it was the recovery of the doctrine of creation out of nothing that facilitated the emergence of the belief, so important for the development of modern science, in the contingency of the world. Certainly Calvin's world is contingent in the sense that it does not have to be, because it is freely created by the will of a personal God. But it is not so securely contingent in the sense that what happens in it does not have to happen as it does. Contingency has, it must be remembered, two senses, referring: (1) to the dependence of the world on God, a sense that was undoubtedly present in Aquinas; and also (2) to the world's non-necessity, particularly in relation to its divine source. Calvin in fact, rightly careful as he is to escape any entanglement in the concepts of fortune or chance, appears also, as we have seen, to deny any concept of contingency. On the one hand, he denies a Stoic necessitarianism, but on the other, by appearing to equate the concepts of contingency and chance, he has rightly or wrongly laid himself open to the same charge. The assertion of divine willing alone is not adequate to escape a tendency to necessitarianism.[34]

---

[31] Calvin, *Institutes*, I.16.3.

[32] Calvin, *Institutes*, I.16.8.

[33] Thomas F. Torrance, *Divine and Contingent Order* (Oxford: Oxford University Press, 1981).

[34] Calvin, *Institutes*, I.16.8. After the equation of the two concepts of chance and contingency, the latter disappears from the discussion.

(2) The immense and rather repetitive length at which Calvin wrestles with the problem of divine agency in relation to the world no doubt has something to do with what Bouwsma has called his anxiety.[35] These were times very much imbued with a sense of Heraclitean flux and the uncertainty of things, as that historian also records. But there are also signs that Calvin was somewhere himself uneasy about the apparently determinist direction of his thought, as his brief appeals to the concept of secondary causation reveal. He does not, however, rule out secondary causes 'in their proper place'.[36] Of the status of these secondary causes nothing is said.[37] In general therefore Calvin is able to give a more satisfying account of the universal providential care of God than of the correlative thesis that human agents are responsible for their actions. The reason for this is to be found in:

(3) In some contrast to the rest of his theology, there is in Calvin's account of the relation of God and the world little substantive part played by Christ and the Holy Spirit. There is in the passages we have reviewed from Calvin only one statement of the christological mediation of divine action in creation.[38] Similarly, the splendid characterisation of the Spirit's universal and life-giving work – 'everywhere diffused' he 'sus-

[35] William J. Bouwsma, *John Calvin. A Sixteenth Century Portrait* (New York and Oxford: Oxford University Press, 1989).

[36] Calvin, *Institutes*, I.17.6 and 9.

[37] It is surely significant that the concept of secondary causality was introduced in order to establish some form of limited autonomy in the creature. But it is problematic. Without a satisfactory concept of mediation, it simply replicates the problems we have met. The question that must be asked is whether the concept of secondary causation is an attempt to ensure the relative autonomy of the creature in the absence of an adequate conception of the mediation of creation and of providence or conservation. Creation trinitarianly conceived is thus the necessary condition of doctrine of creation out of nothing, because without it matter, or some other feature of the universe, becomes the mediator, *and thus eternal*. Secondary causation is therefore either too strong – producing the redundancy of God observed by Blumenberg in Ockham, and later in deism – or it is too weak, and the world becomes once again the determined product of divine monocausality, as for example in Spinoza. Here it is instructive to return to the case of Bishop Berkeley. Berkeley rejected the concept of mediation by created substance on various grounds, among them that substance was unknowable and that it effectively replaced God as the real agent of creation. But his solution, lacking a trinitarian concept of mediation, failed to achieve its end.

[38] See Calvin, *Institutes*, I.16.4.

tains all things, causes them to grow, and quickens them in heaven and earth'[39] – is to be found in the chapter on the doctrine of the Trinity, and does not recur with the same weight in the long treatment of providence. It is at least arguable that the wholesale return to the category of cause in the theology of Edwards has something to do with the intimations of omnicausality in Calvin. And part of the reason is that we meet here somewhat more of a theology of will than of one of love, more of an omnipotent monocausal God than of the one who works through his two hands, the Son and the Spirit.

In concluding this section, however, my concern is to summarise the positive developments in both Luther and Calvin. There is in both of these theologians a major shift away from the language of causality to one of personal action. The achievement is that the doctrine of creation is taken out of the largely philosophical context in which it had tended to be located, where it had become a semi-independent propaedeutic for faith, and returned to the confessed creed. This is the clear outcome equally of Luther's trinitarian reading of Genesis – as well as his close relating of creation with the believer's trust in God – and of Calvin's concern with God's personal and providential oversight of the creation.[40] Thus there is much to be said for the claim that the Reformers contributed to, indeed, achieved with little assistance from their Western predecessors, the recovery, of the doctrine of creation. The heart of this achievement was: (1) that in continuity with Ockham, they did much to re-establish a doctrine of the contingency of the created order on a freely willed act of God, and in this way encouraged the reappropriation of the ontological distinction of creator from creation which had been obscured by doctrines of quasi-eternal forms and hierarchies of causes. There are on this account only two realities, creator and creation. The significance of this is to be found in the reappropriation of the doctrine of the homogeneity of the created order. By this is

---

[39] Calvin, *Institutes*, I.13.14.

[40] It is perhaps worth mentioning at this stage that a link between christology and the abandonment of the scholastic idiom of causality has been observed by Ralph Del Colle to take place in some recent Roman Catholic theology. Ralph Del Colle, *Christ and the Spirit. Spirit-Christology in Trinitarian Perspective* (New York and Oxford: Oxford University Press, 1994), *passim*, though see, for example, p. 132.

meant not that there is no diversity and variety in the creation,[41] but that everything created has the same ontological status, so that, for example, it cannot be taught that the heavenly bodies consist of some ethereal or eternal substance different from that of the earth. Basil of Caesarea and others had long ago made that discovery on the grounds of the doctrine of creation.[42] Galileo's famous observation of the heavens through a telescope was a crucial step in the process of establishing that the heavenly bodies are of the same kind of material as the earth, but he was not as original as is sometimes suggested in secularising accounts of the origin of science. Equally important: (2) the Reformers began a process of replacing a conception of causality, relatively impersonally conceived, or, if not, of creation rather monistically construed in terms of will, with conceptions of agency in terms of trinitarian mediation, and that means agency far more personally conceived. Here they went far beyond their mediaeval predecessors. It follows that the God who creates the world is distinguished from all causes and emanations by the personal and intentional freedom by which he works. In that sense, the doctrine of creation represents the end of causality by virtue of its replacement by a doctrine of creation by personal agency.

IV *The problem of mediation*

The problem left behind by the Reformers, however, derives from the fact that they were less successful in developing an account of the world's continuing relation with God the creator. What was lacking was a satisfactory conception of mediation, by which is intended, as will by now be evident, a trinitarian one. Tradition, as in the Apostles' Creed, and even in the confessions of the rule of faith that are quoted by Irenaeus, attributes creation to the Father, salvation to the Son and life in the Church (etc.) to the Spirit. Dogmatically, that not only encourages modalism, but also draws attention away

[41] The abolition of the mediating function of the Platonic Forms means that there can be a re-establishing of the diversity of things, in their own right, because the focus of attention is turned away from the eternal world to this one. 'God saw *everything* that he had made, and behold, it was very good.'

[42] Basil, *Hexaemeron*, i.3; v.1; vi.5.

from the New Testament affirmations of the place of Jesus Christ in the mediation of creation as well as of salvation. That is perhaps the reason why the doctrine of creation is so often merely monotheistically, perhaps better unitarianly, construed. Rather, it should be said that creation, reconciliation and redemption are all to be attributed to the Father, all realised through the work of his two hands, the Son and the Spirit, who are, of course, themselves substantially God. There is mediation, but it is through God, not ontological intermediates. This tends to be lost when any other mediator conceived independently of the 'two hands' – Platonic forms, Aristotelian causes, Lockean or Newtonian substance – becomes the central focus of attention. Accordingly, although there is a danger of abstraction in so doing, I shall take first the christological dimensions and then the pneumatological, using as a starting-point in each case some remarks of Robert Jenson.

In the first, he argues that the Cappadocian rearrangement of Origen's way of understanding the hypostases – 'making the hypostases' mutual relations structures of the one God's life rather than risers of the steps from God down to us' – cleared away the realm of intermediate beings between God and the world.

> The Trinity as such is now understood to be the Creator, over against the creature, and the three in God and their relations become the evangelical history's reality on the Creator-side of the great biblical Creator/creature divide. Across the Creator/creature distinction no mediator is needed. [Or alternatively, the incarnation is the mediation, not the logos as such.][43]

The final sentence, placed in parentheses because it is a footnote in Jenson's book, makes the essential point. The incarnation – the act of free divine interrelation with the created world – provides the model of mediation that we need. Christology, not the ontologically intermediate being represented by some (Origenistic) conceptions of the Logos, but the Son of God in free personal relation to the world, indeed

---

[43] Robert Jenson, *The Triune Identity. God According to the Gospel* (Philadelphia: Fortress Press, 1982), pp. 106f.

identification with part of that world, is the basis for an understanding of God the Father's relations with his creation.

Before the Cappadocians, Athanasius had already seen the point of this in his argument that Jesus Christ is himself the creating Word, incarnate in human flesh to complete the work of creation. To be sure, this expresses a causal relation in the sense that it brings something about, in particular the reordering of relations between creator and creation. But it suggests a very different conception of the relation of God and the world from that found in the work of the earlier Schoolmen. It is not mediation through immanent patterns of causality because, as Irenaeus pointed out in opposition to the intermediate beings of the Gnostics, God's action through the Son is action by God in person. The reappropriation of that position begun by the Reformers in their trinitarian reading of the Old Testament can be taken seriously because the incarnation demonstrates the utterly free relatedness of God to that which he has made, and so provides an instance and paradigm of a form of *mediated* action that requires no *intermediaries*.

The methodological point that God's action in the incarnation founds a way of understanding divine action in general can be supplemented by the drawing out of its ontological implication: that the stability and reliability of the world in general depends not on some intermediate being or beings – the point of Berkeley's polemic against the concept of substance – but directly on God.[44] Such a suggestion of divine omnicausality,

---

[44] Thus in early modern philosophy, 'substance' performs the same function as the hidden essences and other scholastic beings that modern thought believed itself to have exorcised. Michael J. McLymond, 'God the Measure: Towards an Understanding of Jonathan Edwards' Theocentric Metaphysics', *Scottish Journal of Theology* 47 (1994), 43–59, shows that Edwards knew the way that the wind was blowing. He notes (53) that Edwards' idealism was a reaction to mechanistic and materialistic world-views, especially that of Hobbes. Edwards' view: 'there is no such thing as mechanism, if that word is taken to be that whereby bodies act upon each other, purely and properly by themselves' (*Scientific and Philosophical Writings*, p. 216) is glossed by Jenson's comment, 'Edwards' critique of mechanism is an encompassing piece of demythologizing: there are no little self-sufficient agencies besides God, natural entities are not godlets, and therefore the world harmony is not self-contained' (Robert Jenson, *America's Theologian. A Recommendation of Jonathan Edwards* (New York: Oxford University Press, 1988) p. 25). Edwards is thus understood to be seeking to secure the world for divine involvement in opposition to the eighteenth-century notion of a self-contained universe.

however, can be saved from the nearly pantheistic implications that appear to follow from Berkeley's and Edwards' view that everything comes directly from God. The divine causality must be understood not only as direct, but also as mediated. Edwards' statement, cited above, that 'that "something" is he by whom all things consist' should, but in his case apparently does not, take us to the eternal Son and wisdom of God. To be adequately construed, this mediated upholding, albeit without intermediaries or intermediate being(s), must be understood christologically, so that we should also take quite seriously the implications of the New Testament belief that creation coheres in Christ, or exists through him. It is stable and reliable because it is upheld in being by Christ, through whom the creation has its being. By means of a christological account of mediation, then, we are able to give some account of the stability of the creation which avoids the difficulties of both scholastic and early modern accounts.

But that supplies only one of two desiderata. The other is that some space be given to the created order, that is to say, some account of its distinctive being as creation, as other than but not apart from God – what could be called its autonomy, its ability to be itself, according to the law of its own particular being. We can make a beginning of this christologically. Let us take the humanity of Jesus as a test case, for it enables us to ask the question how this particular part of the created order is maintained in its integrity while yet being dependent on God's agency. If we ask how it is that the humanity of Jesus of Nazareth is maintained in its autonomy, the answer is in part pneumatological. If Jesus' humanity was in no way imperilled by its being that of the Word, that is because of the action of God the Spirit. The Spirit is the one who mediates the action of God the Father in such a way that the life of the Son, while deriving from the Father and dependent upon him, is given space to remain authentically human.

An account of the proper autonomy of the world must run in parallel with this, but we shall preface that by indicating something of the inadequacy of traditional accounts. That is highlighted by a second remark of Robert Jenson, this time on the conception of the work of the Holy Spirit that has dominated Western theological history. According to him, Augustine's rendering of the three persons of the Trinity functionally indistinguishable left the Western Church with a highly problematic account of the causal[45] relations of God and the world. 'Augustine was left with the standard position of Western culture-religion: on the one hand there is God, conceived as a supernatural entity who acts causally on us; and on the other hand there are the results among us of this causality.'[46] The resulting displacement, by what are effectively semi-mechanical conceptions of grace, of free personal action by the Spirit has had numerous deleterious effects in theology, and it can be argued that among them are the various conceptions of divine omnicausality that have distorted understandings of divine action in the world. Let us therefore look briefly at what might derive from renewed attention to pneumatology.

The resurrection of Jesus from the dead has been traditionally attributed to the Holy Spirit, and I will take it as a working hypothesis that this is an illuminating basis for consideration of action by the Spirit. The transformation of the corpse of Jesus into the conditions of the world to come is an instance of causally efficacious, but freely willed, personal divine action. It has a number of features, however, which make it more satisfactory than either patterns of causality operating immanently, as in the Thomist account, or the rather monocausal accounts of Ockham, Calvin and their successors. First, it leaves room for an otherness, a space, between that which causes and that which is caused. Action by the Spirit is in no way assimilable to models of logical implication (see John 3 and Ezekiel 37), but is free, unpredictable and efficacious. It respects the reality of the other by enabling it to be that which it was created to be, in a free act of divine transformation rather than the exercise of causal power. But, second, it does not run the risk of Ockhamist arbitrariness or the mere exercise of *potentia absoluta*. The resurrection of Jesus represents the consistency of the divine action, and in a number of respects: consistency with the outcome of Jesus' obedience, as its affirmation and completion; and with the divine purposes for the creation, whose recapitulation and perfection are inaugurated in the ministry of Jesus.

---

[45] Thus does our central problem recur in yet another place.
[46] Robert W. Jenson, 'The Holy Spirit', *Christian Dogmatics*, edited by C. E. Braaten and R. W. Jenson (Philadelphia: Fortress Press), volume 2, pp. 126f.

Crucial here is the eschatological action of the Spirit, his enabling of created things to become what they are by anticipating what they shall be, a function inaugurated and instantiated by the resurrection of Jesus from the dead. Having said that, however, we must remember that there is eschatology and eschatology. On the one hand, there is that, whose father is perhaps Origen of Alexandria and whose greatest exponent is perhaps Augustine, which sees the end of creation as a return to the perfection of its beginning. This tends to be associated with, if it is not actually the outcome of, a Neoplatonic and emanationist view of things, according to which it is the destiny of creation to be, so to speak, rolled back into the being of God.[47] The inadequacy of this is shown by the consideration that if creation is God's self-communication, his word, then its destiny is to return to him void, for it does not become, in its own right, anything more than it once was. It simply returns whence it came as what it once was: nothing. That is to say, it has no truly eschatological teleology. On the other hand, if the Spirit is indeed the perfecting cause of creation,[48] whose function is to bring the world through Christ to a completeness which it did not have in the beginning, there is rather more to be said. The destiny of things on this account is to be presented before the throne in their perfection, not without the human creation, indeed, but transformed in such a way that their true otherness is not only respected but achieved. This is the work of the Lord who is the Spirit.

In sum, we conclude that the Reformers and their predecessors have enabled us to move to a conception of creation which exorcises some of the more unfortunate elements of Neoplatonism from the tradition. It is better if we do not speak of creation as divine self-communication, which is more appropriately used of God's self-giving in Christ. This is because a general rather than particular divine self-communication runs the risk of an essentially Neoplatonist, emanationist, and finally pantheist absorption of the creature in the creator. In other

---

[47] J. W. Trigg remarks that Origen's 'doctrine of creation out of nothing ultimately provides for an eschatology more consistent with Platonism than the new heaven and earth of the Bible' (*Origen. The Bible and Philosophy in the Third Century Church* (Atlanta: John Knox, 1983), p. 110).

[48] Basil of Caesarea, *On the Holy Spirit*, XV.36 and 38.

words, if we understand the creation rather than Christ as the locus of God's giving of himself, we are in danger of losing the essential otherness of creation from the creator, that which it needs to have if it is truly to be itself in distinction from God.[49] The point of stressing a trinitarian way of construing the relation of creator and creation is that it enables us to understand both the past and the continuing creative divine agency towards the world without closing the space between God and the created order. The doctrine of creation has to do, that is to say, with the establishment of the other in its own distinctive reality: not divine self-communication, but divine constituting of the world to be truly other, and so itself. If that be causality, then we can continue to use the concept, but only if that carries connotations of personal, willed, intentional, consistent and loving agency.[50]

[49] This point might hold also against Moltmann's tendency to conceive creation out of nothing as an act of divine *kenosis* or self-emptying.

[50] I am grateful to Paul Metzger for pointing out some errors and raising some questions which have helped me to clarify some of the points made in this chapter.

CHAPTER 9

CHRISTOLOGY

Two dogmas revisited: Edward Irving's christology[1]

I *Two modern dogmas*

Two dogmas continue to die hard, despite attempts to destroy them, and it may be that they have good reason for refusing to go away. The first is that what has come to be known as 'christology from above' tends to produce a docetic conception of the person of Christ, or at least one in which the humanity of Jesus receives so little emphasis that it becomes little better than a cipher. If an eternal being or hypostasis – to put the matter in the almost tritheistic language that is sometimes used – takes to himself a body, can the resulting being be truly human? Does not the eternal origin inevitably call the tune, undermining the genuineness of the human actions?

It is questions such as these which continue to give cause for suspicion, even to their friends, of some of the formulations of the Alexandrian theologians. While it is unfair, for example, to charge Athanasius with anticipations of Apollinaris, his language is undoubtedly unguarded at times, as when, for example, he speaks of the Word as wielding his body like an implement (*organon*).[2] To that extent, Sellars is justified in commenting that the humanity of Jesus lacks historical particularity in Athanasius.[3] It is not that the saviour is less than human: he took a body 'of no different sort from ours',[4] and Athanasius' soteriological teaching depends upon it. It is rather

---

[1] First published in the *Scottish Journal of Theology* 41 (1988), 359–76.
[2] Athanasius, *Inc.* 42; cf. 17.
[3] R. V. Sellars, *Two Ancient Christologies* (London: SPCK, 1954), p. 44.
[4] Athanasius, *Inc.* 8.

151

that there is a relative lack of interest in what we might call the lineaments of the human story.

The same is true of the christology of Cyril of Alexandria, albeit in a rather different way, especially if Meijering's comment is justified that it did not really matter for him whether the incarnate Lord was that particular man or not.[5] Coming after Apollinaris, however, Cyril is in general more guarded than Athanasius, insisting both on the full humanity and on the unity of action of the one historical person.[6] It is worth noting, however, that the tendency to reduce the humanity to a rather passive role – it is more accurate to speak so than of docetism – is by no means universal among those with a 'high' incarnational christology. Irenaeus, the real intellectual predecessor of Athanasius, is virtually unfaltering in his characterisation of the humanity of the saviour and of the unity of his person.[7]

The second dogma is the reverse side of the same coin. Return to the historical Jesus, it is often proclaimed, and the balance will be redressed. I have argued elsewhere that there exists much confusion about what is meant by 'the historical Jesus'.[8] If, moreover, we look at the historical roots of the matter in the christology of the Antiochene tradition, the essence of the problem will become clearer. When a beginning is made with the human story, two tendencies, one typically ancient, the other typically modern, will emerge. On the one hand, the story will be seen to be linked with the action of the eternal Word, but in such a way that the unity of the one historic Christ appears incapable of satisfactory conceptualisation. The human life is no longer the life of God among us, the death no longer the suffering of the eternal Son, bearing for us the consequences of our fallenness.

On the other hand, the humanity may indeed be conceived as the life of divinity, but it is much more like that of a divinised

---

[5] E. P. Meijering, *God, Being, History* (Amsterdam and Oxford: North Holland, 1974), p. 126.

[6] See, for example, his *Second Letter to Nestorius*.

[7] The one possible exception commonly quoted is his apparent anticipation of a Nestorian direction in *Haer.* III.19.3, where he speaks of the word being 'quiescent' during the incarnate life.

[8] Colin E. Gunton, *Yesterday and Today. A Study of Continuities in Christology* (London: Darton, Longman & Todd, 1983), pp. 54ff.

man than that of God made man for our salvation. A good example is provided by Schleiermacher's treatment of the humanity of Christ. Schleiermacher not only sits light to the Jewish particularity of Jesus, being in general embarrassed by the Old Testament;[9] he also believes that the developed God-consciousness of Jesus was never really diminished – for it was in that that the divinity was centred – and that there can have been no real conflict in the life of the saviour.[10] On such a conception, it is difficult to find much place in christology for what is so central to both gospels and epistles: the temptations, the Gethsemane experience and the death of Jesus. Historical particularity suffers, on this account, more seriously than in any Alexandrian christology from above. Equally, it can be added, it suffers in other versions of the liberal Jesus. Was not Tyrrell justified in his famous jibe about the reflected liberal Protestant face? Could we not say the same thing about contemporary ideological christologies; those, for example, moulded by existentialism, feminism and Marxism?

Where, then, shall we go? We have seen that there are continuing problems with some forms of incarnational christology and worse problems – worse, because they deprive christology of the transcendent perspective which will save it from ideology – with the leading alternatives. The need is for an incarnational christology which will yet do full justice to the historical particularity of Jesus and the detailed lineaments of his story. I want to suggest that the area where we should look is our understanding of the place of pneumatology in christology. And that brings us to the central figure of this chapter, Edward Irving, the Scottish theologian who now, just over one hundred and fifty years after his death, is becoming the focus of renewed interest. In the following, there is no claim to present an exhaustive scholarly account of Irving's christology; rather I shall draw on some of the things he has said in order to point a way to a reconsideration of the problems of christology.

[9] F. D. E. Schleiermacher, *The Christian Faith*, translated by H. R. Mackintosh and J. S. Stewart (Edinburgh: T. & T. Clark, 1928), pp. 62 and 115: 'the Old Testament appears simply a superfluous authority for Dogmatics'.

[10] Schleiermacher, *The Christian Faith*, p. 382: 'His development must be thought of as wholly free from everything which we have to conceive as conflict'; for the implications for the reality of the temptations, cf. p. 414.

II *Jesus Christ as divine act*

We approach Irving's contribution with the help of a return to an Alexandrian type of question: how can it be conceived that the Word became flesh without ceasing to be Word but, equally, without depriving the historical person of Christ of real humanity? We cannot, necessarily, construct theories of how this happened, but can and must ask how best we may express conceptually the kind of action that is envisaged. Here, as Prestige shows, the notion of *kenosis* or self-emptying is important in Cyril's christology, not in the sense in which the concept was being used by some of Irving's near contemporaries, but to express the condescension of the Word in his wholeness to the human condition. 'We assert that the very Word out of God the Father, in the act by which He is said to have been emptied for our sake by taking the form of a slave, lowered Himself within the measures of manhood.'[11] There are two preconditions for the adequacy of such a statement. The first is that in some sense or other the incarnation must be conceived to be an expression of the very nature of God and not, in Rahner's way of putting it, a merely external miracle. Athanasius, it will be remembered, achieved this by asserting the Word's essential nearness to the created world.[12] The second is that the outcome be a real and not a docetic or passive humanity. The later Fathers attempted to guarantee this aspect of the matter by developing the doctrine of *enhypostasia*. The doctrine makes the point that although, for soteriological reasons, it is not enough to say that the humanity of Jesus simply emerges out of history by ordinary means (it is *anhypostatic*), it is yet a true humanity, for it is established as the humanity of the eternal Word. The incarnation, that is to say, is what happens when the eternal Son and Word of God becomes flesh in the person (*hypostasis*) that is Jesus of Nazareth. But as we have seen, the device does not appear, on its own, to have guaranteed an adequate emphasis on the true humanity of Christ.

Let us look at Irving's treatment in the light of those two

---

[11] Cyril of Alexandria, *C. Nest* 63C, cited by G. L. Prestige, *Fathers and Heretics* (London: SPCK, 1940), p. 165.

[12] Athanasius, *Inc.* 8.

preconditions of a satisfactory theology of the incarnation. First, how does Irving conceive the incarnation to be the expression of the nature of God the Word? His answer has three aspects in particular. (1) His christology overall has a robustly supralapsarian character which sets the incarnation firmly in the context of eternity. Irving is strongly set against what has come to be called 'dishwater Protestantism', the doctrine that the incarnation is, so to speak, God's second attempt to make something of the world when the first failed. The Fall of man was, indeed, the 'immediate' and 'also the formal cause of the incarnation; that is to say, what gave to the purpose of God its outward form and character ...'.[13] But its eternal cause was deep in the heart of God, in the reality of the Lamb slain from the foundation of the world, to the evidence of which Irving adds the testimonies of John 17.24 and 1 Peter 1.18–20. Irving appeals to the early Church and the Reformers to support his claim that 'it is a great purpose of the Divine will which God was minded from all eternity to make known unto his creatures ... the forgiveness and love which He beareth to those who love the honour of His Son ...' (p. 12).

(2) The event of the incarnation is understood in trinitarian terms, and it is worth pausing to observe that the same is the case with all of Irving's writings on christology, a feature which gives them the breadth and comprehensiveness which is the mark of all great theology. 'He submits Himself unto His Father to be made flesh; His Father sendeth the Holy Spirit to prepare Him a body ... and thus, by creative act of Father, Son and Holy Ghost, not by ordinary generation, Christ is constituted a Divine and human nature in one person' (p. 159, see also pp. 160f.). Some of the writing is so powerful that it is worth quoting at length:

> My Christ is the Trinity manifested; ... I have the Father manifest in everything which He doth; for He did not His own will, but the will of His Father. I have the Son manifested, in uniting His Divinity to a humanity prepared for Him by the Father; and in making the two most contrary

---

[13] G. Carlyle, editor, *The Collected Writings of Edward Irving in Five Volumes* (London: Alexander Strachan, 1865), volume 5, p. 10. Subsequent page numbers in parentheses in the text are references to this volume.

things to meet and kiss each other ... I have the Holy Spirit manifested in subduing, restraining, conquering, the evil propensities of the fallen manhood, and making it an apt organ for expressing the will of the Father ... (p. 170).

Irving's theology of the incarnation is a classic instance of the principle *opera trinitatis ad extra sunt indivisa* (the actions of the Trinity in the world are undivided), yet it does not lapse into the characteristic Western failing of resolving the threeness of the Godhead into a modalistic expression of the underlying One.

(3) The incarnation is the outcome of the historic condescension of the eternal Son to human estate (p. 161), 'the Eternal Son ... humbling Himself to the human soul' (p. 126). It is a *kenosis* or self-emptying, but one understood as the expression of the inner dynamic of the Trinity, not as the sloughing off of certain attributes. The incarnate one is thus truly God, not a mythological epiphany nor a temporary visitor in human dress: 'in every act of Christ the Divine nature acteth and the human nature acteth; the former by self-contraction unto the measure of the latter ...' (p. 134). The humbling, self-emptying, is radical, and to understand that is to begin to understand the character of Irving's christology. Its outcome is that he completely escapes the tendency to Nestorianism that is found in some patristic christology, as he is himself aware:

> The person, the *I* who speaketh, acteth, suffereth in Christ is not the Divine nature, nor yet is it the human nature, alone; but it is the Divine nature having passed into the human nature, and therein effecting its will and purpose of acting or of suffering. I totally reject ... the language of those divines who say, 'Now the Divine nature acteth, now the human nature acteth'; language which I hold to be essentially Nestorian ... (p. 134).[14]

The radical self-involvement of the Son in the person of

[14] Compare here Cyril's similarly anti-docetic christology: 'Moreover we do not distribute the Words of our Saviour in the Gospels to two several subsistences or Persons ... To one Person, therefore, must be attributed all the expressions used in the Gospels, the one incarnate *hypostasis* of the Word, for the Lord Jesus Christ is one according to the Scriptures' (*Third Letter to Nestorius*, 8).

Christ thus enables Irving to share the rejection of monothelite christology, and to show why such an apparently obscure heresy must be resisted:

> There is a double operation, a twofold will ... one with the Godhead ever consubstantial, and out of the absolute into the manhood condescending, in order to suffer and to act: the Godhead ever emptying itself into the manhood: the manhood not containing the Godhead, but consenting with harmony to the mind of the Godhead (p. 134).

For the sake of the gospel of salvation, anything which confuses the being of creator and creation must be resisted. Yet, equally and for the same reason, the two must come together in Jesus. In common with the Fathers, Irving holds that only God can save lost humankind; and yet unless he does it as man, whole man, the point of the incarnation disappears.

III *Jesus Christ as human being*

But already we are beginning to impinge upon the second condition for an adequate christology, and at the same time the second main aspect of Irving's teaching, his treatment of the humanity of Christ. The first thing to say is that to the radical condescension and *kenosis* of the incarnation of the Son there corresponds an equally radical construal of the humanity of Jesus. There is, once again, some powerful writing:

> For he condescended to dwell in concert and communion with flesh; to look up through fleshly eyes; by fleshly senses to converse with the great wickedness of the earth; and, through the faculties of the human soul, to commune with every impious, ungodly and blasphemous chamber of the fallen intellect and feeling of men ... For the Divine and Almighty Creator to empty Himself of Himself, to take the limitation of a creature, and bind Himself under the appointed law of the action and suffering thereof, is very wonderful; but for the Holy Creator, the thrice-holy One, by dwelling therein to bring Himself into actual communication with, real sense of, and sympathy in, all the wickedness of this

world, passeth all humiliation which can be conceived (pp. 269f.).

It was the total nature of the condescension which was to bring Irving under the condemnation of the Church of Scotland and which is, for the same reason, of most positive interest to us today. For underlying the above citation there is the doctrine which Irving defends at length here and elsewhere, piling argument upon argument, that at the incarnation the Son did not assume the perfect, unfallen, flesh of Adam, but our fallen human nature.[15] Irving's arguments range over every aspect of the case, and once again reveal the breadth of his systematic theology.

The first group of arguments engages with what can be called the ontology of the matter. If Jesus is born in human history to a human mother, then his body necessarily consists of matter that partakes of the fallenness of the world. The argument here is matter of fact: 'That Christ took our fallen nature is most manifest, because there is no other in existence to take' (pp. 115f.). Here the argument has a strongly anti-docetic and, in particular, anti-Apollinarian thrust:

> if Christ had not a reasonable soul, His human feelings and affections were but an assumed fiction to carry the end which His mission had in view; and His sufferings and His death were a phantasmagoria played off before the eyes of men, but by no means entering into the vitals of human sympathy, nor proceeding from the communion and love of human kind ... and bringing up again the fallen creature to stand before the throne of the grace of God ... (p. 118).

Moreover, rejection of the view that Christ took our fallen human flesh involves a devaluation of the work of the Holy Spirit, both in relation to the believer and in our understanding of the person of Christ. That, too, is an anti-docetic argument in that it is concerned to establish the complete involvement of God in our human condition.

The fact that such a theology met with the response it did shows how deeply problematic is much of the christology of the

---

[15] Not, it would appear, altogether unsuccessfully in the long term: Barth makes favourable reference to Irving's doctrine in *Church Dogmatics* 1/2, p. 154.

Western tradition. The teaching that Christ took *unfallen* human flesh dates back a long way, and is represented at its worst in the dogma of the immaculate conception, in which a double cordon sanitaire is erected between the saviour and ourselves. How, then, can he really have assumed that which is to be healed? Once again, we meet the moments of truth in the modern concern to dispute traditional dogma in the name of the humanity of Jesus. As we have seen, however, Irving's way was not to deny the tradition, but to go back beyond its distortions to its roots. We now move to his second set of reasons for teaching the radical involvement of the eternal Word in our human condition. As the above citation shows, the main concern is soteriological. Irving's argument is a version of the classic patristic teaching that what Christ does not assume, he does not heal.

Irving's arguments in this area are closely related to the first set, and concern the nature of salvation. Any view of Christ which makes him less than fully human both takes him out of our sphere and leads to what Irving calls a 'stock-exchange divinity', in which the divine Christ settles a balance held against us by being loaded with the debts we have run up. The two themes are interrelated in the following passage:

> This scheme of supposing Christ to have been laden, as it were, with a body that had the sins of many bodies imputed to it, doth take Him out of our sphere again, and destroy the application unto us, of those things shewed forth in Him; for the sinner might turn upon us, and say, that example of the sinfulness of sin, which you educed from Christ, is not applicable to me, who have but my own sin to bear (p. 218; cf. p. 146).

Once again we meet a Cappadocian type of argument for the fullness of the humanity. In order to redeem the human will from bondage, the Son must 'take up into Himself the very conditions of a human will ...' (p. 23). If Christ did not have a fallen body, how could the sufferings that were part of his ministry really touch him (p. 213)?

Conversely, the fullness of the humanity is the means to a positive understanding of the atonement not as a bargain, but as the restoring of human life to its true end. '[I]f Christ took upon Himself our fallen and corruptible nature, and brought it up through death into eternal glory, then is the act of the will of Christ not to lay down, but to assume or take up humanity into Himself . . .' (p. 148). Underlying all this is a conception of the corporate nature of humanity: that we stand or fall together. Here Irving is able both to take the implications of the cry of dereliction seriously – something that is virtually impossible on Schleiermacher's account – and to point to the relevance of Jesus' suffering for the doctrine of the atonement. In the first place, it reveals sin to be something other than the quantitative matter that his rival theology supposes. Sin 'is not, as it were, the accumulation of the sins of all the elect' – stock-exchange divinity again – 'but the simple, single, common power of sin diffused throughout, and present in, the substance of flesh of fallen human nature' (p. 217). Accordingly, in the second place, Irving is able to develop a correspondingly corporate conception of salvation which yet avoids the objectionable aspects of both traditional penal theory and Aulén's later understanding of the atonement as victory. It is, we might say, Aulén without myth, for the cross is conceived as a victory, but as one not over mythological hosts of evil so much as over the disseminated enslavement to which human being is subject. 'His flesh is the fit field of contention because it is the same on which Satan had triumphed since the fall. Here, then, in the flesh of Christ, is the great controversy waged.' And why is his flesh the 'fit field'? 'Because it is linked unto all material things, devil-possessed, while it is joined in closest, nearest union unto the soul, which in Christ was God-possessed, in the Person of the Holy Ghost' (p. 161). For Irving, the fallen flesh which Christ bore represents in a strong sense the whole of the created order in its fallenness. As in Adam's body 'the whole earth stood . . . represented . . . so likewise the whole substance of organised flesh and blood . . . stood represented in the body of Christ which the Holy Spirit had formed from the Virgin's substance . . .' (p. 154).

We are now on the threshold of the next section of the chapter, but it is worth pausing to note a third set of arguments connected with Irving's insistence that Christ took our fallen human flesh. He is very conscious of the ethical implications of different doctrines of the humanity of Christ. Unless the fallenness of the flesh is accepted, then perfectionism and pharisaism are likely to result: 'You will say, "Stand off: I am holier than thou"' (p. 127). Similarly, the Church's estimate of itself is at stake: 'if Christ may not follow the creature down the precipice ... it is a thing past Divine Power, and unto Divine holiness repugnant, to descend into the gulf, and labour among the wretches there'. And so, 'Holiness becomes distance; love keepeth asunder ... the church ... removed away into a sanctimonious distance ... '.[16]

IV *The action of the Holy Spirit*

From the furore that resulted, it might have been thought that Irving had taught that Christ was actually sinful. He did not, and his account of the humanity of Christ brings together both the concern voiced at the beginning of this chapter for the due expression of the particularity of Jesus' human life and another of the strengths of Irving's theology. If Jesus was as radically involved as Irving makes him in the mess of human fallenness, how far can it be asserted that he remained sinless? The answer lies in the manner in which the Holy Spirit is conceived to be involved in the incarnation and life of Jesus. We have already seen something of how according to Irving the flesh of Jesus takes form through the operation of the Spirit – 'His Father sendeth the Holy Spirit to prepare Him a body.' The Spirit is likewise central to an understanding of Jesus' life. Throughout, it is not some immanent drive, of the kind that would appear to be implicit in Apollinarian or Eutychian christologies, as well as the Western ones which sometimes echo them, that keeps the saviour unfallen, but the humanising activity of the Holy Spirit. '[T]he Holy Ghost was the author of His bodily life, the quickener of that substance which He took from fallen humanity ...' (p. 126).

At this stage, two points of clarification will assist in understanding the strength of Irving's position. The first is made by Bishop Kallistos of Diocletia, that Irving is building on a distinction made by Nestorius, 'between the levels of *nature* and

---

[16] Edward Irving, *The Last Days* (London: R. B. Seeley & W. Burnside, 1828), pp. 510f.

person. The human nature that Christ took at the incarnation was subject, like our own, to the effects of original sin; but on the level of personhood, in his freely-willed acts of personal choice, Christ was utterly and entirely sinless, his whole life being one continual victory over sin.'[17] The second is that to base Jesus' free choice of the good pneumatologically rather than christologically has two important advantages. In the first place, it prepares the way for a demonstration of the human relevance of Jesus' sinlessness. As he was free by virtue of his relation to the Spirit, so may be the ones who live in him. In the second place, because the Spirit is God's transcendent other-ness to the world, drawing it on to its eschatological destiny, Jesus' obedience to the Father through the Spirit can be seen as the free response to an other, rather than as the programmed outcome of an immanent directionality. The matter of the Spirit's transcendence will concern us later. In the mean time, we return to Irving.

The outcome of Irving's pneumatological emphasis is that he is enabled to find the humanity of Jesus not in some supposed reconstructed story underlying the gospel accounts, but in the narrative set out in the actual text. Crucially, the temptations are understood in their full reality. Because it was fallen flesh, it was 'liable to all the temptations to which flesh is liable: but the soul of Christ, thus anointed with the Holy Ghost, did ever resist and reject the suggestions of evil' (p. 126). Irving is able to do justice also to other central features of the story. Those who would hold that certain strands of New Testament christol-ogy take an adoptionist form make much play with the appar-ent incompatibility of passages which appear to place the decisive acts at the conception of Jesus, at his baptism or at his resurrection. Irving does not hold an adoptionist position, yet can make sense of the diversity of patterning within the one overall story.

What, for example, is the point of the baptism? It was to show both that Christ shared the same flesh as others, and so needed to fulfil all righteousness (p. 131; cf. p. 235), and that he was there anointed to 'prophetical office'. The fact that his body

---

[17] Bishop Kallistos of Diocletia, *The Humanity of Christ. The Fourth Con-stantinople Lecture* (Anglican and Eastern Churches Association, 1985).

was in the beginning formed by the action of the Spirit does not preclude an anointing for a specific ministry later, as it tended to do for Augustine, the fountain-head of the Western theology which Irving is attempting to reshape. 'For it is very foolish of us to believe that He received the Holy Spirit when He was already thirty years old ... but ... as He came to the Baptism without any sin at all, so He was not without the Holy Spirit.'[18] The difference between Augustine and Irving is that the former tends to conceive the Spirit substantially, so to speak as a *substantial* possession of Jesus, while the latter conceives him as a *personal other* in free relation to Jesus. He can accordingly be true also to Luke's 'He "grew in stature and in wisdom and in favour with God and man"'. He truly passed through the various stages, from childhood up to manhood, not merely as to His body, but as to His mind; and in order to enable Him to speak as never man spake He must have a special power of the Holy Ghost, as well as to enable Him to heal all that were oppressed with the devil' (p. 131). From his baptism onwards, therefore, Christ 'walked in liberty, He rejoiced in power, He triumphed in victory ... until the time He fell, as it were, plumb down from that elevation into the agony of the garden and the abandonment of the cross' (p. 236). Because of his obedience to the Spirit's leading, Jesus is *real man*, and 'Thus He shewed us an example, that we should follow His steps; and hereby He became the great prototype of a Christian, as He had been the great antitype of all the holy men under the law' (p. 133).

According to Irving, then, his relation to the Spirit is the means whereby Jesus is enabled to be both truly human and, so to speak, prototypically human. But there is a third dimension, too – a 'third measure of the Spirit, which quickened Him in the tomb, with which also our bodies shall be anointed when we shall be quickened in the tomb ...' (p. 237). Irving thus distinguishes between the birth and baptism, on the one hand, and the resurrection, on the other, in respect of their manner of bearing to mankind the significance of Jesus. Appealing to Acts 2 and Hebrews 5, he argues that Christ's priestly office derived from baptism. It is only after the resurrection that Christ himself baptises with the Holy Spirit, and so becomes

---

[18] Augustine, *On the Trinity*, XV.26.46.

high priest to those who follow. Only after passing through the full *recapitulatio*, and that includes the trial of God-forsakenness – for Irving holds that in the agony of death the Spirit left Jesus 'that He might know the hour and the power of darkness' (p. 133) – does he become the *giver* of that Spirit who during his earthly life *gave* him to the world.[19]

V   A Spirit christology?

We now move to a review of some of the problems and possibilities inherent in Irving's christology. We begin by returning to the matter of *kenosis*. As we have seen, there are in Irving's theology of the incarnation more than a few traces of what has come to be called kenotic christology. As a *theory*, kenotic christology holds that in order to become incarnate the eternal Son divests himself of some aspects of his divinity in order to be, so to speak, made compatible with the human experience. Is Irving's christology in that sense kenotic? The answer is, surely not. He is not writing as he does in order to find some way out of the supposed incompatibility of eternal Son and human Jesus, but speaking of the human life as the outcome of the Son's self-giving. In that respect, the incarnation is the *expression* of the Son's eternal reality and not an exception to it, as kenotic theories, with the possible exception of P. T. Forsyth's, tend to teach.

But the question can still be asked: is Jesus any longer a divine Christ, and in what sense? Irving is remarkably sensitive to the issue, and careful about his expression:

> I am unfolding no change in the eternal and essential divinity of the Son, which is unchangeable, being very God of very God; but I am unfolding certain changes which passed upon the humanity, and by virtue of which the humanity was brought from the likeness of fallen sinful flesh, through various changes, unto that immortality and incorruption and

---

[19] This point is of great importance in view of the difference between Eastern and Western Churches over the *filioque*, because the failure of the West to give due weight to the part played by the Spirit in the economy of salvation has much to do with the structure of its trinitarian thinking. Although Irving does teach a version of the *filioque*, there is little doubt that the whole trend of his theology is against it.

sovereign Lordship whereunto it hath now attained, and wherein it shall for ever abide (p. 133).

Not only is Irving thus careful to maintain the dialectic between time and eternity, but he realises that it can be maintained only on a trinitarian ground:

> Your Trinity is an idle letter in your creed; but it is the soul, the life of mine. Your Christ is a suffering God; I know it well: my Christ is a gracious condescending God, but a suffering man. In your Christ, you see but one person in a body: in my Christ I see the fullness of the Godhead in a body. My Christ is the Trinity manifested ... (p. 170).

The latter passage, with its sometimes strikingly contemporary allusions, is the heart of the matter, and for two reasons. First is the matter of the identification of the divine in Christ. What are we demanding when we ask for a divine Christ? Ought we to expect anything beyond the *incognito* of God in the matter, but acknowledge that it is *the human life as a whole that is to be confessed as the presence of God made man*? Is the weakness of much christology, both ancient and modern, not to be found precisely in wanting to have too manifest a divinity, in wanting to see it poking through all or some of the time before it can be confessed?

The second reason is also brought out by Irving's perceptive introduction of the Trinity. His christology is sometimes referred to as a 'Spirit christology', but that is precisely what it is not, as a glance at instances of that jejune genre will demonstrate. The essence of Spirit christology, as it appears in the writings of G. W. H. Lampe, is that it is unitarian. The effect of the doctrine is to introduce a uniformity, a monochrome character, to the conception of divine activity. On Lampe's understanding, God as Spirit acts immanently within the created order,[20] the significance of Jesus being that he is in some sense or other a special or definitive instance of the general operation of the Spirit-God within the created order. Like Irving, Lampe teaches the continuity between the action of the Spirit in Jesus and in the believer. 'By the "Christ-Spirit" is

[20] G. W. H. Lampe, *God as Spirit* (London: SCM Press, 1977), for example p. 96.

meant the indwelling presence of God as Spirit in the freely responding spirit of man as this is concretely exhibited in Christ and reproduced in some measure in Christ's followers.'[21]

In one respect, to differ from Lampe is simply to assert a contrary view of the meaning of the Christian dispensation. There is, it can be said, an absence in this bland theology of, to use Forsyth's words, the cruciality of the cross – of the seriousness of the human condition and of the means of its healing – and a corresponding flattening of the distinction between the orders of creation and redemption. Similarly, Lampe tends to find the basis of salvation in the created order itself, rather than in a personal God who is other than and Lord of the creation. But, in that respect, Lampe knows what he is doing and to disagree is to assert considerations which he would simply reject.

In another respect, however, it is possible to advance considerations which bring the underlying problematic to the surface. A determining feature of Lampe's discussion is that *Spirit* is a word to characterise the immanence of God. In that he would seem to owe more to the influence of modern immanentism, perhaps mediated through Hegel, than to the Bible to which he appeals. As we have already seen in Irving's treatment of the relation of Jesus to the Spirit, the Spirit is a transcendent reality: the presence of God *to* the world but as other than it. (It is Jesus and the Old Testament anticipations of the incarnation that are God's *immanence*.) The Spirit may operate within us, but he is not identified with us, as Jesus is.[22]

That consideration gives rise to another. It is wrong to see Lampe simply as a modern theologian capitulating to the spirit of Hegelian and other philosophies of immanence. Why, we may ask, is there such a drive in modern Western theology to unitarianism in various forms, either deist or immanentist? May not the reason lie in the fact that since Augustine theology has always tended in a modalist direction, conceiving the real God as the pure being underlying the distinctions of the persons who, when examined critically, behave like the Cheshire cat?

---

[21] Lampe, *God as Spirit*, p. 114.
[22] Some qualification of this point about the transcendence of the Spirit was made in chapter 7 above.

Irving, as we have seen, is thoroughly trinitarian, like Calvin before him, although, unlike Calvin, he avoids shipwreck on the rock of Augustinian predestinarianism. His advance is to be seen in the injection of features largely lost in the West since Augustine. The latter is notoriously weak on the Spirit, subordinating the eschatological freedom of a person to a timeless function in a Platonic triad.

By contrast, Irving develops a conception of a distinctively pneumatological form of divine action, without sundering the unity of the one action. But that is not all. The economy of salvation on Irving's account takes shape as a result of the will of the Father, and it is the strong note of Cappadocian *monarchia* which frees him to be incarnational in a way in which most Western theologians are not. Because the Father is the active (*energetic*) source of the economy – rather than, as 'memory', a timeless repository of being – it follows that the Son need not be conceived as being divine *in the same way* as the Father. He is divine, we might say, according to his own hypostasis, a hypostasis having its shape by virtue of its relations to Father and Spirit, but having the distinctive shape manifested by self-giving, obedience, *kenosis*. That is the reason why the humanity of Jesus is not foreign to but an expression of the deity of the Son, in all of what I have called its lineaments:

> So that what the Virgin bore is to be called very God; what was laid in a manger is to be called very God. What was circumcised; what sought knowledge of the scribes and doctors in the temple; what grew in wisdom and in stature, and in favour with God and man; what was in subjection to His parents; what was baptised in Jordan; what was tempted of the devil; what went about doing good, healing all that were oppressed with the devil; what was crucified; what died – all these actings and sufferings are proper unto God in that human nature, which is as much of Him as the Divine nature is of Him (p. 134).

It is as human that Jesus expresses the divinity of the eternal Son and so makes known the Father.

All this, it must be remembered, was written in the first third of the nineteenth century. It was not in every way original. Apart from its anticipations in the thought of the Fathers and of

Calvin, it had received one very significant anticipation. As the recent researches of Alan Spence have shown, Irving's christology repeats some of the features of that of John Owen in the seventeenth century.[23] Did Irving read Owen? There seems little reason why he should not have done. A pertinent question for us, however, is why neither Owen nor Irving has been read seriously during the last century and a half. In England, they have tended to be buried under a deluge of ill-informed if not positively malicious Tractarian misrepresentation of the Reformation tradition.[24] But would the history of Anglo-Saxon christology since Irving have been so depressing if their unique insights had been appropriated more carefully? If they had, might we not sooner have obtained release from the constraints of the two dogmas from which this chapter took its original orientation?

[23] John Owen, *A Discourse Concerning the Holy Spirit* (London, 1674), *Works*, volume 3 (Edinburgh: T. & T. Clark, 1862), pp. 160f.: 'The only singular and immediate *act* of the person of the Son on the human nature was the *assumption* of it into subsistence with himself.' 'The Holy Ghost ... is the *immediate, peculiar, efficient cause* of all external divine operations ...' See Alan Spence, 'Inspiration and Incarnation: John Owen and the Coherence of Christology', *King's Theological Review* 12 (1989), 52–5.

[24] See Alister McGrath, *Justitia Dei* (Cambridge: Cambridge University Press, 1986), volume 2, pp. 125ff., for Newman's unscholarly misrepresentation of Luther. 'It seems to us that Newman did not read Luther at first hand. If this conclusion can be shown to be false, then, reluctantly, we are forced to draw the more serious conclusion that Newman deliberately misrepresents Luther' (p. 127).

CHAPTER 10

THE ATONEMENT

R. W. Dale on the centrality of the cross[1]

I *Two signs of the times*

However perilous it is to attempt to read the signs of the times, those who fail to read them are threatened with dire penalty; and so, by way of introduction, here are two observations, no doubt rather banal, about the way things seem to be going in our world. The first is that after decades of relentless secularism, at least in what can be called the official ideology of our era, there are signs, even in pragmatic England, of a dissatisfaction with things, if not of anything so definite as a spiritual hunger. Yet there is little sign that those supposedly responsible for these matters are prepared for the situation. To many, and certainly to intellectuals who are generally sympathetic to Christianity, what they are offered seems to be more like a stone than bread, if not a form of betrayal. For the most part, official representatives of Christianity are greeted with contempt rather than welcome when they try to articulate some vision for our times. Although much of the blame can be attributed to the incapacity of the press to take seriously anything less than the sensational, I do not think that this is by any means the whole story.

The feeling was summed up by the journalist who asked some years ago why bishops talked of politics when it was their calling to speak of redemption. Those who know anything of R. W. Dale will realise that this is a false dichotomy. The writer of a major,

---

[1] Delivered as the Dale Lecture, Mansfield College, Oxford, 23 February 1995, under the title, 'The Cross and the City. R. W. Dale and the Doctrine of the Atonement'.

perhaps great, book on the atonement,[2] he also left his mark on the civic life of the great city of Birmingham: at once the cross and the city were encompassed in his concerns. The book was designed, as we shall see, to defend the centrality of the historic cross in face of criticisms of Christian theology directed mostly from those who were within, or more or less within, the fold.[3] When contemporary apologists[4] essay a defence of the faith in today's rather different conditions, the cross figures somewhat less prominently. That, I think, and not the inherent offensiveness of the cross, is the chief source of a widespread suspicion that politics has in many cases taken the place of redemption. May we not, with Dale, have both the cross and the city? That is a topic to which I shall return at the very end of the chapter.

The second feature of our time is perhaps less immediately exciting, but, in view of developments in some of the lands recently emerging from official atheism, may have long-term influence on the way we understand and articulate the faith. It concerns our relations with Eastern Orthodoxy. For the last millennium at least there has been a major rift between the Churches of East and West. The Churches of the East take their theology uncompromisingly from the Eastern Fathers, especially perhaps Athanasius, the Cappadocians and Maximus the Confessor. The doctrinal centre of the disagreement between the divided confessions lies in the Western addition to the creed, under the influence of Augustinian theology, of the *filioque* clause. I do not plan to review that complicated, though important, topic here.

But there is another major difference between the traditions, and it is over the doctrine of salvation. The Western tradition, formed as it was in part by lawyers such as Tertullian, tends to centre on images of legality – of sin as breach of divine law – and

---

[2] R. W. Dale, *The Atonement* (22nd edition, London: Congregational Union of England and Wales, 1902). References to this work will be in parentheses in the text.

[3] Depending on where the unitarians with whom he engaged are to be placed. 'It is true ... that in writing the Lectures, the men who were most distinctly and vividly present to my mind were those ... whose faith in the Atonement has given way under the solvent of what is described as "liberal" thought. And yet I hoped that I might be able to reach some who are hostile to Evangelicalism ...' (p. xv).

[4] And perhaps it is apology that is the problem.

thus correlatively on salvation in terms of penance, forgiveness and the rest. Now, clearly law is part of the overall scheme, in so far as sin must in one of its aspects be understood as a breach of divine law which brings upon the breaker the associated consequences. It would also be false to suggest that these aspects have no place at all in Eastern thought. Athanasius, certainly in his early days, understands sin in part as breach of the divine law.[5] But – to simplify somewhat – salvation for the East is centred not so much on the cross understood as in some way a satisfaction of the demands of the law as on the whole life, death and resurrection of the Son of God. This in turn is conceived less as an execution, or whatever, than as the Son's self-offering to God the Father, a sacrifice whose outworking is the divinisation of the believer. That is a major difference. Western theology, rightly in my view, has continued to be suspicious about divinisation; yet, at the same time, it has found it difficult to escape from an over-dependence on legal categories without depriving the cross of its centrality. I shall hope to show in this chapter that Dale has things to say that will enable some conversation to take place between the two traditions, and indeed, some reconciliation of the two focuses of the teaching.

II *Dale in his context*

What is the heart of the problem? Christianity in all its forms, with the possible exceptions of the most 'radical' and 'atheist', teaches that, in some way or other, the human race has fallen into a condition from which only God can save it; and that his action centres in some way or other on what is sometimes called the Christ event: those actions and passions which constitute the career of Jesus of Nazareth. Once that is said, however, agreement ends. There is disagreement about the nature of the fallenness and its symptoms; about the relation of salvation to human createdness and destiny; and in particular about the way in which we should describe, and the kind of significance we should attribute to, different aspects of the career of Jesus. Do we focus on his life and example, his incarnation, his death, his resurrection and ascension, or some combination of them all?

---

[5] Athanasius, *Inc.* 5f. Death gains a legal hold on the human race.

The struggle in which R. W. Dale was engaged was a characteristically modern one. Against the modernist tradition which sought on various grounds to divert attention from the death of Jesus as an atoning act, and stress instead the effect of his loving example on the believer – in what is called a subjective or exemplarist theory of the atonement – Dale wished to stress the centrality of the death of Christ, as, indeed, a function of the love of God, but also as implying some notion of judgement.

That struggle continues in the life of modern Christianity, and it could be that in certain respects it is unending and insoluble, at least in the respect that such deeply different presuppositions operate on the two sides of the divide that even conversation is difficult. But what accounts for so deep a gulf between different groups of those professing the same faith? One stratagem here is to blame everything on the acids of modernity, or more specifically on the Enlightenment, which have supposedly eaten away at the fabric of traditional belief. There is something in that; but only something. Two of the Enlightenment charges against traditional Western Christianity require an answer. The first centres, predictably, on the way in which the language of law had come to predominate in Western accounts of the atonement. Suggestions that Jesus had been burdened with a penalty considered *quantitatively* raised a number of questions about both the justice of God and the possibility of the transferability of penalty. Can another go to prison for my offence, and – and this is the point – if he does, what difference has it made to me? Am I *saved* in any sense that has direct bearing on who and what I am?

The charge is that the atonement as orthodox Western Christianity taught it is more to do with remission of penalty than with new life in Jesus Christ, and that brings us to the second criticism of the traditional approach. It is alleged to bear an air of externality, as if something – a 'transaction', reminding us of Irving's jibe about 'stock-exchange divinity' – is taking place outside the moral agent and above his head. Let me put it another way. Salvation is to do with relationships: with God, other people and the world.[6] Its necessity arises from the

---

[6] I would not necessarily want to deny that in certain respects it has to do with our relation to ourselves also, but that is an aspect which has been far too prominent – a fire that is hot enough already, to use a well-known metaphor.

fact that in various ways our relations with our creator, our world and one another have gone awry. One of the symptoms of the disrupted relation is, as we have seen, breach of divine law, and there should therefore be ways of understanding the legal aspects of atonement theory which save it from many of the objections of its critics. In so far as law has to do with the relationships of creator and creature, some sense can be made of those relationships being restored through Christ's bearing the consequences of our offence. But so long as that law and its penalties are considered in any way merely objectively and mathematically – largely externally – the problems remain. I may be relieved that someone else has paid my fine, but the action may well affect not a whit my relations with my neighbour or the kind of person that I am. That is to say, we cannot evade the ontological dimensions of the atonement. What has it to do with human being as well as human action – or rather with human being as the source of forms of righteous action? Our question remains: is there a less flawed way of expressing the matter?

Before I move to a review of Dale's contribution to the answering of these two crucial objections, let me say something about his approach to the atonement in general. Dale is interesting on the history of the atonement because his systematic antennae are sensitive; he knows what the problems are. He is also impressive in the strength of his grasp of the history of doctrine and his hold on the tradition. While by no means seeing the history as merely a struggle between heroes and villains, he points unerringly to the roots of later problems, caustically rejecting that tendency which reigned from Origen at least to Bernard of Clairvaux and held that in some sense the human race was held justly under the power of the devil (pp. 274–7). Yet at the same time he rightly attributes the hold this position had not to stupidity, as the modern is so often tempted to do, but to a tenacious concern that the objectivity of the atoning act be maintained (pp. 277f.). It is his firm hold on the need for objective atonement of some kind that enables Dale to understand what happened in the Middle Ages and beyond. This was in essence a shift away from a view that the cross freed the sinner from the clutches of the devil to one much more centred on metaphors of legality.[7] Crucial to the development was the achievement of Anselm of Canterbury, whose theology of satisfaction was to be the determining influence behind much of the theology of atonement of the Reformers and their orthodox successors. Here Dale is again interesting, because he acknowledges, as we shall see, the value of the development, and for similar reasons acknowledges its proper hold on the objectivity of atonement. But he is also critical of many of the emphases. We shall learn the reasons for his judgements when we have first traced his response to liberal criticisms of the orthodox belief.

III   *Dale's theology of the cross*

At the outset, Dale is uncompromising in demonstrating at length and in detail the centrality of the cross for the biblical writers, and, indeed, for the historical Jesus. There is, he argues, no biblical basis for any theology which does not see the cross as definitive for relations between God and the human race. An analysis of the New Testament teaching takes up a large part of the work, and is not without interest. It is also, I believe, for the most part right, even though modern historical scholarship might have some queries about how much can be so confidently traced back to the teaching of Jesus himself. But we can, I hope, agree with Dale that:

> It seems very difficult to attribute any religious authority to the New Testament writers and yet to refuse to accept a theory of the Atonement. The rudiments of a theory are contained in all the terms by which they describe the nature and purpose of the death of Christ. 'Christ died for the ungodly;' He 'suffered, ... the Just for the unjust;' these words must either remain non-significant for us, or else we must make our choice between interpreting them as meaning that the Death of Christ had a vicarious, or perhaps a representative, character, or as meaning nothing more than

---

[7] There was the attempt of Abelard to do something very different, but that has to await a later era for real influence.

that in some general way his death was intended for our advantage ... (p. 12).

In this respect, and rightly, Dale refuses to give an inch to the challenges of modernism. But in other respects he concedes that there is a case to answer. The key is to be found in the way he handles the central question of the concept of law, where he realises that there is law and there is law, and the use of one form of language is not necessarily identical with that of the other. There is, first, law that is understood as requiring quantitative, mathematically calculated punishment for every infringement. According to this, the concept of law requires some form of equivalent penalty, visited upon either the culprit or some other. Dale will have nothing to do with this, because it infringes what he takes to be the central message of the Bible, that the cross is primarily a function of and inseparable from the love of God. He strains every intellectual effort to make clear the distinction between a God of transforming love who yet takes seriously human offence against the right order of things and a God who must keep the legal or moral accounts balanced.

> There are very many persons who believe that the idea of an objective Atonement was invented in order to satisfy the exigencies of rigid theories concerning the Divine justice ... Theology ... was merciless in its judgment of human nature, exaggerated the evil of sin ... It ascribed to God its own gloomy and uncompassionate spirit, and conceived of Him as filled with fierce anger against the human race. Then it became necessary to discover some means of allaying His wrath, and therefore the Death of Christ was represented as the ground on which the sins of the world are forgiven (pp. 267f.).

Dale traces the history of theology in order to show how these misunderstandings came to be so prevalent. Although some tried to purge Anselm's theory of satisfaction of its offensive character, there are many sorry episodes in both Catholic and Protestant theological history, among them Turretin's conception of the retributive justice of God (pp. 291f.) and the 'exaggerated and degraded form' which Reformation teaching received in Grotius (p. 294).[8] Dale recognises that the very persistence of such themes shows that there is something positive to be said for them. '*The history of the doctrine is a proof that the idea of an objective Atonement was not invented by theologians*' (p. 299, Dale's italics). But as some of the pejorative language makes clear, he is by no means content with a major deficiency to be found in many of the theologies he reviews. What is wrong? Two points recur from time to time in Dale's argument. The first is a repetition of what he takes to be a commonplace, that atonement without remaking the sinner in the image of Christ is inadequate. This is an implicit reference to the problem of an atonement externally conceived. We shall see later how he deals with what I have called the problem of externality. But the second is more important for this stage of the argument: that all this must be understood primarily as a function of the love of God rather than of his justice punitively conceived. According to Dale, the root of all the inadequacies to be found in the history of the doctrine is indicated at the beginning of the lecture in which they are considered. Speaking of the criticisms often made of theologians, he says that 'It is imagined that in their speculations on the character of God, and on His relations to mankind, they forgot that He has revealed Himself as our Father, and that Love is the life and glory of all His moral perfections' (p. 268). Thus the heart of Dale's criticism of the objectionable concept of law is that although it may do justice to the centrality of the cross, it fails to understand it primarily as a function of the love of God.

Alongside all this, as we move to a more acceptable concept of law, we must set the argument of the ninth and penultimate lecture in which Dale is very much alive to the penal dimensions of the doctrine of the atonement, dimensions which have their place because of the connection between breaches of the

[8] Dale's summary of the history is to be found on p. 297. It appears that 'for nearly a thousand years many of the most eminent teachers of the Church were accustomed to represent the Death of Christ as a ransom by which we are delivered from captivity to the devil; that for nearly five centuries the most eminent teachers of the Church were accustomed to represent the Death of Christ as an act of homage to the personal greatness and majesty of God; that during the last three centuries the Protestant Churches have represented the Death of Christ as having a relation neither to the devil nor to the personal claims of God, but to the moral order of the universe'.

law and the moral necessity of punishment. Dale is aware of the
deficiencies of any merely utilitarian or reformatory conception
of punishment:

> If ... the justice of punishment consisted in its fitness to
> produce a favourable moral impression on the sinner, God
> would be free to inflict or to remit the penalties of the Law
> without regard to any other consideration than the moral
> disposition of the person by whom the precepts of the Law
> had been violated. The severity of punishment would have to
> be measured, not by the magnitude of the sin ... but by the
> difficulty of inducing the sinner to amend (pp. 373f.).

The only just reason for punishment is desert (p. 378). Like
Anselm, Dale holds that a God who simply remitted penalties
without other consideration would not be God. To say in effect
that evil is not evil is in contradiction of what he calls the law of
righteousness, the order of things set for human life within the
created order.

Dale's defence of the appropriateness of the penal dimension of the atonement against unitarian critics of the doctrine
regains some of the ground. He also shows that their unitarian
theology is their weakness, because it prevents them from
understanding the atonement fairly. If Jesus is merely a man,
then all he can in this context be conceived to be suffering is an
unjust punishment. But that is not what the doctrine teaches.
Against those who accuse orthodox Christianity of teaching
that Jesus is punished by God *as a man*, Dale stresses that the
divinity of Christ is the heart of the matter. 'It was the death of
the Son of God, of God manifest in the flesh'; and, anticipating
Moltmann's use of the text, but in a rather different way,
'Immediately before His Death He was forsaken of God' (p.
360). What is the connection between the death of the Son of
God, abandoned by God the Father, and the remission of sins?
Dale makes a point which is not often made, referring to those
biblical passages which attribute to Christ the functions of the
divine judge. '*The penalties of sin are to be inflicted by Christ*' (p.
362, Dale's italics). The one who dies is the one who exercises
the divine function of judgement. Thus in so far as there is
substitution, it is at least in part by virtue of Christ's divinity that
we must understand it to take place. We might say that this is a

matter of such nice judgement that it amounts to no difference
at all. But it does, as is made clear by Dale's historical assessment of his own Western tradition and his perceptive allusions
to the early theologians of the East.

So far as the West is concerned, this Protestant theologian is
pleased, and right, to prefer a mediaeval Catholic conception
of the atonement to that of Luther. The much-maligned
Anselm of Canterbury, so often thought to be among the
begetters of the punitive conception of atonement, is here
shown to belong more among the heroes than the villains.
(This in itself shows that we must beware of regarding the
Western tradition as monochrome or uncritical of its own
inheritance.) Dale's contrast between the mediaeval and the
Reformer may be questioned, but it redounds remarkably to
the credit of the former.

> Luther represented the Death of Christ as the endurance of
> the suffering due to the sins of our race. On Anselm's theory,
> Christ has secured our salvation because in His Death He
> clothed Himself with the glory of a unique righteousness, for
> which God rewards Him. On Luther's theory, Christ has
> secured our salvation because in His Death He clothed
> Himself with the sins of the human race, so that God
> inflicted on Him the sufferings which the sins of the race had
> deserved (p. 290).

Notice the contrast between the negative – our sins being
inflicted on Christ – and the positive – his 'being clothed with
the glory of a unique righteousness'. That is surely to take up
the theology of the Letter to the Hebrews, of the one who
'through the eternal Spirit offered himself without blemish
before God ...' (9.14). Except, as we shall see, it is only to take
up part of Hebrews' theology.

There seems to be little doubt that it is the reading of the
Eastern Fathers that has helped Dale, as it has helped other
Congregationalist and Reformed theologians from Calvin
onwards, to exercise this independence of judgement. In
particular, he recognises the suggestions of a more adequate
conception in such theologians as Gregory of Nazianzus. In the
passage Dale cites at length, Gregory expresses his outrage at all
theories that in some way or other conceive the blood of Christ

as in some way a quantity – a ransom paid to either God or the devil. The passage concludes: 'Is it not clear that the Father received the sacrifice, not because He Himself demanded or needed it, but for the sake of the Divine government of the universe (δί οἰκονομίαν), and because man must be sanctified through the incarnation of the Son of God?' (pp. 273f.).[9]

Dale's point is this. It is a function of the love of God to remove those factors affecting human life which render obedience to divine law impossible. This involves bearing the consequences of those breaches of obedience which have led to human incapacity to be truly human apart from the grace of redemption. What is thus removed is not a penalty conceived as a quantity, but that which blocks the human relation to God. On this understanding, the law is wholly salutary. It is the creator's dispensation for the good ordering of life on earth. The moral law, we might say, is there for human benefit, including, indeed, freedom. But the latter consideration means that any conception of atonement or redemption must take seriously human responsibility for the breach of relations, and that entails the moral necessity of *some* conception of judgement vicariously borne.

It is thus that Dale engages with the accusations that atonement is immoral. His solution, as we have seen, is *christological*. The one who dies under divine judgement is himself the one who exercises it. It is thus the divine judge who undergoes judgement, not a human substitute who bears a penalty equivalent to that which others have merited. To that extent, Dale's conception is an anticipation of Barth's great treatise, 'The Judge Judged in our place'.[10] It shares similar weaknesses, and to those we shall come. But first we must ask whether in so conceiving the atonement Dale has also solved the problem of the externality of the atoning history to the atoned. Has he shown that the consequence of the death of Christ is new life for the atoned? When he turns to answer the charge – implic-

---

[9] It is at this place that we can introduce a far more positive contribution of Luther to the tradition. In his view of the righteousness of God as that according to which he justifies rather than punishes the godless, Luther himself reached the heart of the point. God's justice is that which brings about salvation *by a means other than* punishing offence. There is in Luther's theology a real tension between his theologies of justification and of the atonement.

[10] Karl Barth, *Church Dogmatics* 4/1, §59.2, pp. 211–83.

itly, for he does not so express the problem himself – we find further influence of the patristic tradition on the nineteenth-century Congregationalist. That is scarcely surprising. Once a theologian adopts what can be called a transformational rather than juridical or transactional theory of the atonement, some kind of positive relation to the patristic doctrine is only to be expected. In order to make clear, however, the direction of his answer, I want to turn aside to one of the representatives of that tradition to show something both of the patristic doctrine of salvation and of what, I shall suggest, also underlies Dale's less than satisfactory resolution: the reason why, as I hinted before, he won back only some of the ground occupied by his modernist opponents.

IV *Sacrifice and divinisation*

If we examine Athanasius' conception of the atonement, we shall be able to understand something of the fount from which Dale has drunk. In the first place, Athanasius remains relatively untouched by the Western preoccupation with law. His main interest, especially in the later writings such as the *Discourses Against the Arians*, lies in the self-offering of Christ which achieves a cleansing of human sin. The Word of God takes flesh not to save us from the penalties of the law but to 'offer Himself to the Father, and cleanse us from all sins in His own blood, and [to] rise from the dead'.[11] Notice the stress on self-offering, something we have already noticed in Anselm, who, in this respect as in some others, betrays influence by the Eastern Father.[12] Moreover, the final clause, referring as it does to the resurrection, suggests an emphasis on the whole life of Jesus[13] not so stressed in Dale, who, as we have seen, was, rightly and necessarily, defending against modernist attacks the centrality of the once-for-all significance of the death of Christ. It is here that we might take further lessons from the Eastern tradition.

[11] *Ar.* 2.7. *Four Discourses against the Arians*, translated by Henry Wace and Philip Schaff (Oxford: Parker & Company, 1892), p. 352.
[12] *Cur Deus Homo*, I.4, gives a similar reason for the incarnation: God's unwillingness to allow his creative work to come to nothing.
[13] See, for example, *Ar.* 1.46, on Christ's anointing with the Spirit so that we might be anointed also.

There has been much Western criticism of what is sometimes called the 'physical' view of salvation in the Eastern Fathers, and, indeed, there is sometimes a suggestion in Athanasius that the problem with human life is not its fallenness so much as its *alterability*.[14] But the advantage of the Athanasian approach is this. Although he is quite clear that breach of the law is a factor in human fallenness, the important feature, certainly in his early *On the Incarnation,* is the ontological change brought about by Adam's sin. That is to say, what matters primarily is not that we break the laws of God, but that in some way our humanity is diminished by our rejection of God's grace – diminished, that is, irreversibly, apart from Christ. And the atonement reverses the movement to dissolution by relating the atoned back to God, the source of life. It is the restoration of relations that is at the heart of Dale's conception also. He notes, citing his words from a secondary authority, that although 'Athanasius speaks of Christ as *paying the debt in our stead* which we had incurred by sin',[15] 'Athanasius, however, had far larger and deeper conception of the nature of Christ's redemptive work than this metaphor would suggest' (p. 278, and n. 1).

There is another place where the two are interestingly alike, though this time, in my view, wrong. It is here that we come to the second of the two concerns outlined at the beginning of the chapter, the relation between the Eastern and Western church traditions. The outcome of the atonement was, for Athanasius, and has been for his tradition since, divinisation.[16] The problem with this is: too soon, and, perhaps also, too far. There need be no objection to the claim that the end of salvation is to enable us in some way or other to share the life of God, or indeed in some measure to anticipate this in the present. But many forms of the doctrine of divinisation overstep the limits of the distinction between the biblical conception of communion and Platonic participation in deity. But before we speak of that there is something else to be said, and here there is little doubt that Athana-

[14] In contrast with Adam, 'the Lord being unalterable and unchangeable, the Serpent might become powerless in his assaults ...' *Ar.* 1.51 (Wace and Schaff, p. 336).

[15] See *Inc.* 20.

[16] *Ar.* 2.59: '"The Word became flesh," that He might make man capable of Godhead' (p. 380).

sius has lost something that is to be found in his great predecessor and influence, Irenaeus.[17] What is the end in view,
divinisation or the perfection of our created humanity? Irenaeus' attacks on the Gnostic denial of the value of life in the
flesh and his associated eschatology of human maturity suggest
that the concept of deification may without it represent too
great a concession to Gnosticism, or dualism if we wish to be
more polite.[18] If we move too rapidly to speak of a directedness
to immortality, we lose something of what the atonement has of
relevance to us under the conditions of continuing human life.

It is the question of humanity that needs to be asked more
insistently; the humanity both of Jesus and of ourselves. Why do
I think that Athanasius is wrong? The clue is to be found not in
exchanging arguments about the precise meaning of the concept of divinisation, but in examining what this theologian
makes of the humanity of Christ. Divinisation, it can be argued,
is used of Jesus in such a way that the authenticity of his
humanity is endangered. What does Paul mean, asks Athanasius, when he speaks in his letter to Philippi of the exaltation of
Jesus? The answer is that it consists in the divinisation of his
human nature.[19] Now it seems to me that this is just wrong, and
that the exaltation means in biblical terms the resurrection and
ascension of Jesus Christ to a position of mediation and
authority *in his continuing humanity*. (This is the place where we
return to the Letter to the Hebrews, whose theology of the self-
offering of Christ depends upon a strong emphasis on the
eternal significance of the *human* saviour.)

---

[17] I owe to Douglas Farrow the point that although the Eastern doctrine of
deification is often thought to be implicit in Irenaeus, there are reasons for
doubt. 'Irenaeus was interpreted as teaching what quickly became the central
motif of eastern theology: "God became man that man might become God."
Behind that dictum which does *not* properly represent his view of things,
stands the opposition between Creator and creature that he was fighting in the
gnostics – an opposition that can only be resolved by collapsing the space
between the two' ('St Irenaeus of Lyons. The Church and the World', *Pro
Ecclesia* 4 (1995), 333–55 (341)).

[18] There are other grounds for asking whether Athanasius may have lapsed
into a dualism not present, at least to the same degree, in Irenaeus. Rebecca
Lyman, *Christology and Cosmology. Models of Divine Activity in Origen, Eusebius and
Athanasius* (Oxford: Clarendon Press, 1993), pp. 150–9, suggests that contemporary asceticism may have led Athanasius into a rather world-denying
anthropology.

[19] *Ar.* 1.45.

Why is this important? I shall come to this in the final section of the chapter, but first a hint. Our conception of the end – in both senses – of human life will bear on our conception of life in the earthly city. What does the death of Christ mean for the earthly city, for our continuing to live in the flesh? It can be said that both of our traditions are weak in articulating this, as the history of the relations of Church and State in both Rome and Byzantium witnesses only too well. Something has gone amiss, so that the Church whose calling is in some way to attract the hostility of the world through its very powerlessness has chosen to do so by its wielding of the sword. The cross has led too rapidly to the other world, in an improperly realised eschatology, and not by way of the crucified humanity of Jesus. Politically, the Church has for the most part evaded the road to glory taken by Jesus himself.

Here there is something to be said for the law. We may not like the rather quantitative Western conception of legality, but do need to take account of law as God's dispensation for the living of life in the world. We should be glad of this. Recent history is making it only too clear that both positivist conceptions of law and those attributing its origin to immanent processes, as in Marxism, for example, are recipes only for a Hobbesian war of each against all. Without a transcendent framework for social order, we are lost; that may be a slur on human autonomy, but it is a true characterisation of human finitude and fallenness. To that negative point can be added a more positive, and somewhat more gospel-oriented, view, that one of the outcomes, according to the Reformers, of embracing the gospel is that we are able to love God's law: gladly to affirm it as a framework for our living. The concept of divinisation can call attention so much to the elevation of our bodies to some higher realm that it neglects their being reshaped in the image of God made man in Christ. That is to say, like a merely transactional or penal doctrine of the atonement, it too can neglect the relational core of the conception: that it is a matter of so reordering the relation of God and the fallen creation that new forms of life and behaviour are enabled to take shape. The renewed relation to God must be understood in part in terms of a correlative worldly orientation, or something is lost. And so we return to Dale.

The final lecture of *The Atonement* is in some ways the least satisfactory one of the book. Concerned with 'the relation of the Lord Jesus Christ to the human race', it rightly attempts to complete what the book is designed to develop: a theology of the atonement which conceives it in transformational rather than legalistic terms. If I am right in my criticism of Athanasius, the key to the matter is that of humanity, and in particular the relation between the human life – the recapitulation – of Jesus Christ and human life in the present. But Dale looks only or primarily to the divinity of Christ to express the relation between him and the human race. Like many nineteenth-century theologians, Dale sees the attraction of pantheism, though it is a pantheism of Christ the creator. 'We truly live only as we live in Christ. Our highest life is life derived from Him' (p. 419). His expression of it, which includes an appeal to the only New Testament text making explicit reference to what came to be called divinisation,[20] shows his awareness of the perils of pantheism. But he is insistent that this universal relation to Christ is not at the expense of human freedom:

> Every form of Christian perfection ... is a 'fruit of the Spirit,' an expression in our personal life of the perfection of the life of Christ. In the spiritual, as in the material sphere, man is a free personality surrounded by a vast and immeasurable Power which is not his own, but through which his history may become bright with the glory of the noblest achievements ...
>
> Scientific men, having their imagination filled with the vastness of that universal and indestructible energy ... have gone on to affirm that the human will is but one of its Protean manifestations. Devout mystics, overpowered with awe and wonder by the energy of the life of God, in which, and in which alone, they were conscious that they were living, have gone on to affirm that the will of God is the only active force in the universe ... In ancient and in modern times materialism has suppressed the personality and the will of man in the presence of the aweful forces of the physical universe. In ancient and in modern times mysticism has

---

[20] 'In Christ, we are "made partakers of the divine nature" (2 Pet. 1.4)' (Dale, p. 417).

suppressed the personality and the will of man in the presence of the living God. The Christian philosophy of human nature might perhaps be roughly defined as a form of Pantheism in which the moral freedom of man and the moral freedom of God are resolutely and consistently vindicated (pp. 417f.).

Dale has, with his sure systematic grasp, perceived the problem. There is a community of oppression between scientistic materialism and religious mysticism. If the atonement is to be truly atonement, the reconciliation of creator and creature, it cannot be at the expense of the reality of either: creator must remain creator, and therefore the one whose will must be done, and the creature creature, one who can only be truly a creature in dependence on divine grace. Unfortunately, he lacks the equipment to ensure that it will remain grace and not an overwhelming of the human with the divine, and that is precisely the problem with doctrines of divinisation. At stake is genuine humanity, so that more attention is needed to the place of the humanity of Christ, as the one who intercedes at the right hand of the Father, and of the Holy Spirit who realises that intercession by enabling humanity to be truly itself.[21]

V *Return to the city*

And so we return to where we began. The link between the cross and the city is to be found in the humanity of Jesus. It is as man that Jesus engages with the powers of darkness and wickedness in high places. It is his human body that is, to use Irving's words, 'the fit field of contention' between God and evil.[22] But the victory is inseparable from the suffering of the cross. It is here that Dale is strongest, and here, because they suspect that we evade that challenge, that I think some mod-

---

[21] This is the weakness also of Barth's treatment of this topic in the fourth volume of the *Church Dogmatics*. There is a sense in which his stress on the self-humiliation of *God* in the incarnation militates against an adequate stress on the incarnation and cross as a human act.

[22] Edward Irving, *The Collected Writings of Edward Irving in Five Volumes*, edited by G. Carlyle (London: Alexander Strachan, 1865), volume 5, p. 161: '... because it was the same on which Satan had triumphed since the fall. Here, then, in the flesh of Christ is the great controversy waged.'

erns are rightly contemptuous of the modern politicising of Christianity. The jibe of 'physician, heal thyself' is difficult to answer. Unless there is an authentic Christian polity, centred on and derived from the life, death and resurrection of the 'proper man', all talk of liberation runs the danger of being but empty rhetoric. It is only when the cross calls us back to our own need for the grace of justification and sanctification – and from all forms of the Pelagianism that is so rife in modern Christian thinking about both of the cities – that the Church is at all likely to have anything to say to and do for the secular city.

CHAPTER 11

THE CHURCH

John Owen and John Zizioulas on the Church[1]

I *The Spirit and the Church*

It would be possible, as an exercise in cynicism, to write a history of the Church as the story of the misappropriation of the doctrine of the Holy Spirit. Crudely expressed, it would go like this. The Holy Spirit, we are promised, will live within the Church, informing and inspiring her worship, faith and life. What is a promise, however, has been turned into a claimed possession, so that, fallen creatures as we are, we have confused what we, the Church, have done with the action of the Spirit.[2] Thus it is that those whose ecclesiology is of a clericalist hue will sometimes tend to identify the Church with what the clergy – or perhaps the bishops – say and do. To this side of things belong the theologies which suppose the almost automatic disposal of the gifts of the Spirit by an institution. If, on the other hand, our theology is more congregationalist in emphasis, as mine is, the danger is that we shall ascribe like authority to the decisions of church meetings, or worse, as has too often happened, to the private judgement of individuals. In both cases, the tendency is the same: to *identify* the work of the Spirit with churchly or individual Christian judgement.

The roots of the problem lie far back in the history of the

[1] 'The Transcendent Lord. The Spirit and the Church in Calvinist and Cappadocian. The 1988 Congregational Lecture' (London: Congregational Memorial Hall Trust, 1988). The opening section has been revised to lessen the repetition of themes from other chapters.

[2] James Whyte, 'The Problem of Authority', *King's Theological Review* 7 (1984), 37–43, is a good treatment of the way appeal to the Spirit is used to justify in a circular manner the correctness of decisions made by ecclesiastical authorities in the past.

Church, and it can be argued that differences in this area of
doctrine are crucial for, if not actually determinative of, the
present ecumenical disorder. The schism between East and
West, which culminated in the eleventh century, centres on a
divergence in the theology of the Spirit. Does the Spirit
proceed from the Father or from the Father and the Son?
Behind that apparently technical dispute there lies a history of
progressive divergence between two Christian communities
who are separated at least in part because they understand
differently the person and work of the Spirit, and consequently
the nature of the Church. The schism between East and West
was succeeded, some few centuries later, by the Reformation, a
split within the fabric of Western Christendom itself; and this
divergence, too, centred on differences about the way the Spirit
is conceived to work towards and in the Church. I believe that
the Reformation and the subsequent fragmentation of Western
Christendom is the result not of Protestant intransigence
and indiscipline, but of a weakness inherent in the Western
tradition.

Such a diagnosis is supported by the fact that a further compli-
cation has been introduced by those who would develop radically themes that they believed to have been begun, but not
developed, by the Reformation. Since the Enlightenment, there
has developed a view of things, a view now largely dominant in
Western culture, which teaches that the human mind is the true
source of meaning and authority. Such doctrine can be interpreted as deriving from a secularisation of the tendency of which
I spoke at the beginning of the chapter. The Church has often
been tempted, I suggested, to identify her activity with the work
of the Spirit. That doctrine has now been secularised and, so to
speak, democratised. 'Where the Spirit of the Lord is, there is
liberty' (2 Cor. 3.17); now, it is sometimes suggested, where the
spirit of autonomous humanity is, there is not only liberty but
the true action of God. The action of autonomous humanity is
the action of the only divine spirit we know. That spirit of human
self-aggrandisement has at times infected Churches in the
Reformed and Free Church traditions. At their best, they have
been fine examples of witness to the freedom which is the gift of
the Spirit under the gospel; at their worst, they have been lamen-
table: exalting individual human judgement over the godly dis-

cipline, and so succumbing, in their own way, to the spirit of Enlightenment modernity.

One does not have to look further than the repeated outbreaks of pentecostal enthusiasm in the history of Western Christianity to realise that there is something deeply amiss with the way in which the doctrine of the third person of the Trinity has been understood, taught and lived. The problem derives, I believe, from the failure to give to the Holy Spirit the kind of personal identity or particularity that is required if we are to speak of him and identify his action in the world. If we do not find adequate means of identification, the danger remains that we shall identify his work apart from the work of the Father and the Son, and in terms of what we happen to find attractive or appealing at the present time. We have seen in chapter 7 some of the historical causes of the problem as they were characterised by Robert Jenson, and an argument that from there many contemporary problems take their origin.[3] Central is the contention that many of the characteristic weaknesses of the Western tradition derive from a failure to maintain the personal transcendence of the Holy Spirit. The reason is that if we cannot conceive the Spirit as the free Lord, then we may succumb to the temptation of identifying him with some immanent causal force: with our ecclesiastical or political institutions, or with some private experiences and beliefs. It may profit us here to listen to the way in which one Orthodox theologian understands the doctrine of the *filioque* to distort the institutional shape of the Church. It is something of a parody, but one with elements of truth. The doctrine, he says, is:

> one reason why in the Roman Catholic Church there has been such infrequent mention of the presence and activity of the Spirit. Christ the Word, transmitting his power to Peter and his successors ... and withdrawing at the Ascension to some remote and transcendent place, keeps the Spirit also with him. The character of a juridical society has been imprinted upon the Church, a society conducted rationally and in absolutist fashion by the Pope while neglecting both the active permanent presence of the Spirit within her and within all the faithful, and also the presence of Christ bound

[3] Above, pp. 109ff.

indissolubly to the presence of the Spirit. The Pope, the bishops, the priests occupy the place of the absent Christ who is not present through the Spirit in the hearts of the faithful ... ; the faithful are not the images, the visible signs of the invisible sacramental and pneumatic presence of Christ ...

Staniloae, however, is nothing if not even-handed, and Protestant sins are, again with much truth, shown to be the other side of the same coin:

Protestantism has also experienced this same weakness, for, having rejected the direction of a vicarial hierarchy it has lost even that unity which was maintained by largely human means. From the *filioque* Protestantism has at times deduced a separation of the Spirit from Christ and, consequently, having preserved the idea of the transcendence of Christ, it has substituted the presence of the Spirit for the presence of Christ ...[4]

Whatever we make of that, it is difficult to deny that there have been distortions of dogma which had a deleterious impact on the way Churches have understood and organised themselves.

In the body of the chapter I hope, beginning with one great Congregationalist theologian and in conversation with those Greeks who are so important as authorities for Orthodox ecclesiology, to say something about how we may conceive the action of the Spirit in one central area of his work; that is, in relation to the Church. We cannot order his movement, but we can seek to discern his person and work, and so come perhaps to a clearer realisation of where the heart of the matter is to be found. In the next section, as the topic is developed, I hope to hold two themes in constant interaction: the freedom, transcendence and particularity of the Holy Spirit; and the nature of the Church as community; for it is there that we must seek an identification of the Spirit's particular work.[5]

---

[4] Dumitru Staniloae, *Theology and the Church*, translated by Robert Barringer (New York: St. Vladimir's Seminary Press, 1980), pp. 107–8.

[5] It is much to be regretted that the interpretation of the account of the day of Pentecost in Acts 2 has been so dominated by the wind, the fire and the apparently ecstatic behaviour of the apostles. The Lord is not in the wind and fire (1 Kings 19!) but in the creation of community, and that is the real point of the symbolism.

II *John Owen: the transcendence of the Spirit*

One of the motive forces behind the Reformation was a concern to establish the Church as a communion of saints in face of its apparent decline into an establishment of specialists in religion dispensing grace to a passive laity. Luther's doctrine of the priesthood of all believers must be understood in that sense, whatever distortions it has since come to suffer. In more recent times, it has been argued, particularly on the Continent, that the continuation of state Churches after the Reformation, and their employment of process of law in maintaining themselves, effectively prevented the fulfilment of Luther's theological programme; for the realisation of the nature of Church as community is precluded if it continues to be an externally and legally organised institution.[6] It is, however, to English Congregationalism that we owe some of the first attempts to come to terms with the problem; and to John Owen in particular two major contributions.

The first is to be found in his treatment of the doctrine of the Holy Spirit. What Owen offers is a doctrine of the transcendence of the Holy Spirit, whose importance is that it runs counter to theology's tendency to conceive the Spirit as an essentially immanent force: as something *within* an already given person or institution qualifying its existence. But if the Spirit is in some way identified with an aspect of our being, then the danger we have already met threatens. In the Old Testament the Spirit of the Lord is often characterised as a mysterious power, blowing unpredictably on parts of the created order. It is never identified with any part of the created order. New Testament developments of the particular personalness of the Spirit build upon this conviction of freedom and otherness. The wind blows where it wills (John 3); but the Spirit also searches the deep things of God (1 Cor. 2.10), and aids the believer who cannot find the words in which to pray (Rom. 8).

---

[6] See Martin Rade, 'Der Sprung Luther's Kirchenbegriff und die Entstehung der Landeskirche', *Ausgewählte Schriften*, edited by Christoph Schwoebel (Gütersloher Verlagshaus Gerd Mohn, 1988), volume 3, pp. 151–66 (p. 155): 'fehlt auch jeder Vertiefung der ausdrücklich aufgestellten oder vorausgesetzten Definition der Kirche … nämlich der *communio*, der "Sammlung" des "Volkes" '.

Many such texts suggest an 'over-againstness' of the Spirit which is rarely captured in theological treatments, but which must be held in view if we are to identify the distinct personal being and action of the Spirit.

It is clear from Owen's *A Discourse Concerning the Holy Spirit*[7] that he was in no danger of underestimating the transcendence of God the Holy Spirit, and so of mistakenly identifying any human work with that of the Spirit. He is insistent on the distinction between the Holy Spirit and all other spirits[8] and, correspondingly, on his distinct *hypostasis*:

> *for he to whom all personal properties, attributes, adjuncts, acts, and operations, are ascribed, and unto whom they do belong . . . is a person, and him we are taught to believe so to be.*[9]

Nor does Owen commit the complementary error of supposing that there are three gods, or of speaking as if such were the case, but yet he has a freedom sometimes lacking in Western theologians to attribute distinct modes of being and action to the Spirit. The Holy Spirit has for him a distinct identity whose delineation works to prevent any confusion with that which is not God – an identity perhaps most manifest in Owen's account of his relationship to Jesus the incarnate Son. In Owen's christology the Spirit, again in a way almost unique in Western theology, is held to perform a wide range of actions in relation to the human nature of Christ: he is the 'other' over against Jesus, freeing him to be the true Messiah of God. In his pneumatology proper, among the terms Owen uses to characterise the distinct being and action of the Spirit are, it must be noted, freedom and authority.[10] The exercise of these and other qualities, 'manifest him to be a *voluntary agent*, and that not only as to what he acts or doth in men, but also as to the manner of his coming forth from God . . .'.[11]

Owen's second great contribution is to be found in his ecclesiology. Again, I will outline only briefly what seem to be the main features of his work, concentrating on what he has to

[7] John Owen, *A Discourse Concerning the Holy Spirit. Works*, volume 3, edited by W. H. Goold (Edinburgh: T. & T. Clark, 1862, 1st edition 1674).

[8] Owen, *A Discourse*, p. 60.

[9] Owen, *A Discourse*, p. 69. The italics are Owen's.

[10] Owen, *A Discourse*, p. 107.

[11] Owen, *A Discourse*, p. 116.

offer in the way of a theology of the Church as community.[12] That for Owen the being of the Church consists in its character as community is clear from the use that he makes of Aristotelian terminology in marking out the nature of the Church. Speaking of what he calls the 'visible church-state', he distinguishes between:

> (1) The *material cause* of this church, or the matter whereof it is composed, which are *visible believers*. (2) The *formal cause* of it, which is their voluntary coalescency into such a society or congregation, according to the mind of Christ. (3) The *end of it* is, presential local communion, in all the ordinances and institutions of Christ . . .[13]

According to this conception, it is the actual believers as they are constituted a community who make a Church, not some supposed invisible underlying structure. The community is the Church. That passage comes from a relatively early writing, and in the later *True Nature of a Gospel Church*, Owen expands the idea somewhat:

> By the matter of the church, we understand the persons whereof the church doth consist, with their qualifications; and by its form, the reason, cause, and way of that kind of relation among them which gives them the being of a church . . .[14]

What is interesting about the later formulation is the fact that the Aristotelian terminology now takes a back seat, so that terms deriving from classical trinitarian theology – *person, cause, relation* – may come to the forefront. The result is that Owen's doctrine of the Church is an echo of the Greek theology of the Trinity according to which God *is* what the three persons are in relation to one another. The outcome is an ecclesiology in which the Church is understood by analogy with the Trinity. It is not a direct reading down from a concept of God to the nature of the community. Rather, the Church is understood

---

[12] The following points are taken from *The Promise of Trinitarian Theology* (Edinburgh: T. & T. Clark, 1991), chapter 4.

[13] Owen, *An Enquiry into the Original, Name, Institution Power, Order, and Communion of Evangelical Churches. Works*, volume 15, p. 262.

[14] Owen, *The True Nature of a Gospel Church and its Government. Works*, volume 16, p. 11.

with the help of the concepts used in a doctrine of God, so that
its being – the kind of entity that it is – is articulated with the
help of theological ideas, in some contrast with the widespread
tendency to treat it by analogy with an army or a state. In that
way, we are helped to understand the Church as the community
which is called to echo at its own level the kind of being in
relation – communion – that God is eternally. It is, on Owen's
part, an immense achievement.

What does he lack, and why? He appears to me not to have
brought together the two insights that he has achieved. In his
treatment of pneumatology, there is much on the work of the
Spirit as the creator of faith, and the rest – on the Spirit in
relation to the individual, or the Christian in general; and yet
very little on the Spirit as the creator of community: as the One
by whose agency God the Father realises the communion of
saints on earth. And there is a parallel inadequacy in his
treatment of the Church. Before I say what it is, a brief
historical digression is in order, and it will enable me to outline
the main burden of this chapter. It is that we should, among all
the other things that we say of the Holy Spirit, give a central
place to his being the transcendent and free Lord who creates
community by bringing men and women to the Father through
Jesus Christ and so into relation with one another. The Spirit is
not some inner fuel, compulsion or qualification – in fact he is
nothing impersonal at all – but the free Lord who as our *other*
liberates us for community.[15]

What is here historically interesting, as Geoffrey Nuttall's
account of seventeenth-century Congregationalism indicates, is
that Owen and his contemporaries operated in their ecclesiology with precisely the two concepts I have been commending:
community and freedom. We will pause to examine his report,
because it is so illuminating. In the first place, it is clear that our
Congregational forebears did not simply have a theory of
community, but practised their church life as if that were at the
centre of their being. 'In the Congregational churches', Dr
Nuttall writes, 'order is never far removed from fellowship: it

---

[15] In a recent book, Tom Smail has argued that the Spirit brings us to the
Father *of* but not *by* ourselves: as, we might say, the enabler of our freedom.
The Giving Gift. The Holy Spirit in Person (London: Hodder & Stoughton,
1988).

must express fellowship or it is nothing.'[16] Nor, as sometimes appeared to be the case when it was viewed from outside, was this merely a fellowship within individual congregations. 'Just as fellowship within the local, visible, gathered church of the saints could be so real, so vital and so self-authenticating that there was the less need to be concerned with the charge of schism, so the fellowship between the churches could be so serious and affectionate that there was the less need for organised and regular synods or associations.'[17] In these days of the proliferation of dreary meetings, one is tempted, however unspiritual the urge, to indulge in a bout of historical nostalgia.

That, however, is not the point, for we must hurry on to show that for these Churches fellowship was not won at the expense of freedom – for it is a modern heresy that hell is other people – but was rather a function of it.

> The faith they knew was an eager, free and full surrender to the Lord, and in the Lord to one another.
>
> William Bartlett ... defined 'visible Church-state' as 'a free society or communion of visible Saints, embodied and knit together by a voluntary consent'; and in his definition John Rogers included the condition, 'all her Members freely, and voluntarily, embodying without the least compulsion'.[18]

Their freedom was a function of their relations with one another. It was, moreover, a theologically grounded conception of freedom with which they operated: 'it was indeed the Lord who gathered them out of the lands ... At the same time, their response to what they believed to be the divine commands ... was a voluntary response, was given with "a willing mind".'[19]

I stand to be corrected by those who know more of him than I do, but it seems to me that the theology of the Church in terms of free congregating, which plays so large a part in Owen, is not sufficiently safeguarded from a later collapse into an individualistic and merely secular concept of freedom. Yet unless our notion of freedom is controlled pneumatologically;

[16] Geoffrey F. Nuttall, *Visible Saints. The Congregational Way 1640–1660* (Oxford: Blackwell, 1957), p. 94.
[17] Nuttall, *Visible Saints*, p. 100.
[18] Nuttall, *Visible Saints*, pp. 106f.
[19] Nuttall, *Visible Saints*, p. 108.

unless, that is to say, our concept of churchly freedom is the freedom given by the Spirit who creates community, we shall be in danger of a collapse into the kind of individualistic autonomy that encourages us to think that we do it all by ourselves, and which, as I have already suggested, sometimes marks later times. In search of the connecting link which Owen lacked, I turn now to the theology of some of the Cappadocian theologians, both ancient and modern, hoping to take further the process which the Reformation and its successors began.

III *Cappadocian ecclesiology*

As we saw, it was from the Greek Fathers that, directly or indirectly, John Owen appears to have received some of the concepts which enabled him to develop his interesting theology of the Church. An examination of their work, however, suggests that they did more to lay the groundwork of an ecclesiology than to develop one. The work of Gregory of Nazianzus, for example, is remarkable for its lack of ecclesiological content. In his discourse on the Holy Spirit, only one small part of a great list of the actions and attributes of the Spirit is relevant to ecclesiology, and that only vaguely. The *Oration on Pentecost* is similarly lacking in ecclesiological content. Basil is little more to the point, simply listing in his treatise *On the Holy Spirit* 'the ordering of the Church' among the gifts of the Spirit.[20] Yet there are to be found in these theologians the two gifts that Owen received and developed. The first is what the contemporary Greek theologian John Zizioulas, who consciously aligns himself with the Cappadocian tradition, has claimed to be a new concept of being. As the title of his book suggests and the contents expound, the theologians of the Trinity developed a conception of *Being as Communion.*[21] For God, to be is to be a communion of distinguishable but inseparable persons, a conception which bore fruit, as we have seen, in Owen's theology of the Church.

Second, the Greek trinitarian theologians developed the

[20] Basil of Caesarea, *On the Holy Spirit*, XVI.39.
[21] John Zizioulas, *Being as Communion. Studies in Personhood and the Church* (London: Darton, Longman & Todd, 1985).

conceptuality which enabled them to distinguish between the types of action characteristic of the different persons of the Trinity without rending the unity of the divine action in and towards the world. Basil is thus able to elaborate the distinctive functions of the Spirit,[22] and, while affirming that the Holy Spirit is 'inseparable and wholly incapable of being parted from the Father and the Son', to distinguish 'the original cause of all things that are made, the Father; the creative cause, the Son; the perfecting cause, the Spirit'.[23] From the notion of the Spirit as perfecting cause, there is, as we have seen,[24] much to be learned. But what we gain from the Greek Fathers for this stage of our argument is not so much an ecclesiology as, first, a theology of communion or community which enables us to focus ecclesiological questions; and, second, a conception of the Spirit of the kind that we require if we are to think together the Spirit and the Church, to draw concrete links between the Holy Spirit and the community of faith.

But why is it necessary that we should so attempt to think? The reason is to be found in many of the phenomena that have proved so problematic in the theology and life of the Church: the weakness of the tradition in understanding the action of God the Spirit in Church and world, and the fact that the Church has historically found it difficult not to assume that her actions are the actions of God the Spirit. Our concern, that is to say, is both theological and practical: with the way the Church is understood and with the way she takes shape in the world. And underlying that is the question of institutionalism: or, more precisely, in our context, that of the relation between the Spirit and the institution.

The protest against the Church as an institution is to be heard on many lips: often, of course, for simplistic and individualistic reasons, but not only that. Why is it, we may ask, that a faith at whose centre is the notion of freedom should have taken shape in the world in ways widely regarded as a threat to freedom? John Zizioulas has argued that the Church is rightly regarded as a threat to freedom in so far as it takes the form of a historically given reality: something, we might say, imposed

[22] See *On the Holy Spirit*, XV.36.
[23] *On the Holy Spirit*, XV.38.
[24] Above, chapter 7, section IV.

upon us by the past. We return to the point made earlier about the near incompatibility of a legally defined Church and a Church that is a community. An institution is not, as such, a community, because its existence is independent and logically prior to the persons who become part of it. A community is constituted by its members by virtue of their free relatedness to each other, as we have seen Owen suggesting. By contrast, an institution is a given reality to whose being the particular persons who join it are, if not irrelevant, at least secondary.

Now, without doubt the Church needs to be an institution in the sense that it must – theologically must – be a historically given reality. That 'must' derives from its relation to God's past and completed action. The Church has a past, and that past is one of the realities that make her what she is. The Church was *instituted* – became an institution – when Abraham was called to be the one in whom all nations of the earth would be blessed. That institution was realised in Jesus Christ whose ministry, death and resurrection achieved the instituting of the body – his body – which is the historic Church. It has often enough been remarked how close in some New Testament expressions is the relation between Jesus and the Church: by persecuting his followers, Saul was persecuting *him*.[25] In the Pauline writings, Christ is variously the body which is the Church and the head from which the body takes its shape. In both cases, there is nearly but not quite an identification of the Church with Christ, enough to make it understandable that the Church has sometimes been claimed to be the extension of the incarnation. But that is precisely where the difficulty emerges. If that is all that we have to say, we may come very near to making claims for some kind of absoluteness of the Church as it institutionally is: the sort of claim that invites satire and ridicule by virtue of its patent incredibility in the light of the direction that Church history has often taken.

In support of his contention that a Church conceived merely as institution is a threat to human freedom, Zizioulas has argued that institutionalism derives from an overweighting of ecclesiology to christology at the expense of the doctrine of the

---

[25] The Lord's question – 'Why do you persecute me?' – is repeated in all three varying accounts of Saul's conversion (Acts 9.4; 22.7 and 26.14).

Holy Spirit. In so far as anything is *merely* historically given, it is the vehicle of 'nature' and so inimical to freedom. He remarks that even Jesus has to be liberated from past history. To achieve that liberation is the work of the Spirit: 'it is to liberate the Son and the economy from the bondage of history. If the Son dies on the cross, thus succumbing to the bondage of historical existence, it is the Spirit that raises him from the dead.'[26] In so speaking, Zizioulas makes possible a number of crucial moves, all of them involving important distinctions that are rarely made in ecclesiology. First, he draws on the Cappadocian way of distinguishing between the work of the Son and the work of the Spirit in the economy of salvation: 'the contribution of each ... bears its own distinctive characteristics ...'.[27] What, then, are the distinctive characteristics of the work of Son and Spirit? In the economy, the Son represents God's immanence in history: he becomes flesh, history. The Spirit, contrary to what is often assumed, is God's transcendence. He is God's *eschatological otherness* from the world, God freeing the created order for its true destiny – and so, to use Basil's terminology, its perfecting cause. As we have seen, the Spirit liberates the crucified Jesus from the power of death and so enables him to be free for the present and future.

The second distinction is directly ecclesiological, and follows from what we have said about the Church as institution. As the Son institutes the Church – gives it immanent historical existence – it is the function of the Spirit to constitute it, to free it from institutional*ism.* As Zizioulas points out, without some such distinction the tendency is to regard the Spirit as rather like fuel for a vehicle. The vehicle – the Church as institution – is there, given, and the Spirit makes her move. In such a case, the community becomes secondary to the institution, because what is sought is the movement of an already-given reality. What does it mean, then, to say that it is the function of the Spirit to constitute the Church? Let us return, briefly, to Owen. We can agree with him that the formal cause of the Church – the reason for its being the kind of entity that it is – is the 'voluntary coalescency' of visible believers into a society. But if that is all

[26] Zizioulas, *Being as Communion*, p. 130.
[27] Zizioulas, *Being as Communion*, p. 129.

that is said, may not the outcome be a kind of ecclesiological Pelagianism, according to which we begin to forget the kind of freedom that we have, and behave as if we do it all ourselves? Of course, Owen was not unaware of the point: the congregation gathers freely by virtue of election and according to the mind of Christ. But without some explicitly pneumatological determination of our conception of freedom, I believe that the danger of a merely secular concept of freedom becomes unavoidable.

The link that must be made is between the Spirit as the source of freedom and the being of the Church as community. First, then, the general question of how God can be conceived to be the source of our freedom. Negatively, so to speak, the Western tradition has rightly affirmed, against all forms of Pelagianism, that we are not free unless set free. The atoning death of Christ on the cross is the necessary condition of any human liberation, and our justification through the cross the sole gateway to the life that flows from a renewed relation with our maker. Where our tradition has been less strong is in marking out the shape that new life in freedom takes in the Church, and it is perhaps no accident that the Churches of the Reformation have themselves been as subject as Rome to the temptations of institutionalism. We must therefore ask the second and more particular question: how is the freedom won for us to be realised in the present? That has clearly much to do with the Holy Spirit, but how is that to be understood in churchly terms? It is here that we must consider the work of the Holy Spirit in constituting the Church.

I want to begin a development of that theme by referring to the Achilles' heel of Calvinist, and indeed all Western, theology, the doctrine of election. As we have seen in chapter 6, according to Barth, the doctrine of election is above all gospel, good news: that God elects us into reconciled fellowship – communion – with himself. Yet it has become in our history the opposite of gospel, the bad news that before all time human beings have been gratuitously foreordained to be either sheep or goats, and mostly goats. Barth's reordering of the doctrine in a more universal direction has been a liberation, and has already aided in the reconciliation of historically separated Christian communions. And yet the heavily christological treatment he has given the doctrine has brought problems: still, the impression is given, election is something taking place entirely in our past, something that, far from liberating us, appears to have determined our future apart from us, albeit in a somewhat more promising direction. Suppose that, without wishing to deny the christological dimensions – that God chose us in Christ – we consider the place also of the Spirit who makes holy by calling God's people into the community that is the body of his Son. Earlier doctrines made the mistake of seeing election as a causal force, determining our present from the eternal past; that is the root of the offence the teaching has so often caused. And yet are we not bound to say that we do not make ourselves Christians, because it is God the Spirit who enables us personally and freely to be joined to the community of faith? It is when we know the Spirit as the transcendent other, who comes from the Father and calls us into the body of which the Son is the head, that we may gladly accept our election as the source of our liberation.[28]

The Spirit, then, liberates by calling us into relation with Christ through the medium of the community of his body. He liberates us, that is to say, by bringing us into community: by enabling us to be *with* and *for* the brothers and sisters whom we do not ourselves choose. The Spirit respects our liberty, because he is not an internal, immanent causality forcing us into the Church, but a personal 'other' coming alongside us to set us free for others, just as he was alongside Jesus in his temptation in the wilderness. We may accordingly walk away from our election, paradoxically to choose the slavery that is life apart from Christ. But the positive gift of freedom is to be free in and for community: because to be free *is* to be in community: anything else is a denial of what it is to be human. It is worth observing here that the logic of Paul's talk of freedom is churchly. 'Now the Lord is the Spirit, and where the Spirit of the Lord is, there is freedom. *And we all ...*' (2 Cor. 3.17f.).

[28] 'The speaking of the Gospel is the event of predestination in that the gospel gives what it speaks about, but this eschatological efficacy of the gospel is the Spirit. We must parody Barth: the Holy Spirit is the choosing God' (Robert W. Jenson, 'The Holy Spirit', *Christian Dogmatics*, edited by C. E. Braaten and R. W. Jenson (Philadelphia: Fortress Press, 1984), volume 2, p. 138).

The heart of the constitution of the Church by the Spirit is to be found in worship. Every act of worship that is in the Spirit is a constituting of the Church. The Church is more than an institution because it is a community that must, ever and again, take place: it must be constituted in the present as the people of God. To achieve such a constitution is the Spirit's eschatological work. When true worship takes place, there is a sharing in the worship of heaven and an anticipation of the life of the age to come. It is then that the Church truly *is*. According to the classic pattern of Reformed worship, the community is called to worship when the gospel is proclaimed in the opening words of Scripture (a summons regrettably today often replaced by more secular forms of greeting). The matter can be understood pneumatologically: through the Word the Spirit constitutes as the community of worship the institution – a group of people standing in a particular historical relationship to one another – which stands before God.[29] The Spirit lifts the community to the Father through the Son: and therefore we must say that the Church is constituted as the Spirit, through the word of the gospel – the risen Christ becoming concrete in the present – calls the community into being.

Similar points can be made in relation to the sacraments. Daniel Hardy has remarked that every baptism is a reconstitution of the Church. That is a profound truth. When another becomes incorporate in Christ through the Spirit, there is a new creation (2 Cor. 5.17). Paul's claim should not be taken individualistically, so as to suggest that there is in the individual an inner change, invisible and having no empirical results. 'In Christ' means for him in the community of the Church. The new creation, the reconstitution, takes place because by virtue of the baptism there is a new community. It is still the one body of Christ, the people called to be the children of Abraham and so instituted in God's past election: in that sense, the same. But

---

[29] We must not, it should be noted, stress the constituting of the Spirit at the expense of the Word's instituting. According to the Fourth Gospel, worship is in spirit and in truth; in the Spirit and in the Son. We may observe too that the author of Revelation is in the Spirit on the Lord's day when he is addressed by the risen Lord and granted a share even while in exile in the life of the Church and the worship of heaven.

the relationships that constitute the community are changed, so that there is also a new reality. That reminds us again that for the Church to be the Church it has constantly to be constituted anew, and it is the work of the Holy Spirit to achieve that constitution: to make it ever and again the people of God and body of Christ as he calls into it new members. So it is with the Lord's Supper. If the close connection between communion and community that is so important for Paul (see 1 Cor. 11 in particular) is to be recovered, it will be by a reappropriation of the pneumatological dimensions of the celebration. The Lord's Supper and the *koinonia* of the body of Christ take place as the Spirit constitutes the Church around the table of the Lord. Only by some such emphasis shall we escape the tendency to turn the celebration into the reception of individual doses of religion.

There is to be found in the Letter to the Ephesians a recapitulation of our central themes. That great book, the climax of New Testament ecclesiological thinking, celebrates Christ as the end to which all creation moves. The mystery of the Church is that it is called to serve that end of the reconciliation of all things in Christ. It is here that we return to Basil's conception of the Spirit as the perfecting cause of the divine creation: 'to unite all things in him, things in heaven and things on earth' (Eph. 1.10). The eschatological destiny of the creation is a kind of community: the bringing of all the creation to the Father in Christ. The Church is called to be the community that plays a central part in the perfecting through Christ of the created order. But the perfecting is the work of the Spirit. Pneumatological themes recur in the letter: the Holy Spirit is the 'guarantee of the inheritance' (1.14, cf. 2.18). Crucial in the progress of the argument is the fourth chapter, whose theme is clearly pentecostal: the gifts of the Spirit are given for the building of that community which is called to praise God in worship and life and so to achieve in its worship and work anticipations of the reconciliation of all things in Christ.

In conclusion, I would reiterate that the Spirit is not some force or possession operating causally within the believer or the institution, although sometimes our language suggests that way of thinking. As the Spirit of the Father who comes to us through the Son and lifts us up into the life of God, he is a person, and so acts personally, both respecting and granting freedom by his very otherness. The Spirit is the institution's transcendent Lord, reconstituting the Church by calling into her new members and constituting her anew in each act of worship. There should be no suggestion that the Spirit works automatically or indeed only through the Church: that, too, would be a denial of his freedom and transcendence. But if we in the tired Churches of Christendom are to regain the confidence and freedom to speak and live the gospel, we should not be reluctant to hope, pray and expect that even our institutions shall from time to time be constituted the body of Christ, vehicles of the Spirit's work in perfecting the purpose of God for the creation, 'to unite all things in Christ, things in heaven and things on earth' (Eph. 1.10).

IV *Coda*

Talking about the Holy Spirit is an odd activity. We are saved not by theology, but by God the Father through the Son and in the Spirit. Yet the way in which we theologise about the Spirit necessarily has a bearing upon the shape our lives take in the Church, and, consequently, the shape the Church takes in the world. Theology's part is in aiding the traditions to merge and interanimate each other, so that in due time we may liberate the immense thought and energy that is expended in merely ecclesiastical matters for the Church's living in and for the world. In this chapter, accordingly, I have attempted two chief tasks. First, I have tried to show that one of Congregationalism's major theologians has taken neglected themes from patristic theology, and so laid the groundwork not only for a more adequate theology of the Church but for future ecumenical conversation. Second, by building upon that foundation, I have sought to point to a neglected area of our theology which has important implications for the way in which we understand and order our life in the Church and the Church's mission in the world. If we look to the Holy Spirit not simply as the fuel for the given institution but as the one without whose continued and repeated work the Church cannot be the Church, we may be set free by the Lord who is the Spirit to lift our eyes above the minutiae of institutional and merely ecclesiastical concerns to the Church's true calling, which is, by the praise of God which is both worship and life, to share in the promised reconciliation of all things to him.[30]

[30] I am immensely grateful to Christoph Schwoebel for comments on an earlier draft of this chapter, comments without which it would have emerged in far less satisfactory form.

CHAPTER 12

THEOLOGICAL ANTHROPOLOGY
Reinhold Niebuhr – a treatise of human nature[1]

The movement of human thought, both in history and individual, is a complex and many-sided affair. The way in which Reinhold Niebuhr's work has fed the thinking of many contemporary theologians, moralists and politicians is impossible to quantify. There are, to be sure, laments often heard about his neglect, and it is true that a number of contemporary theological movements would profit from a careful study of his thought, particularly perhaps his warnings against the romantic elements in some philosophies. Yet a stream may continue to water the earth even when it runs for a while underground. A personal reminiscence may be the best way to show how this has operated in one case.

I read deeply into Niebuhr in my formative years, as a graduate trained in classics and analytical philosophy, and beginning the study of theology. Since then returns to him have been only occasional, because, rightly or wrongly, other matters came to take priority. One of them was the preparing and teaching of a course in the history of modern philosophy. As is well known, to teach is often the best way to learn and to probe, and this process was no exception. As time went on, one particular tendency came to seem ever more evident. Both empiricist and rationalist – to use the simplified and partly misleading classification of the historians – had something to say. The latter spoke of the intelligibility of things, of the rationality of the universe and its openness to the enquiring human mind. On the other hand, the empiricist, too, had to be

[1] A slightly revised version of a lecture given to a conference, 'Reinhold Niebuhr Reconsidered', held at King's College, London, 19–21 September 1984. First published in *Modern Theology* 4 (1987), 71–81.

heard. Speaking of the centrality of our sense experience, of the concrete and material way we encounter our world, empiricism made an essential contribution to the development of modern science and culture. Each of them seemed, however, to stress beyond measure one side of the matter. Both streams of thought of the Enlightenment came to appear as heretical versions of the Christian doctrine of creation, the one stressing the world's meaningfulness, the other its relation to the human senses, but both in a way which obscured other aspects of the matter. The source of the error was part theological, part anthropological. To see the world and human life outside their relation to God, as Western philosophy has increasingly done, is not to see them at all.[2]

I now realise that Reinhold Niebuhr was one of those who taught me to look upon the history of culture with those kind of eyes. Looking again at his critiques of rationalism and romanticism in the first volume of *The Nature and Destiny of Man*,[3] I recognise a similar critique of the modern tradition. It is couched in language typical of Niebuhr. Romanticism's 'basic error lies in its effort to ascribe to the realm of the biological and the organic what is clearly a compound of nature and spirit, of biological impulse and rational and spiritual freedom' (I, p. 42). In other words, romanticism ties us too closely to the created order, and risks an obscuring of that transcendence of the finite that is so important to Niebuhr's anthropology. Rationalism, on the other hand, so stresses that transcendence over the world that other factors fall out of the picture. Similarly, in discussion of another pairing, Niebuhr can say that naturalism tends to deny human freedom, idealism human finitude. A Christian anthropology, by contrast, denies excesses on both sides, conceiving human beings as nature *and* spirit, immanence within the creation *and* transcendence over it. That is where both our promise and our peril are to be found.

Niebuhr's analysis of the human condition is so familiar that

[2] For an extended account of the critique, see my *Enlightenment and Alienation. An Essay Towards a Trinitarian Theology* (London: Marshall, Morgan & Scott; and Grand Rapids: Eerdmans, 1985).

[3] Reinhold Niebuhr, *The Nature and Destiny of Man. Vol. I. Human Nature. Vol. II. Human Destiny* (London: Nesbit, 1941). Future references will appear in the text in parenthesis as NDM I or II. Further page references will take the form of page numbers in parentheses in the text.

it would not be profitable to embark on a detailed exposition
and analysis. What I want to do, rather, is to cast light on this
important thinker by attempting to place him in his context in
a long tradition of Western thought about the human condition. Niebuhr is both a product of and a contributor to this
tradition. As we have seen, he undoubtedly transcends it by the
power of his analysis of his predecessors and contemporaries.
But at the same time he is deeply influenced by major epochs
and thinkers within it, thus perfectly illustrating his own characterisation of our finitude and transcendence.

I　*Rebellious son*

I want to begin by developing the hint contained in the title of
this chapter, that Reinhold Niebuhr, with his anthropological
concentration, is a child of the Enlightenment, if, indeed, one
so rebellious that the weight of his relationship derives from
what he denies. The Enlightenment is that era in which the
anthropocentrism of our modern culture came to birth. The
story is well rehearsed. Descartes, seeking a certainty he had not
attained in his conventional education, turned within to the
certainties of the mind. It was the individual mind, not the
outside world or the tradition, that was to be the source of
truth. It was, of course, an era of great confidence in human
possibilities. The discoveries of the developing natural sciences
gave the feeling of a new age of liberty, in which the trammels
of obscurantism and authority would be thrown aside. More
than that, the expectations centred increasingly on human
achievement, on what lay within human power.

Other thinkers and agents built upon Descartes' foundation,
differing from him in detail but not in basic direction. John
Locke, much contrasted with Descartes because of his empiricism, was one with him in this: that he held it within the power
of reason to develop a system of morals, and thus implicitly
denied the need for any authority deriving from outside the
human mind. It was in ethics above all that the confidence most
survived criticism. In other respects Kant, the greatest mind of
the age of reason, found that his confidence in the power of the
mind to penetrate the mystery of being was curtailed by Hume's

destruction of metaphysics. But not in ethics: here the mind was godlike in its capacity to formulate and decide. What was once received upon authority from 'outside' now has its source in the new lawgiver, the human mind: 'every rational being ... must be able to regard himself as also the maker of universal law in respect of any law whatever to which he may be subjected ...'.[4]

Here we could not be much more distant from Reinhold Niebuhr's robust refusal to countenance any form of human self-divinisation. Yet there are parallels between Kant's thought and his which make the matter worth pursuing. In the first place, for Kant, too, man is a synthesis of nature and spirit. The *Groundwork* makes this quite clear. On the one hand, viewed from without, the human agent can be explained in terms of causes which fully determine his or her reality: naturalism, as Niebuhr would describe it. On the other hand, viewed from within, there is in practical reason the capacity to transcend that finiteness. Indeed, there is a kind of infinity inherent in the lawgiving function, a strong version of idealism. In the second place, there is in Kant, despite the apparent optimism of the earlier work, an equivalent of the Christian doctrine of original sin. One has only to look around the world, says the Kant of *Religion Within the Limits of Reason Alone*, to see that moral optimism is nonsense.[5] Human actions everywhere serve to show that there is operative within the human mind a propensity to evil that can only be healed by a kind of redemption, although it is scarcely what has traditionally been conceived by the Christian Church. It is a kind of philosophical reorientation, a Christ in us but without the corresponding Christ for us.[6]

Kant's moral philosophy has been enormously influential in forming the liberal theological tradition, and it is clear that he and Niebuhr addressed themselves to the same question in a not dissimilar context, both of them aware of the limitations of

[4] Immanuel Kant, *Groundwork of the Metaphysic of Morals*, translated by H. J. Paton in *The Moral Law* (London: Hutchinson, 3rd edition, 1956), p. 83, marginal pagination.
[5] Immanuel Kant, *Religion Within the Limits of Reason Alone*, translation of second edition, 1794, by T. M. Greene and H. H. Hudson (New York: Harper Torchbooks, 1960), pp. 28f.
[6] Kant, *Religion*, particularly pp. 55, 77f.

modern optimistic moralism. But Niebuhr's analysis is vastly superior. In the first place it is more coherent, and for two reasons. First, Kant's account of the radical evil in human nature coheres ill with the philosophical optimism that marks other aspects of his work. And yet the doctrine of radical evil, though it is often seen as an aberration, is testimony to Kant's wish to be true to things as they are. Second, there is a radical dualism in Kant's view of human nature. Matter is mechanistic, mind autonomous and free; and the two may meet, but never in a comprehensible way. Because Niebuhr has a doctrine of creation, he is spared both the mechanism of matter and the divinisation of mind. The problem for him is not the philosophical puzzle of relating two incompatible levels of being, but the moral and theological one of the relation of sin, grace and freedom. The centre-stage is held not by the dualism of spirit and matter, but by the fallenness of both nature and spirit from their proper relation to the creator and sustainer of all things.

And that brings us to the second strength of Niebuhr's analysis. Where the age of reason turned to the god within, Niebuhr sought the content of life in a broader land, in our relation to God on the one hand and to society on the other. Kant's recommendation is that it may be necessary to turn away from Christ to consider the dictates of conscience. Niebuhr's centre, as Paul Lehmann has shown, is other: the Christ for us and the Christ in us are the centre of his thought, according to his own account, which we must believe.[7] The oft-made criticism of Reinhold Niebuhr, that he lacks a doctrine of redemption corresponding to his account of sin, is thus far unjustified. But it is certainly true that it is given less attention, even in NDM II, and that the form of Niebuhr's christology is decisively shaped by his anthropology. He therefore remains in the tradition whose direction (with assistance from Augustine) was set by Descartes, as the famous opening words of NDM suggest.[8] But he set out to transform it by bringing to the centre of theological and philosophical thinking aspects of our human

[7] Paul Lehmann, 'The Christology of Reinhold Niebuhr', *Reinhold Niebuhr. His Religious, Social and Political Thought*, edited by C. W. Kegley and R. W. Bretall (New York: Macmillan, 1961), p. 253.

[8] 'Man has always been his own most vexing problem. How shall he think of himself?' (NDM I, p. 1).

reality that had been overlaid by centuries of an optimism which, seen with the eyes he gives us, appears unbelievably optimistic. His concern is anthropological, but seeks to transcend anthropocentrism by a robust theocentric, if in some ways elusive, framework. Rebellious sons, however, still belong in the family.[9]

II *Western theologian*

Like Reinhold Niebuhr, the Enlightenment lived in part from what it denied, and that was Augustinian Christianity as it shaped and was shaped by the Middle Ages. Niebuhr's doctrine of sin can be understood in large part as the revival of certain central aspects of Augustinianism. In many ways Augustine himself was a very anthropocentric thinker: witness, for instance, the deep effect of his own struggles on the shape of his theology and the dominance of psychological categories in his theology of the Trinity. But of chief interest for us is his place in the development of the doctrine of sin in the West.

Western theology was from the first more concerned with such matters than Eastern. It is certainly false to say that sin does not feature in the theology of the East and that the latter tradition's concern was with bodily corruption and not with sinfulness. But the decisive part played by lawyers like Tertullian and church leaders like Cyprian in the West set a distinctively different direction. To a tendency to think in legal categories was added Augustine's own preoccupation with sin and forgiveness. The story is not in every way an elevating one. Augustine's anthropology generated a deep historical pessimism which was undoubtedly the root of many of the worst features of mediaeval Christendom, in particular its development of reactionary political institutions and the use of repressive measures against dissenters. (That is why it *is* possible to read Niebuhr one-sidedly and in a reactionary manner. But such a reading involves abstracting the Augustinian pessimism

[9] This analysis is supported by two of the points made by Professor James Gustafson in the lecture he gave to the same conference: that Niebuhr belongs in part to the American Liberal Protestant tradition, and that his understanding of myth is more anthropological than theological.

from its context in Niebuhr's broader thought.) But I want here to centre attention on what happened in and around Augustine's time with the development of the dogma of original sin.

A context is provided by Paul's analysis in the Epistle to the Romans. Two features are noteworthy. The first is that for Paul sin is not of interest in itself. The account of human sinfulness, leading to the assertion in Rom. 3.23 that 'all have sinned and fallen short of – or lost – the glory of God' is prefaced by an assertion of the power of the gospel in salvation and completed by the theology of justification, redemption and expiation that dominates the early chapters of the epistle. Adam typology is absent from his analysis, which is dominated by a positive soteriology and not by a pessimistic account of human incapacity. The second feature is that when Adam typology does appear, it is not of interest in itself, but to stress the grace abounding that is Jesus Christ. Whatever is said of Adam is more than overweighed by the 'how much more' of the gospel: 'where sin increased, grace abounded all the more ...' (Rom. 5.20). To use the familiar Lutheran terminology, law is subordinated to gospel, and expounded only in order to provide a backcloth for the latter. It is an essential backcloth – for without it gospel is not gospel – but it is not of independent interest.

When we come to Augustine and his successors, matters are subtly different. They are not, of course, entirely so, and the difference must not be exaggerated. Augustine's opposition to Pelagius was on evangelical grounds: if Pelagius was correct, then it was not necessary for Christ to have died. But accounts of the discussions of the matter of original sin in the fifth and sixth centuries indicate a considerable shift of balance. In the first place, a dominating factor is provided by considerations drawn from the practice of infant baptism. If baptism is for the remission of sins, and infants are baptised, then infants must be sinful. What is significant in all this is the negative weight given to baptism. It ceases to be understood as initiation into the new people of God, and instead is dominated by considerations of the removal of some inherited stain or burden. The often scarcely concealed assumption is that the primary feature of the human condition is membership of the mass of perdition, doomed to destruction: an undoubted Manichaean streak.

Baptism, membership of the Church, removes from this mass. The paradoxical feature of this is that both sin and salvation come to be understood individualistically, for salvation is of individuals out of the doomed mass: salvation from the world instead of for and into it. In the second place, the link between the individual and the mass is increasingly centred on his or her relation to the historical Adam. 'Augustine', wrote N. P. Williams, 'asserts that "sin", which for the moment seems to be synonymous with "concupiscence" ... originated in the transgression of Adam. This "sin" has become ingrained into human nature and is transmitted by physical heredity.'[10] The link between 'concupiscence' and Adam meant that another impetus was given to the tendency to conceive sin in individual and often in sexual terms. It is through the process of sexual reproduction that the taint is passed from generation to generation.

Niebuhr's achievement in relation to this tradition is twofold. The first aspect concerns his analysis of the individual as a sinner. Gone are all those features of the tradition which somehow suggest that sin is a function of our physical or sexual constitution. Of course, Niebuhr is aware of the moments of truth in the tradition: 'The distinctively Christian doctrine [is] that sin has its source not in temporality, but in man's wilful refusal to acknowledge the finite and determinate character of his existence ...' (NDM I, p. 189). And sensuality, as the refusal of transcendence of the finite, is indeed one of the chief features of human sin. But Niebuhr refuses to see the root of our problems in our physical and sexual natures. What he has done is to expunge the traces of Manichaean thought which undoubtedly survived in doctrines of original sin, and to stress instead the parallel side of Augustine, the 'existential' dimensions of sin rather than those transmitted genetically. In principle, Augustine believed, it is possible to live without sinning. In practice, no one succeeds in doing so. And why not? Why do people not do what they are capable of doing? Because they do not want to.[11] It is this analysis, paradoxical but inescapable, that Niebuhr believes to be the strength of the realistic assess-

[10] N. P. Williams, *The Ideas of the Fall and of Original Sin. A Historical and Critical Study* (London: Longmans, Green & Co., 1929), p. 327.

[11] *De peccatorum meritis et remissione*, II, vif.

ment of the human condition generated by Augustinian thought. 'Sin is natural for man in the sense that it is universal, but not in the sense that it is necessary .... Sin proceeds from a defect of the will ... ' (I, p. 257). Niebuhr accepts the paradoxes and apparent logical absurdities which flow from this doctrine. His justification for it is that it is continually fruitful in throwing light 'upon complex factors in human behaviour which constantly escape the moralists' (p. 264). And these factors are chiefly seen in the light of the double truth 'that the will is free in the sense that man is responsible for his sin, and ... is not free in the sense that he can, of his own will, do nothing but evil' (p. 259).

But the 'existential' analysis is made in the light of other considerations. It is here that Niebuhr places himself firmly in the Reformation tradition, itself a mixture of Augustinian and anti-Augustinian strains. Human life is to be viewed from the standpoint of the justice of God and not merely by an analysis of immanent features (NDM I, Ch. 1, section III).

> Without the presuppositions of the Christian faith the individual is either nothing or becomes everything ... His inclination to abuse his freedom, to overestimate his power and significance and to become everything is understood as the primal sin. It is because man is inevitably involved in this primal sin that he is bound to meet God first of all as a judge, who humbles his pride and brings his vain imagination to naught (I, p. 98).

We meet God first of all as a judge, but second and more especially as justifier. 'The doctrine of atonement and justification ... is an absolutely essential presupposition for the understanding of human nature and human history' (p. 159). It is only in the light of the Christ for us and in us that all these things can be said and, in a measure, understood. In Niebuhr's Augustinianism, Adam speculation has been replaced by an analysis of the human condition less dependent upon literalist interpretation of the Scriptures, more oriented to judgement and forgiveness. But there is a real continuity. The individual remains helpless, freely but universally sinful, only to be rescued by the justifying grace of God. There is a straight line from Augustine through Luther and Calvin to Reinhold Niebuhr.

III *Modern theologian*

A little while ago, reference was made to Niebuhr's twofold development of the Augustinian tradition of theological anthropology. The first aspect we have now seen to lie in his bringing to the fore of what could be called Augustine's existential analysis of the plight and salvation of the individual. In combination with Adam speculation, that analysis had led to serious deficiencies: in particular, as we have seen, its individualism and tendency to think of baptism in negative terms, as removal from the mass of perdition. Corresponding to such a conception there came to birth a view of the Church as the place where there were gathered those who were saved *from* the world, the receptacle of brands plucked from the burning. To parody crudely, the world is the place where are to be found *individuals* on the way to destruction; the Church the recourse of those individuals whose destiny is elsewhere: it is an otherworldly and exclusive vision.[12]

It was part of Reinhold Niebuhr's early experience in face of the distinctive problems of modern industrial society to meet up with the fruits of such a view of the Church: a society left to go to the devil and a complacent churchmanship concerned with religion but not with justice. It is the strength of Hans Hofman's 1956 study of Niebuhr's theology to show that here lay the heart of his achievement. 'Niebuhr is sure that the relatedness between God and the individual man wholly excludes any possibility of a mystic or private tête-à-tête with God. What God says to man personally brings man into relatedness with the whole world around him and gives him his place in it.'[13] The individual remains at the centre of the analysis – perhaps too much so – but never in isolation. Niebuhr's threefold account of human nature, says Hofman, refers 'not to immanent human traits but to the position of

---

[12] This involves great oversimplification, but nevertheless it is difficult to escape the moment of truth in Dietrich Ritschl's claim – though he was making it in a different context – that in certain respects there is little dogmatic difference between Augustine, Bultmann and Billy Graham. *Memory and Hope. An Inquiry concerning the Presence of Christ* (London: Collier–Macmillan, 1967), p. 34.

[13] Hans Hofman, *The Theology of Reinhold Niebuhr*, translated by Louise Pettibone Smith (New York: Charles Scribner's Sons, 1956), p. 150.

man as it is determined by the relationships with which he deals in his activities and aims'.[14] It is the centring of anthropology in relationships rather than to a supposed descent from a historical Adam that marks Niebuhr as a distinctively modern theologian, and a little must now be said of what this means.

The rethinking of the doctrine of sin was made necessary by the development of the critical method in the eighteenth century. The rejection of the view that Adam was a particular man who fell and transmitted his fault to all succeeding generations pushed theology in two directions. The first was, in effect, to deny the doctrine of sin largely or altogether; and we know what Niebuhr made of that. The second was to develop an alternative analysis concentrating less on the physical, more on the social and relational aspects of the matter. The latter way was taken by the father of modern theology, F. D. E. Schleiermacher. Schleiermacher is particularly perceptive about the corporate nature of sin: it is 'not something that pertains severally to each individual and exists in relation to him by himself, but in each the work of all, and in all the work of each; and only in this corporate character can it be properly and fully understood'.[15] It is on these grounds, and not on a tracing back to Adam, that Schleiermacher bases his doctrine of original sin, which now comes to mean the sin that afflicts us by virtue of our social origins: 'the sin of the individual has its source in something beyond and prior to his own existence'.[16] Adam and Eve then become, on his account, symbolic expressions of a relationship subsisting timelessly between the human person and God, but rooted in the corporate historical experience of the human race.

Although Niebuhr's references to Schleiermacher are mainly critical, it can be seen that he belongs in the same tradition, in both its strengths and weaknesses. Indeed, the strength of *Moral Man and Immoral Society* is its depiction of the way in which groups behave, of how they take up and demonise, so to speak,

[14] Hofman, *The Theology of Reinhold Niebuhr*, p. 155.

[15] F. D. E. Schleiermacher, *The Christian Faith*, translation of second edition by H. R. Mackintosh and J. S. Stewart (Edinburgh: T. & T. Clark, 1925), p. 255.

[16] Schleiermacher, *The Christian Faith*, p. 279. It is not surprising that Schleiermacher was a social reformer in a way that many of his liberal successors were not.

the unselfish possibilities of the individual.[17] The critique of the group returns in NDM, in which the process of argument goes something like this. The heart of sin is pride, and is exacerbated by the anxiety and insecurity which lead the human agent to attempt to put himself in the place of God. Pride of power and pride of knowledge lead inexorably to moral and spiritual pride, and the outcome is that religion provides the final battleground between God and human self-esteem (I, Ch. 7, III). Supervening upon the pride of the individual is the pride of the group. Groups develop wills of their own, so to speak, and their pretensions exceed those of the individual. Their final danger is to present themselves as 'the source and end of existence'.

What should be the attitude of Christians to this? Not the one that has frequently been displayed: of escaping from the challenges of society or recommending reactionary and oppressive measures to keep sin at bay. Here Niebuhr is decisively different from the extremes of Augustinian pessimism. The grace which flows from judgement and justification should be conceived as a grace which enables a transformation of individuals not out of the world but in Christ. Niebuhr here cites with approval a remark of James Denney, 'I would rather be saved in Christ than lost in God' (NDM II, p. 117). Just as pride is the heart of the problem, the solution is to hold to a conception of grace which continues to nullify the pretensions of pride. Views of the Church which in any way identify it with the Kingdom of God fail to hold true to biblical conceptions of grace. Niebuhr wants a more open and dialectical view of the relation between Church and society, and, in an anticipation of preoccupations of more recent years, comes towards the end of NDM with a discussion of 'The Kingdom of God and the Struggle for Justice' (II, Ch. IX). 'Love is ... the primary law of [the individual's] nature; and brotherhood the fundamental requirement of his social existence' (II, p. 253). Here Niebuhr is critical of his Reformation heritage, holding that it has sometimes encouraged too individualistic a conception of justification. Rather: 'Justification by faith in the realm of

---

[17] Reinhold Niebuhr, *Moral Man and Immoral Society* (Edinburgh: T. & T. Clark, 1980).

justice means that we will not regard the pressures and counter pressures, the tensions, the overt and the covert conflicts by which justice is achieved and maintained, as normative in the absolute sense; but neither will we ease our conscience by seeking to escape from involvement in them' (II, p. 294). There is in Niebuhr's view of Christianity an incipient theology of its function as a liberator for involvement in the structures of society.

IV   *Conclusion*

I have argued that Niebuhr has made three major contributions to the Western theological tradition. First, he has begun with the Enlightenment's preoccupation with the meaning of human life, and radically revised it in the light of a renewed Augustinianism. Second, he has brought to the centre and filled with new life certain aspects of the Augustinian and Reformed conception of human bondage. Third, he has criticised Western individualism with a view to establishing the bearing of the Christian gospel on society where it had seemed to operate as an escape from the world. There do, however, seem to be places where the spell of Augustine has proved too strong, and it is with one or two of these that I wish to conclude.

The thought of Augustine is marked by a very strong dualism of time and eternity, and with a corresponding tendency to see the temporal order as itself the place of disorder and decay. This emerges not only in the doctrine of sin we have outlined, but also in a relative incapacity to conceive time and space as the locus of the presence of God: the eternal tends to be sought through a movement out of and above time into the eternal realm. In this respect, christology is less of a problem – or was, before the modern age – than the doctrine of the Spirit. Christ has his place as a timeless, sacramental means of ascent to the eternal world. But the Holy Spirit? That has always been the weakness of Western theology, for there it becomes a matter of being able to identify events in time as the eschatological presence of God. Niebuhr's most sympathetic commentators tend to agree that this is his weakest point. Thus Hofman asks how 'the "being in Christ" [can] be conceivable without an understanding of the doctrine of the Holy Spirit' (p. 246), and Lehmann observes that 'faith in Christ not only apprehends but also obeys. Sin is overcome, not merely "in principle" but also "in fact".'[18]

How does this lack of a fully trinitarian breadth affect the anthropology? First of all, there tends to be a dialectical rather than a trinitarian conception of human being. The *simul justus et peccator*, and not the new person in Christ, tends to remain the dominating conception. Redemption is not the primary reality, as it is for Paul. Grace never quite succeeds in abounding more than judgement. Second, there is the lack of an adequately churchly dimension, and it reveals itself in the following way. Attention has already been drawn to Hofman's observation that for Niebuhr man is a kind of middle term between God and society. But that term *man* is problematic not only to those who would object to the masculine form of the word. It tends to operate in Niebuhr rather as an abstraction. It is noteworthy how much of the analysis of NDM falls short of the subtlety of Schleiermacher's analysis. Almost the whole of those works is concerned with the individual, who continues to be the centre from which all questions radiate. In that sense, Niebuhr never escaped the spell of the Enlightenment: his theology remained individualistic, whatever his ethics and politics.[19]

But if we are essentially *relational* beings, will this do? As relational, we take much of our reality from our world and the people in our past and present. There is no 'man' or 'woman' apart from these relationships. The Christian, therefore, exists in various networks of relationships, among them the ecclesial. It is as so related that he or she participates in the realities of the Christ for us and the Christ in us that were of such central importance for Niebuhr. Bonhoeffer saw the Church as the place where Christ takes form in the midst of worldly reality. If he is right, we can no longer be content with the *simul justus et peccator*, for the presence of Christ through the Spirit must be conceived as the sphere in which sin begins to be outgrown in

[18] Niebuhr, *Moral Man*, p. 279.

[19] As John Milbank pointed out to me after the lecture, Niebuhr's conception of the state tends to conceive it as the individual writ large.

fact as well as in principle: whatever the risks of pride and complacency, that has to be the centre, as it was for Paul. Christian reality bears upon the world as the one network of relationships makes real, in interaction with the other, the form of Christ in and for the world.

What is lacking in Niebuhr is detailed attention to the realities made possible by life in the Spirit, because his anthropological concentration rarely allows him to break out into a wider perspective. But it would be unfortunate to end on too critical a note. To conclude more positively, let us return to the beginning of the chapter, and recall that we all belong in a tradition, whose preoccupations and assumptions we absorb during our upbringing and education. European and North American theology has long been dominated by particular ways of asking questions about our 'own most vexing problem'. Reinhold Niebuhr did not wish, in that respect, to leave the tradition, and so it is unjust to treat him too strictly as a systematic theologian and not, as he wished to be regarded, as an ethicist. What emerges from the various historical comparisons that have been made is this: that even so strictly regarded, he has used the tradition of which he was a part to build anew, and we can ask no more of any thinker.

CHAPTER 13

AUTHORITY AND FREEDOM

P. T. Forsyth's *The Principle of Authority*[1]

I *The question in context*

Peter Taylor Forsyth has about him something of the capacity of Kierkegaard to utter the kind of lapidary judgement that both breaks through cliché and comes, upon reflection, to appear to be undeniably true.[2] As a rule they are 'fireworks in the fog', according to one notorious and foolish characterisation, only if their relation to the remainder of Forsyth's thought is ignored. Whether or not Forsyth is a systematic theologian is partly a matter of definition, but there is an overall unity and coherence to his thought of the kind that justifies its claim to be systematic after the manner of Brunner's fine description of Irenaeus: 'if this is what it means to be a systematic theologian: to perceive connections between truths, and to know which belongs to which'.[3] It is fortunate that Brunner's definition does not centre on tight coherence, for one of the things that becomes apparent from the collection of papers in celebration of his thought is that there are some fundamental tensions within Forsyth's corpus. The general contention that I would make is that his is an integrating mind, bringing together in an overall vision, if one

---

[1] First published as 'The Real as the Redemptive: P. T. Forsyth on Authority and Freedom', *Justice the True and Only Mercy. Essays on the Life and Theology of P. T. Forsyth*, edited by Trevor Hart (Edinburgh: T. & T. Clark, 1995), pp. 37–58.

[2] That is not to deny that sometimes his dicta come to appear obviously false.

[3] Emil Brunner, *The Mediator. A Study of the Central Doctrine of the Christian Faith*, translated by Olive Wyon (Philadelphia: Westminster Press, 1947), p. 262.

with at times rather misty outlines, a wide range of intellectual, cultural and practical considerations.

Nowhere is there likely to be a better test of overall consistency than in a theologian's – or, for that matter, in any thinker's – grasp of the relation between authority and freedom. In the modern world they are widely thought to be in some form of opposition: freedom is to be achieved in freedom from authority, at least so far as that is conceived, after the manner of Kant's celebration of enlightenment, in terms of traditional forms of authority. According to this, any authority that is not in some way self-imposed is inherently suspect. On the other hand, the ever-present threat of authoritarian orders arising from the chaos bred by modern autonomy appears equally to make a choice between the two in some way necessary. But the best accounts bring them into some kind of positive relation, and it is here that the real test of consistency is to be sought, for the modern fashion, against which Forsyth repeatedly directs polemic, is right to the extent that they have come at least to appear to represent incompatible values, or at least values to be traded off one against the other.

The first judgement that I want to cite from Forsyth is germane to this enquiry. 'There is only one thing greater than Liberty, and that is Authority.' In the decades after the ruinous careers and defeat of two similar but rival systems of authoritarian politics, each in its own way a reaction to modern libertarianism, we may think that Forsyth had failed to read the signs of his own times. But that would be to mistake his point, for he knew only too well that the drift to those systems of oppression derived from the failure and not the assertion of right authority. He continues: 'The intellectual, and especially the moral, situation of the age raises with ever-growing force what I have called the central question of religion, and therefore of everything – the question as to *authority*.'[4]

That, of course, is one of the many places in *The Principle of Authority* where the words of eighty years ago could have been written today. But the background to Forsyth's treatment of the relation between authority and liberty is provided not only by

[4] P. T. Forsyth, *The Principle of Authority* (London: Independent Press, 1952, 1st edition, 1913), p. 17. Further references to this work will appear as page numbers in parentheses in the text.

the modern predicament. It is also to be found in two other features of the tradition he received: the treatment of freedom in the Augustinian and Calvinist tradition against which the modern world is in such wholesale rebellion, to its manifest impoverishment or worse, and the reaction to it in the liberalism that he found finally so unsatisfactory. So far as the former is concerned, although he clearly belongs in the tradition of Augustine and Calvin, Forsyth is interestingly aware of the weakness of what he had inherited. For example, twice in that book he prefers the notion of helpless guilt to that of total depravity.[5] And, with respect to the latter, there are a number of respects in which, as Ralph Wood has shown, he remains true to the liberal tradition in which he began his theological life.[6] The ways in which he deals with these two aspects of his past provide the keys to his own alternative and in many ways superior treatment.

The tradition of Augustine and Calvin does present a real problem, and its chief flaws could be said to be part of the cause of the widespread belief that authority and freedom are alternatives. The weakness is that isolated by John Oman in *Grace and Personality*, however unsatisfactory the solution he there essayed. The tradition's flaw is to be found in its tendency to impersonality, to the mechanising or naturalising of grace. Any notion of irresistible grace, such as appears to operate in parts of the systems of both Augustine and Calvin, overrides the autonomy of the agent, and generates a form of authoritarianism – of *absolute* dependence – which appears therefore to be hostile to any notion of freedom.[7] Yet Forsyth's solution is different from that essayed by Oman, who tends to make autonomy axiomatic and then rather lamely seek to find a place for grace. Oman's is essentially a modernist solution, while for Forsyth any notion of freedom which does not conceive it as

---

[5] '[T]hat moral helplessness through sin and guilt which used to be misunderstood as total corruption ...' (p. 298).

[6] Ralph Wood, 'Christ on Parnassus. Forsyth Among the Liberals', *Journal of Literature and Theology* 2 (1988), 83–95. I am not convinced by all the aspects of this thesis, for Forsyth seems to me in some areas of his thought to have emancipated himself more successfully than Wood argues from his liberal past.

[7] John Oman, *Grace and Personality* (London: Collins, 1960, 1st edition, 1917).

arising from divine action, and as therefore dependent upon a prior authority, is finally the denial of the gospel of justification by divine grace. Indeed he is a theologian of election, albeit not in the form associated with traditional Calvinism. In this chapter, then, we shall be concerned with the consistency both of authority and freedom in general and with Forsyth's treatment of them in particular. Is there, to use Alec Whitehouse's fine expression, an authority which is the authority of grace?[8] Forsyth certainly believed so.

II *Freedom as limitation and concentration*

A rather obvious way of putting the question of freedom is to understand it in relation to Kant's philosophy of moral autonomy. This is broadly speaking the view that freedom is a kind of empty space in which the moral agent, to be autonomous, must be determined by nothing except the moral law which is at once discovered and imposed, or rather discovered by being imposed, by practical reason alone, apart from any *exterior* determination. Like Jonathan Edwards before him, Forsyth is rightly dismissive of any notion of freedom from determination, the freedom of empty space. Here his analysis is both subtle and wide-ranging. First, he gives reasons for showing that there is no *thought* that is free from determination. To imagine otherwise is to succumb unaware to forces that both determine and imprison in a slavery to immaturity. His first argument depends upon a distinction between the individual and the person. Individuals are those who not only believe that they are naturally free, but also succumb to the very homogenising forces that deprive of true personality:

> It is often to be remarked how the tendency to a ready assertion of the natural self destroys personality ... Personal values are overwhelmed by the fashion of time and place ... The man who does not rise to become a person becomes an item ... He does not live; only some gregarious force lives through him ... He is the slave of his heredity, his environment, his disposition, his mates (pp. 285–6).

[8] W. A. Whitehouse, *The Authority of Grace. Essays in Response to Karl Barth* (Edinburgh: T. & T. Clark, 1981).

Second, he argues that freedom of thought is something that has to be attained. It is a freedom of maturity, the freedom of a formed person in distinction from the rootlessness of the individual:

> Freedom of thought is a hard-won power and glory . . . It does not come like flight to a bird or love to a boy. It is not its emancipation from the past, nor its escape from tutors and governors. But it is thought emancipated from the prejudices and passions of the common natural man, or from that 'collective suggestion', which makes a man the victim of his most ordinary environment . . . Thought truly free is an accomplishment and privilege of maturity . . .[9]

But though Forsyth is interested in the matter of education, and stresses its need in this very context – making youthful judgement a major symbol of a false notion of the freedom of thought – the freedom of intellectual maturity is, as with everything else, the fruit of redemption. We shall hope to glance at his hierarchy of values later.

The second area, that of moral freedom, is, scarcely surprisingly, of more interest to Forsyth than intellectual freedom, although, because he refuses to divide up the person into faculties, its treatment is of a piece with that of the latter. In the tradition of Edwards, though it is Burke that he interestingly cites,[10] he holds that freedom derives from limitation. There are various ways in which freedom is given by being limited, but chief among them is that it is something that has to be given, from without. Above all, it must be given by God, and that means by 'the Christ of the Apostolic Redemption' (p. 251):

> So that if freedom must always be limited to remain free, and if it must be limited at last only by the principle that creates it, then the redemption of Christ must be the last regulative principle in the freedom of a Church, and finally of the world (p. 250).

Notice that Forsyth is not here playing a freedom of redemption against a freedom of creation. It is rather that freedom is

---

[9] Forsyth, *The Principle of Authority*, pp. 287f.; cf. p. 291 for an attack on modern 'anti-traditionalism'.
[10] ' "Liberty", says, Burke, "must always be limited in order to be possessed" ' (p. 235).

the gift of the creator, but that, given that things are as they are, it can now come only through salvation from sin that is slavery. That is the voice of Paul, John, Augustine, Luther, Calvin and Edwards. Freedom is not an empty space, but consists in service to the truth, to what is really there, to the personal authority that is God's.

But because it is service to the real, the limitation of freedom is at the same time its concentration, a word Forsyth uses in connection with the universal significance of the cross of Christ.[11] His primary interest is in the freedom deriving from the cross, that historic source of all creative authority, so that he is therefore able to play a variation on a central Augustinian theme, that freedom is to be understood as obedience (pp. 211, 235). 'Such limitation of freedom is really its concentration, and therefore its power' (p. 259). Limited freedom is not freedom destroyed, but freedom empowered. The more obedient the agent is to the heavenly vision, the more power is released. '*Absolute* obedience is the condition of *entire* freedom' (p. 272). That is not as authoritarian as it sounds, for, as we shall see, obedience to true authority is the way by which the self is established in its true integrity, and, indeed, rationality:

> [W]hen an active element begins to enter our obedience it becomes rational. We not only *feel* the force of our authority, we *see* the force of it. We see reason for it . . . We have the kind and degree of freedom that goes with rational perception.[12]

The way is now open for us to show why it is that for Forsyth, far from being contraries, authority and freedom are mutually involving.

III *Redemptive authority*

The choice that all must make is not between autonomy and authority but between different forms of authority, between

---

[11] Compare a similar use of the word 'condensation' in *The Church, the Gospel and Society* (London: Independent Press, 1962), p. 10.

[12] Forsyth, *The Principle of Authority*, pp. 307–8. Readers of his following sentences will see that for Forsyth this is a partial account only, but his general point remains.

true and false authority.[13] Forsyth argues that autonomy as it is conceived in modern thought is not autonomy at all. Anticipating MacIntyre and Hauerwas, he claims in one characteristic judgement that 'It is a fatal fallacy of all such autonomy that it must regard virtue not as the principle of action but only as its result' (p. 311). And yet, again showing great subtlety of analysis, he presents alternatives in the way in which this is understood which are often absent from discussions of the topic. His arguments in support of his view that modernism is simply mistaken in its notion of authority include the following. First, he asserts that there is a sense in which all authority is external to the agent. To evade that is to fly in the face of reality. The necessary externality of authority provides a constant refrain in his argument. It is clearly one of its defining characteristics:

> An authority must be external, in some real sense, or it is none. It must be external to us. It must be something not ourselves, descending on us in a grand paradox (p. 271).

This is particularly the case with the divine authority with which he is ultimately but by no means exclusively concerned. 'All absolute authority must reveal itself in a way of miracle. It does not arise out of human nature by any development, but descends upon it with an intervention, a revelation, a redemption' (p. 299).

But, second, he shows that there are different forms of externality, those which are, we might say, heteronomous because they are foreign to the being of the person and those which in some sense or other reflect, or, better, constitute personal reality. 'External authority is only mischievous, not when it comes to us from without (for all authority must), but when it represents a kind of pressure which cannot evoke and nourish our moral soul' (p. 290). True authority 'is not foreign, but it is other' (p. 300). The distinction between what is alien and what is other is crucial, and highlights another dimension of the poverty of a modernity which in almost every respect treats the two as identical. In this connection it is worth pointing out that Forsyth understands well that the rejection of

---

[13] 'Liberty is illicit which renounces its own creative principle' (p. 251).

tradition is a rejection of the other, and therefore an impoverishment of the present.

Third, the distinction between the alien and the other is established by developing a conception of inwardness which corresponds and answers to the external shape of authority. The language of pietism – or perhaps of Schleiermacher, if that is different – is drawn upon, so much indeed that there are times and a sense in which Forsyth appears to suggest that the only true authority is an inward authority. 'This authority does not indeed impinge upon the soul's surface, it wells up within the soul's centre' (p. 301). 'The cure for individualism is ... some real authority interior but superior to the Ego itself' (p. 270). 'In the interior of the soul authority and freedom go hand in hand. For here it is soul that acts richly on soul ... Moral influence is entirely a matter of personal authority' (p. 285):

> True authority, final authority, is personal. As it acts on wills, it must be a will. It must have a moral quality. It must be good. It must be the one good thing in the world – a good will. At last it must be the will absolutely good – the Holy. We yield to the holy man; and to the absolutely Holy One ... we should yield nothing less than our whole selves ... (pp. 308–9).

Thus is the Kantian language of moral reason transmuted, overturned, into the language of grace.

It follows, fourth, that the only absolute authority is that of God, and that God's authority is absolutely self-grounded:

> It is a deep remark of Höffding that if there be an absolute authority He can only express Himself in miracle. If He is absolute He can be founded on nothing outside Himself. He is His own norm. He can be proved by nothing ... His supreme revelation must be the supreme miracle ... The absolute is in history ... only by a miracle. That is what we worship as the miracle (and not simply the marvel) of the person of Jesus Christ (pp. 309–10).

It is in this context that Forsyth engages in polemic, rather similar to that of T. F. Torrance in an article written in 1993,[14] against the kind of external, and therefore, he rightly believes, ultimately self-grounded and subjective, authority exercised by the Church of Rome (p. 317). In contrast, 'The authority of the Church is but the weight of its experienced Gospel in a vast plexus and long series of regenerate and corporate souls.' It is therefore a derived but inward authority, flowing from 'God in his salvation renewing the soul . . .' (pp. 290–1).[15] While Rome's authority may also be seen as a derived authority, Forsyth is clear about the difference. True authority can in no way be legal, but can only be exercised as personal authority continually renewed from the source. It is only as such that the Church has authority in society, and Forsyth's vision is a classical dissenting one, reaffirmed most vigorously in recent times by Yoder and Hauerwas. 'The only moral authority that can save society is one that thus asserts itself in the individual conscience by its saved experience of a universal Redeemer . . .' (pp. 298–9).

It is in his stress on the inward and personal locus of authority that Forsyth most shows the marks of the modern. His relations with Kant provide an illustration of his dialogue with modernity. On the one hand, Kant was for him, as he was for Coleridge, something of a liberator from the more abstract forms of Enlightenment rationalism. He provided a way of moving from the priority of the mechanical to that of the personal, from nature to the will. Not only does he teach that the ethical is the real, but he also appears to provide Forsyth with the 'clear distinction between natural life process, however rarefied or spiritual, and the action of the moral consciousness' (p. 201). As we have already seen, there are references to and echoes of Kant elsewhere, as we would expect in a pupil of Ritschl. Yet there is also a clear disagreement:

> But conscience is not a legislator, it is a judge. It does not give the laws either for action or belief, it receives them; it

[14] T. F. Torrance, 'A Machine Grinding out its Dogmas', *Church Times*, 21 May 1993.
[15] Eastern Orthodox theologians like to contrast their conception of authority with that of both Rome and the Reformation. The former is, they say, external and legal, the latter individualist and experiential. Forsyth, along with Calvin and much of the mainstream Reformed tradition, is not individualist.

recognizes the authority of laws from another source, and administers them to the occasions which arise (p. 240).

The locus and weight of the various sources of inner and outer authority have been subtly but significantly changed. How does Forsyth believe that in this way he can have his cake and eat it? Here he attempts an answer to a question which Barth tended to dismiss as improper, thus giving his own theology a sometimes rather authoritarian air. Although there is a sense in which for Forsyth authority is irrational and miraculous, there is also one in which it is rational, and that is its method of operation, which corresponds to the nature of that over which it is an authority: 'it emerges only amid psychological conditions' (p. 300).[16] Corresponding to the form of authoritative divine action there is a form of human experience. We must avoid, he argues, 'spatial metaphors of extension and mutual exclusion' when we are speaking of 'spiritual action and inter-penetration' (ibid.). The conversion that is necessary to the process of redemption 'wears the garb and speaks the tongue of our spiritual and conscious experience' (ibid.).

Forsyth's chief difference from Barth in this respect is that he does not eschew the concept of experience and the use of categories drawn from psychology.[17] His difference from Schleiermacher, however, is that he is far more careful to develop an a posteriori concept of experience, one whose shape is constrained by that which is experienced:

> The first content of my religious experience is not myself as feeling so or so – e.g. dependent (Schleiermacher) – not myself in a certain frame, but God in a certain act, a certain giving, as giving Himself, as thus grasping, saving, new creating me (p. 372, cf. p. 142).

Experience is a medium, not a matrix, or, as he puts it, ground (p. 331). 'Our very response to it is created in us before it is

---

[16] Forsyth shows a sometimes touching hope in the future progress of Christian psychology. But we cannot expect him to have been right about everything.

[17] To read the work of this man, even one mercifully free from the modern compulsion to justify everything with a footnote reference, is to become aware of the catholicity of his reading.

confessed by us ... [I]t is something miraculously created in us by the Bible to respond to divine power acting as grace' (pp. 333–4 – a rather Barthian note there). We appropriate rather than verify (ibid.). Forsyth sets his face strongly against experientialism, and, while feeling free to draw upon William James, accuses him of neglecting the very determinant of experience that makes it what it is (p. 301). 'A Gospel mainly experiential and subjective ... is bound to have its obverse in a greater uncertainty and a freer challenge by contemporary society.'[18] Rather, the authority 'speaks in the midst of our most intimate experience ... ; but its decisive word is not drawn from our experience' (p. 301). Experience is an ambiguous term: 'Sometimes it means the action on us of an objective fact which emerges *in* experience but is not *of* it' (p. 329).

Thus experience, although important, is not the main focus of Forsyth's account; that is the historic cross. For those incapacitated both intellectually and morally by sin and guilt there is no other way to freedom than through authority, and authority of a specific kind, that operating through redemption. It is therefore the nature of the cross and the God there revealed which finally shapes Forsyth's conception of authority and the locus of its action. The notion of the holy is the creative and dominating centre, rather as the notion of love in freedom is the centre of Barth's theology:

> The gospel of Christ's Cross is therefore the final centre of all Authority, because there alone the Holiness of God – the absolute sublimity, transcendence, and victory of the God of the Conscience – establishes itself for ever in the destruction of both guilt and sin (pp. 364–5).

The contrast with Barth is here instructive. While both theologians frequently link revelation and salvation – the cross being the focus of both – there is a tendency in Barth to stress the noetic, while Forsyth stresses the moral. The freedom of God is a notion closely linked in Barth with revelation; the stress in Forsyth is on the moral quality of holiness.

---

[18] 'In various ways religious uncertainty dogs the steps of an excessive subjectivity, such as marks an age that has just discovered the value of experience and can think of nothing else' (p. 348).

IV   *The principle of authority*

It is at this place that there arises a series of questions to Forsyth's theology which take us to the heart of its unique character, as well as of its treatment of authority. All in some way concern the relation between creation and redemption. We can approach it with reference to Daniel Hardy's criticism of Forsyth's ecclesiology, a topic closely related to that of authority. According to Hardy, Forsyth's concentration on the Church as the fruit of redemption makes it difficult for him to have a conception of what he calls created sociality. That is to say, Forsyth has a conception of being in community in the Church, but not an adequate conception of an underlying universal human sociality which might provide a basis for ecclesiology:

> One effect of these views ... is to eliminate what one could call 'general sociality' or created sociality present in the human condition; there can be no such thing as the social transcendental present in human society as an element of nature, because its place is always taken by the specific gift of God in Christ.[19]

Although there may be good Forsythian reasons for questioning that diagnosis, the point for our purposes is that it raises the question of the relation, particularly as it has taken shape in the Western tradition, between reason and revelation. The Enlightenment can from one point of view be understood as the reassertion of the rationality of the created order, both natural and human, against their subservience to the imposed authority of a religion of revealed redemption. It asserted nature against grace, created as against redeemed reason, as we might put it. Forsyth is in strong reaction against this, and rightly so. The words of the original title of this chapter, 'The Real as the Redemptive', adapted from the title of chapter 10 of *The Principle of Authority*, make this very clear. Forsyth is writing in conscious opposition to either Hegel or a disciple making use of the master's principle that 'the rational is the real'. His

[19] Daniel W. Hardy, 'Created and Redeemed Sociality', *On Being the Church. Essays on the Christian Community*, edited by C. E. Gunton and D. W. Hardy (Edinburgh: T. & T. Clark, 1989), pp. 21–47 (p. 40).

concern was not so much to celebrate the authority of God over against that of thought, but none the less to oppose the rationalism that makes truth the immanent possession of the knower.

We think of God, we entertain the idea of God, as we think anything else that is reasonable. But what everything turns on for the truth of the notion is the discovery of a right and a claim on us. It thinks us, it does not merely think itself in us (p. 102).

This overturning of Hegel's immanent rationality in favour of a more transcendent construal goes hand in hand with Forsyth's shift from the centrality of the rational to that of the moral. Rationality has its place, but it is secondary to the moral. He has, to be sure, a far from moralistic understanding of what he means by the moral realities of the gospel, as we shall see. Indeed, his often-quoted confession that he had changed from being a lover of love to an object of grace suggests that the Aberdonian, after the much-discussed conversion, moved from a moralism, or at least a religious stance suggesting that the onus of the faith was on the free agency of the believer, to the passive stance of one for whom to receive was, in view of moral helplessness, the prior requirement. Like Luther, he had come to elevate the passive righteousness of the God who justifies by grace over the active righteousness of those who must make their own salvation.[20] That is true, but it is not the whole truth. It was not only redemption that was of grace for Forsyth, even though the order of creation does receive rather inadequate treatment. The slogan 'the real as the redemptive', inverting Hegel as we have seen him invert Kant, and many of his arguments suggest that he was aware of the fact that the question was one of ontology just as much as soteriology, and that is the case even when he is dealing with soteriology. His is far more than a moralism of the pious soul, for it is a moralism which bases the moral agent in what is a theology of reality. In

[20] He does, however, prefer receptivity to passivity (pp. 103f.). 'The process of thinking ... involves an act of will (that is of obedience).' Here he is classically Calvinist: 'Omnis recta cognitio Dei ab obedientia nascitur' (John Calvin, *Institutes* I.6.2).

that sense, the created order is important for him as more than simply a backcloth to redemption.

What then is the relation of creation and redemption? 'The real as the redemptive.' The message shouted from the rooftops is that Forsyth is revealing himself as a characteristically Western theologian, though a distinctive one, for I can think of no other theologian before him who would use words quite like that. Augustine? Too Platonist; for him the real is, when it comes to the crunch, that world ontologically closest to the creator, the eternal world of forms, first-born of the Trinity's creative work.[21] Aquinas? Too Aristotelian; reality for him is that which is shaped by the creator's all-determining causality. Luther or Calvin? Well, there is a problem, for either of them could be found saying similar things, though none perhaps quite so apparently one-sided. Calvin certainly would suspect something of a lack of balance, perhaps; Book II of the *Institutes* at the expense of Book I. Luther perhaps is in some respects nearer; but it is the reality claim that marks Forsyth's dictum as being of particular interest. Luther, as is sometimes claimed, was too interested in the existential relevance of the gospel to be much interested in what we call questions of ontology. It is rather in his engagement with specifically modern questions that Forsyth shows himself to be particularly himself, though, as I have suggested, also particularly Western.

What does that mean? In the first place, that it would be an odd theologian indeed of the Eastern traditions who could be heard saying anything remotely suggesting the priority of the redemptive in the way that Forsyth was urging. Of all things Western, it is the doctrine of the atonement with which Eastern theologians claim to be most uneasy. They are rightly suspicious of the Western tendency to elevate the doctrine of salvation at the expense of the doctrines of creation and what Barth called redemption: the beginning in Christ and the Spirit from which all things derive, and the end to which in Christ

---

[21] I am assuming that serious theologians would place God at the head of their account of what it is to be real. The question at issue here is how that divine reality bears upon and so shapes the reality that is not God. That may appear to disqualify a number of recent proponents of the art who deny, or affect to deny, the objective reality of God. This is in part a matter of definition, but it seems to me part of the definition of the word theology, proper, that it is the logos of the one we call God.

and the Spirit they move. Does not Forsyth suggest that atonement is in some way prior in the scheme of things to creation and eschatology, and does that not make him a typical Western exponent of salvation theology? Yes, but he is one who attempts, however inadequately, to shape a theology of nature in the light of redemption. In *Christ on Parnassus* he makes the claim that in Christendom, as a fusion of the Hebrew and the Greek, 'The ground plan of Nature was now Redemption. The sphere of nature, which the Greek had leavened with his thought, received now a consecration from God's will and purpose ...'.[22] Forsyth has a doctrine of creation, but it is of creation understood in the light of redemption, and indeed reconstituted by it.

I would contend, therefore, that there is to be found in our theologian something more than a playing of soteriology against other doctrinal loci, even though for him redemption is the centre of systematic theology. One point worth noting is that he contends that salvation is redemption in and with the created order, not out of it, as the Western tradition is so often accused of implying. He could be, and probably is, attacking Ritschl when he says:

> For the whole creation groans for the Redemption, and is included in the process which works to the manifestation of the Sons of God. And the miracles of Christ show that His work is not simply to empower the soul to rise over an inferior creation and beat down Nature under its feet, but that it is also to involve Nature in the grand co-operation of all things in the everlasting kingdom (p. 206).

As he shows in another great book, the justification of God is at the same time the justification of the whole world. And could it be that he has the weaknesses of the Western tradition in mind when he says that 'The curse of orthodoxy ... has been to sever the cross from the whole moral fabric and movement of the universe and make it a theologian's affair'?[23] These remarks, however fragmentary, are further indications of Forsyth's systematic perceptiveness and comprehensiveness.

---

[22] P. T. Forsyth, *Christ on Parnassus* (London: Independent Press, 1959, 1st edition, 1911), p. 85.
[23] Forsyth, *The Justification of God* (London: Duckworth, 1916), p. 192.

They also serve to focus our enquiry about authority. Has our theologian a view of authority so dominated by sin and salvation that he has nothing much to say on the general question of authority, on what we can call created authority? It is clear that in the order of knowing – perhaps we should say, in the case of this theologian, the order of experience – the only way to a theology of authority can be through the strait and narrow gate of the cross. In a human situation characterised by helpless guilt, and therefore moral impotence, the only true authority that can be exercised is the authority through which redemption is achieved.[24] Given the human situation, the real can only be the redemptive, so that Forsyth's ontology is an ontology of the holy as a doctrine of God. The balance of the matter is expressed thus:

> If there is any authority over the natural man, it must be that of its Creator; and, if the New Humanity has any authority above it, that authority must be found in the act of *its* creation, which act is the Cross of Christ (p. 58).

It is further true that a theology of what can be called created authority follows from the basis given in redemption. The God of the cross is the one who is the power of all things. This means that the theology of the holy generates a universal ontology according to which the authority of God is not merely for the Church, but for the whole of society: 'the harmonised judgment and grace of the Cross, at once critical and creative for the whole of society' (p. 405). Here the title of the book, not merely of a chapter, is significant: not *Christian* or *Ecclesiastical Authority*, but *The Principle of Authority*. Forsyth is writing for the whole world. This is clear from the one definition of authority which he essays:

> What we usually mean by authority is this. It is another's certainty taken as the *sufficient and final* reason for some certainty of ours, in thought or action (p. 313).

From the fact that authority is a *principle*, something of universal bearing, it follows that 'The principle of authority is the foundation of education and of religion. And no ethic is

[24] 'Human nature is great and wonderful; it is human will that has the blight and the doom' (p. 260).

possible without it' (p. 307). 'The sphere of authority is not in religion alone (though its final source is there). In all the affairs of life it has its action' (p. 313).

There is, then, to be found in Forsyth a theology of authority in general. Here two points can be made. (1) Not only does divine authority make a claim on society as well as on Church; it is also true that without this authority, society founders. 'The present decay in the matter of public liberty and its vigilance is more than concurrent with the decay of sure faith in a divine authority' (p. 409). Forsyth believes that the loss of the authority of the gospel in Western society is the cause of a deep loss of direction, and he is surely right. His description of the modern West as 'an outworn age trying to narcotise with mere energies its moral fatigue' (p. 393) could scarcely be bettered.

(2) There is to be seen operating in Forsyth's work a kind of hierarchy of authorities, for from time to time he recognises that there is a general authority upon which redemptive authority supervenes, so to speak. He begins by recognising that human beings as a matter of fact live by some authority or other, though he is not entirely convinced that such a natural theology gives adequate guidance to its exponents:

> Most people live under what they hold to be the authority of *all*. They do, or seek to do, what everybody else does. They are most secure in those things which are the universal fashion, in the primal unities, customs or instincts of society, in immemorial convention.[25]
>
> Some again are satisfied with the authority of *most*. They live as politicians do – by majorities ... Their ideal is the popular ...
>
> Others again follow the authority of the *few*. It may be a majority of experts, as in the case of science (pp. 313–14).

It is here that Forsyth begins his acknowledgement of natural patterns of authority. In many things we quite properly accept the authority of others, in varying relationships. Among the quite proper authorities are the expert and the educator.

---

[25] He adds, 'In the religious sphere we are familiar with the principle as "*Quod semper, quod ubique, quod ab omnibus*", or "*Securus judicat orbis terrarum*", or the "*fides implicita*".'

Indeed, democracy is lost without them.[26] But, and this is the key, they must be recognised for what they are; relative authorities. 'True faith releases us by passing us upward from one authority to another' (p. 324). Without the recognition of the authority of the holy God of the gospel, not only the Church but also human society is lost.

V *Conclusion*

As is the case with all writers, historical distance enables us to be aware of the weaknesses of Forsyth's thought. Despite his affirmation of authority as a principle, it is there in little more than outline, and both that and the account of the relation of created and redeemed authority are fragmentary and at times indistinct. Moreover, despite the admirable moves through the development of a theology of experience to counter the impression of a sheer dialectic of freedom and obedience, there is a neglect of the pneumatological dimensions which are indispensable in any account of the relation between divine action and human response. Nevertheless, there is an overall coherence, impressive in its grasp, albeit sometimes a rather intuitive grasp, of the different dimensions – theological, hamartiological, anthropological, cultural and social – which must be taken into account in a truly systematic treatment.

That said, the chapter will conclude with discussions of two of the general points of interest for today in what Forsyth has to say, and they serve as a conclusion to the book also, as comments on tendencies in some modern theology. (1) It becomes evident towards the end of the book that Forsyth's theology is a theology of power.[27] Many of its expressions are offensive, I suspect because they are salutary, if exaggerated for the sake of rhetorical effect. '[W]e are His property much more than His brethren' (p. 253). However, the link between a high doctrine of divine transcendence and human freedom is well made:

---

[26] 'It is the principle of authority, in whatever shape, that must save democracy from becoming easy, casual and corrupt, from mean, grey and gritty mediocrity ...' (p. 307).

[27] 'Faith is not faith in truths, but in powers ...' (p. 259).

What was it that made the tremendous strength of Calvinism? What makes some form of Calvinism indispensable and immortal? It was this, that it cared more to secure the freedom of God than of man. That is what it found in the Cross. That is why it has been the greatest contribution to public liberty ever made ... Seek first the freedom of God, and all other freedom shall be added to you. The Calvinistic doctrine of predestination was the foundation of public liberty; and, deeply, because it was an awful attempt to secure God's freedom in Grace at any cost (p. 255).[28]

There lies its contribution to contemporary debate, and in face of two contemporary approaches to theology against both of which Forsyth is in healthy rebellion. One is the theology of signs and wonders associated with the American evangelist John Wimber, whose theology, according to one recent critique, could be summed up in the slogan 'power without the cross': that is, the power of success, a finally anthropocentric theology justifying Christianity by its works.[29] The second is the recent spate of theologies of the cross, whose assumption appears to be the centrality of some form of suffering God, or at least one whose primary concern would sometimes appear to be the equality of the sexes or the economic development and/ or ecological salvation of the world.[30]

Let us examine the second of these before moving to the first. Against all forms of anthropocentrism, Forsyth's theology is contemptuous, his deity glorious in his transcendent self-sufficiency. This God holds all merely human schemes in derision (Ps. 2.4). Here is a splendid antidote for the utilitarian deity of so much recent theology:

> The supreme value ... felt in God is not His utility. If He slew us we should praise His holy name. It is a question not of His utility to us but of ours to Him, not of His service to us but His right and glory over us ... His greatest mercy is not in

---

[28] That the historical claim of the last sentence may be questionable does not detract from the general theological point being made. Forsyth's strength is to see precisely where the root of the modern predicament is to be found.

[29] See Martyn Percy, *Words, Wonders and Power* (London: SPCK, 1996).

[30] That is not to suggest that these matters are unimportant, but rather to accept Forsyth's polemic against the anthropocentrism and opportunist pragmatism of much modern theology.

sparing us but in seeking and accepting our praise and service. His last word to the soul is not only [note well] 'I save' but 'I claim' (p. 387).

That God has no need of the creation is not to say that he has no concern for it; quite the reverse. Yet the need of the creation is not for self-justification so much as for redemption by holy love. Moreover, and here we come to the other comparison, the same theology holds against a theology of signs and wonders. In one place he specifically says that it is 'God the All-holy rather than the Almighty' whom we meet in his chosen form of action (p. 54). 'All the holiness of God bears down on my soul. Not His power, His influence, but His holiness' (p. 40). It is Forsyth's theocentrism that is so salutary for an era of deities made in the image of man or woman.

Interestingly, where modern theology of the cross, with its patripassianist overtones, tends to transfer the qualities of the Son, or perhaps we should say of the human Christ, to the Father, Forsyth operates in a reverse direction. 'What is true of God is also true of Christ. He is not only Saviour but Lord ... Through the Bible, God with all His power and claim, comes in Christ' (p. 373). The focus is not the suffering of God in Christ, the weight of whose human act would thus be lost, but the efficacious action of God in the suffering of Christ, though not only in that. He who has seen Christ truly has seen the Father, for Christ is he who above all does the work of the one who sends him. Do we not, or should we not, hear Forsyth speaking directly to the condition of the modern Church when he resists the idea of God as an indulgent father – 'whether we take the old Lear or the modern Lear – Père Goriot' – with the words, 'A Cross which is nothing but a revelation of divine sacrifice and service to us is an indulgent and demoralising Cross. It is a piece of undiscriminating charity' (p. 379). The theology of power defined by love is nowhere better expressed than in the following powerful piece of rhetoric:

> God is only God as absolute, eternal, holy love; His love conquers; it is the absolute power over us, and the final power over our world. All things work together for good to them that love God *in His universal, royal, holy, and final purpose* ... Such is the God of the Bible. He reveals Himself,

but it is of His absolutely free and royal choice for His own holy end ... And God ceases to be God when he ceases to be such a God – the absolute, miraculous, personal, holy, and effective King and Lord of us and our world. To curtail his power is to infect Him with weakness; that is to say, it is to make Him a mixture of power and weakness – which again is to make Him a part of the world, and destroy Him altogether as God (pp. 371–2).[31]

(2) The second thing to say is that Forsyth's is a profoundly moral vision, as I have already suggested, which interestingly shares Coleridge's affinity for some aspects of Kant's thought. And the moral vision is closely linked to the vision of power, because Forsyth is concerned finally that God's will be done on earth as it is in heaven. The concern with praxis would satisfy many a liberationist, if the praxis took the approved form. But while Kant's morality finally becomes a rational and para-doxically anthropocentric system, everything requiring assess-ment at the bar of human reason, Forsyth submits everything to the judgement of the God made known on the cross of Christ. The vision is moral rather than moralistic, and from time to time he clearly differentiates between the two. There are a number of aspects to this vision, some less convincing than others.

His main enemy, slightly misconceived, is what he supposes to be the naturalising of salvation in the patristic era. Here he shares the belief, perhaps associated most prominently with Harnack, in a supposedly 'physical' theory of salvation, and with better reason attributes to Anselm the beginnings of an emphasis on personal reconciliation as being the heart of the matter. The most creative contribution he has to make in this regard is his ontology of the holy. It is sometimes complained that his conception of the holy is unclear, but it seems not to be in its general outlines. The holy has some claim to be a fundamental notion, one we cannot do without if we are to understand who God is and who we are – what Coleridge would call an idea – the meaning of which is made clear in the

---

[31] 'We experience Christ as Brother, or as ideal, or as Master, but we do not experience Him as Saviour; or if as Saviour, then not from perdition, not as absolute Owner, King and Lord' (p. 367).

contexts in which it is used. Its function is to express the divine love in judgement and forgiveness that is at the centre of things.

One does see here, perhaps, a salutary correction of the Western tendency, from Augustine through Anselm to Hegel and even at times Barth, to stress the divine rationality as being at the centre of things. It could be said that in his theology Forsyth plays goodness against the other transcendentals of truth and beauty, for he sees truth primarily in the moral transformation made real by the historic cross of Christ. And perhaps that is as it should be. It is the human creation which is made in the image of God, the human creation through whose sin the remainder of the created order is subjected to futility and whose redemption it awaits, the human creation that is called to be conformed to the image of Christ. We are the problem, and through Christ alone the locus of the solution. In that sense, the moral is the focus of the truth of reality, and Forsyth is right, as he is about so much. '[T]he saved conscience is integrated into the justice of the universe' (p. 268). But that is so by virtue of God's authority and the way it is realised in the world.

> Faith is such a delivering power because it has within it such a gracious authority. Everything else, Church or Bible, is authoritative for us in the proportion in which it is sacramental of this final and absolute authority, of the Creator as Redeemer, the authority not merely of God but of a God of grace. Authority reflects a dying king (p. 299).

The last word is thus of the authority of grace, the grace of redemption through the cross of Christ.

INDEX OF SUBJECTS

INDEX OF AUTHORS